MW00333889

# The Bible, Theology, and Faith
## A Study of Abraham and Jesus

How can academic biblical interpretation fruitfully contribute
to Christian belief and living in today's world? This book
offers a synthesis of some of the best in pre-modern, modern,
and post-modern approaches to biblical interpretation, and
locates the discipline within a self-critical trinitarian rule of
faith, where historical criticism, systematic theology, ethics,
and spirituality are constructively combined.

R. W. L. Moberly reclaims biblical and patristic principles of
what is necessary for meaningful and truthful speech about
God to be possible; he engages with contemporary ideological
suspicions directed both to scripture and to its interpreters;
and he offers an account of God and humanity in relation to
both Old and New Testaments. Hermeneutical theory is given
practical shape in in-depth studies of Genesis 22 ('The
Akedah'), the journey to Emmaus (Luke 24), and the
christology of Matthew's Gospel, studies which should be of
interest to both Jews and Christians.

R. W. L. MOBERLY is Lecturer in Theology at the University
of Durham. Author of *At the Mountain of God* (1983), *The Old
Testament of the Old Testament* (1992), *From Eden to Golgotha: Essays
in Biblical Theology* (1992), and *Genesis 12–50* (1992), he has been
an Anglican priest since 1982.

# Cambridge Studies in Christian Doctrine

*Edited by*
Professor COLIN GUNTON, *King's College London*
Professor DANIEL W. HARDY, *University of Cambridge*

*Cambridge Studies in Christian Doctrine* is an important series which aims to engage critically with the traditional doctrines of Christianity, and at the same time to locate and make sense of them within a secular context. Without losing sight of the authority of scripture and the traditions of the church, the books in this series will subject pertinent dogmas and credal statements to careful scrutiny, analyzing them in light of the insights of both church and society, and will thereby practise theology in the fullest sense of the word.

# The Bible,
# Theology, and Faith

### A study of Abraham and Jesus

R. W. L. MOBERLY

*University of Durham*

CAMBRIDGE
UNIVERSITY PRESS

PUBLISHED BY THE PRESS SYNDICATE OF THE UNIVERSITY OF CAMBRIDGE
The Pitt Building, Trumpington Street, Cambridge, United Kingdom

CAMBRIDGE UNIVERSITY PRESS
The Edinburgh Building, Cambridge CB2 2RU, UK     www.cup.cam.ac.uk
40 West 20th Street, New York, NY 10011–4211, USA     www.cup.org
10 Stamford Road, Oakleigh, Melbourne 3166, Australia
Ruiz de Alarcón 13, 28014 Madrid, Spain

First published 2000

Printed in the United Kingdom at the University Press, Cambridge

*Typeface* TEFFLexicon 9/13 pt    *System* QuarkXPress®   [SE]

*A catalogue record for this book is available from the British Library*

*Library of Congress Cataloguing in Publication data*

Moberly, R. W. L.
The Bible, theology, and faith: a study of Abraham and Jesus / R. W. L. Moberly.
    p.   cm. (Cambridge studies in Christian doctrine)
ISBN 0 521 77222 2 (hardback) – ISBN 0 521 78646 0 (paperback)
1. Bible – Hermeneutics.    2. Faith.    3. Bible. O.T. Genesis XXII – Criticism,
interpretation, etc.    I. Title.    II. Series.
BS476.M576    2000
230′.041–dc21    99–056885    CIP

ISBN 0 521 77222 2   hardback
ISBN 0 521 78646 0   paperback

To *Patricia*
*Dorothy and Ken*
*Fiona and Stephen*
*Johanna and Alan*
*Karen and Andrew*
*Sally and David*

in lasting gratitude

# Contents

*Preface*

This book has grown in an often fragmentary and not very well-planned way, with vision usually only clear in retrospect not prospect. Although I hope that the final product has achieved coherence in such a way as to render unimportant the convoluted processes of its growth, a scholar trained in pentateuchal criticism never feels entirely confident about such matters. But while my earlier recensions may safely be relegated to oblivion, I wish to record with gratitude my indebtedness to at least some of the many formative influences on the various stages of my work, without whom it would not have become what, for better or worse, it now is.

The Theology Department of Durham University, superbly located in Abbey House, continues to be a most congenial context for work. I am able both to savour the views of Palace Green and the cathedral, and still attend sufficiently to my computer screen. A relaxed and supportive atmosphere lends itself to good conversations over coffee or lunch or *en passant* on the staircase. I am enriched by being here.

A preliminary first draft of the whole was read through by Stephen Barton, Chris Seitz, and Dan Hardy, who offered the kind of constructive criticisms for which every writer hopes; Stephen in particular has been an invaluable conversation partner and has contributed immeasurably to the development of my thinking. Particular chapters received valuable comment both from colleagues, Kingsley Barrett, Jimmy Dunn, Loren Stuckenbruck, Francis Watson, and Tom Wright, and from two of the best of my Biblical Theology students, Geoff Burn, and Lynda Gough. The Durham Old Testament and New Testament postgraduate seminars patiently sat through much of the material (at times feeling slightly bemused?) and made many a sharp contribution. Colleagues in the Scripture Project at the Center of Theological Inquiry, Princeton, have mulled over much of the material and given me a clearer sense both of its strengths and of its shortcomings.

I am increasingly aware, however, that many of the essays and books which have most influenced me are not mentioned in these pages at all, or are only mentioned in a cursory way disproportionate to their real significance; and likewise with numerous conversations along the way. I hope that some of my friends and also others may recognize their traces in my thinking and writing, and know that their influence has been so profound that it is a part of me and I can no longer separate it out.

I am grateful to Dan Hardy for suggesting Cambridge Studies in Christian Doctrine as a suitable location for my manuscript. Kevin Taylor at Cambridge University Press has always been helpful. Even his insistence that the manuscript be shortened, which I received with less than enthusiasm, was appropriate; despite my mutterings (and the loss of much footnote engagement with recent scholarly debate) I have to admit that the final version (whatever its defects) is an improvement on its predecessor. It has been a pleasure to work with Jan Chapman as copyeditor. And I am grateful to Nathan Macdonald for compiling the indices.

Although my thinking about the issues of this book has been going on for many years, the actual research and writing has taken place in a time of acute personal difficulty – in the aftermath of the death by cancer of my beloved Meredith on 7 July 1994, 114 days after she gave birth to John-Paul. My incapacity through grief, together with the exacerbation of my long-running M.E., could have rendered my personal and professional life unfruitful for a long time. But in addition to the wonderful support from my colleagues at Abbey House, the critical difference was made by those friends who were willing to help with the overnight and weekend care of John-Paul and who became a support system for both him and me. Their steady friendship and practical care channelled hope and healing in the valley of the shadow, and continued throughout the time in which this book was written – until the advent of Jenny last autumn brought new wonder and joy. It is to these friends that the book is dedicated, as a small token of a gratitude I cannot sufficiently express.

**1**

# The Bible, the question of God, and Christian faith

There are many ways in which one could approach discussion of the Bible and its interpretation. One could look at classic models of the past. One could study particular twentieth-century scholars, such as Bultmann, von Rad, or Childs, who have made landmark contributions. One could offer a history of the subject with a view to highlighting some aspect. One could try to survey the burgeoning plurality of methods and results in contemporary biblical study. I propose to do none of these, but rather to develop an account of biblical interpretation in relation to the question of God in three stages. First, I will offer a very broad brush sketch of certain aspects of biblical interpretation within which to contextualize my general concerns. Secondly, I will expound and analyse two significant and different contemporary accounts of how biblical interpretation operates (or should operate). Thirdly, I will set out my own specific hermeneutical assumptions which inform the handling of the biblical text in the rest of the book.[1]

## Situating the argument

### (1) A basic tension

The scholarly study of the Bible is a difficult discipline. Many of the difficulties relate to age-old questions, such as the relationship between faith and reason, or appropriate method in reading ancient texts, questions which are renewed in every generation. However, the particular form in

---

1. I realize the dangers inherent in the kind of generalizations which will regularly feature in this argument, for it is rarely difficult to think of exceptions and qualifications, and one cannot do justice to the complexities of hermeneutical debate in one chapter. I ask for the reader's patience with the broad brush strokes of this whole chapter.

which the questions are renewed varies, and if one does not attend to the particularities of context no satisfactory account can be given.

My concern in this book is the interpretation of the Bible as the foundation, and primary resource, of Christian faith and theology. To have this concern is common among biblical scholars, and is a primary reason why many people choose to become biblical scholars. Yet the status of the concern is problematic in many ways. Biblical scholars who have agreed that the Bible should be related to Christian faith have constantly disagreed as to how that relating should be carried out. In recent years there has been a strong resurgence of Jewish scholars engaging in biblical study, and the varying possible relationships between Jewish and Christian agendas (in which the Bible itself is differently defined) is a live topic. There are those who wish to study the biblical texts as interesting ancient texts with no commitment to, or interest in, their continuing status as Jewish and Christian scripture. Some see the continuing significance of the Bible as a matter for cultural analysis of one kind or another but with little or no reference to historic discussions of faith and theology. Some question whether the concern to relate the Bible to faith today is not likely to prejudge prematurely or foreclose certain issues and to make analytical scrutiny of the text ultimately subservient to apologetics. All these questions are a matter of lively debate at present.

I take it as axiomatic that a scholarly study of the Bible as a resource for Christian faith must always do at least two things (and similar concerns, *mutatis mutandis*, will characterize also many Jewish scholars). On the one hand, it must learn, and not retreat, from the insights of modern *Wissenschaft* (even though it may wish to reconceive some of them). Most obviously, in terms of biblical study as a scholarly discipline, the impact of critical historical awareness has been immense. When the biblical text is used as a source for the life and thought of certain segments of the ancient world, then in principle it is handled as any other source would be handled, subject to the familiar agenda of such matters as philology, compositional context, genre, historicity, and a historically nuanced evaluation of interesting and often controversial assumptions, prescriptions, and practices within the text.

On the other hand, the Christian faith (in all its apparently endless diversity) offers a particular understanding of God and humanity, and a particular way of living, which centres on the figure of Jesus Christ. This faith is rooted in the Bible as a privileged and unique account of the nature of God and humanity and of the significance of Jesus for both. The way of living which arises from this, which has endured (in multifarious forms, and with constant abuses) to the present day, is one to which many millions have testified as a way, indeed *the* way, of truth. If this faith and life is to continue as a genuine and significant option – an option which, humanly speaking, can hardly be taken for granted – then it must constantly be nourished from its primary resources, the most foundational of which is the Bible, and so it remains vital for the Christian scholar constructively to integrate the Bible with the life and faith of the Christian Church.

How should these two requirements be held together? First and foremost, it is important to see that most easy polarizations – such as the Bible as a book like any other book versus the Bible as a book unlike any other book, or what the Bible historically meant versus what the Bible homiletically means, or the Bible as ancient religious ideologies versus the Bible as purveyor of timeless truths, or the scholar as the disinterested pursuer of truth versus the scholar as partisan advocate and apologist – are best abandoned. Their occasional heuristic usefulness in highlighting a certain kind of contrast is more regularly outweighed by their imposition of a distorting and deceptive oversimplification of complex and intertwining issues. This may perhaps be seen through brief preliminary reflections on three issues: the contextual nature of reason, the relationship between Bible and Church, and the problem of speaking about God.

### (2) Reason and life

Modern biblical criticism arose within a cultural context in which reason was as highly esteemed as it could be. The rational and disinterested pursuit of truth, empirical (as opposed to dogmatic) in method, open (as opposed to hidebound) in attitude, and judicious (as opposed to partisan) in assessment, is something that it seems should hardly need defence against detractors, for once such an outlook has been well acquired there is something self-evidently right about it.

Yet one thing that seems common to many diverse moods and movements of the present time, which is a factor in the designation 'postmodernity' (however one understands the term), is a critique of reason. This is a critique which is not (except in its more bizarre manifestations) advocating unreason, but rather which insists that reason cannot be abstracted from the totality of life. On the one hand, the use of reason is inseparable from the use of language, and languages are social constructs of immense historical and cultural complexity. On the other hand, the use of reason is not fully separable from personal and cultural context: the questions one asks, and the answers which satisfy, always relate to the various wider contexts of which each person is a part. None of these factors deny the importance of reason within human life. But they do mean that discourses about reason can no longer treat reason as though it were somehow disembodied and not subject to the particularities of life which are part of the human condition. Empirical methods and judicious assessments remain important. But they operate within particular traditions of life and thought, and there are many contexts of life in which other approaches and qualities are also necessary (what may judges and scholars need in order to flourish as businesspeople or lovers?).

Since a sense of an inseparable relationship between reason and life was a fundamental presupposition of classic Christian theology – in shorthand, the complementarity of knowledge and love – the present climate of thought is in many ways suitable for a rediscovery of certain historic Christian insights and for reformulating discussions of 'faith and reason' and of 'Bible and theology'. To be sure, there are important differences between the self-reflexive turn in contemporary epistemology and the linkages of reason and life in the premodern period, and I do not wish to obscure these. Nonetheless, the changing intellectual and social climate creates new similarities, as well as new differences, between Christian and other concerns.

### (3) Bible and Church

There is an obvious problem which affects Christian (and *mutatis mutandis* Jewish) study of the Bible. On the one hand, the content and self-definition of all the mainstream branches of the Christian Church is provided, at the very least, by the Bible in conjunction with the theological formulations of the patristic period – the creeds and councils with their trinitarian and incarnational understandings of God, Christ, humanity, and salvation. To accept the validity of these doctrines (however much they may need reformulation and reappropriation) is part of the official definition of what it means to be a Christian – at least for the Roman Catholic and Orthodox churches, and also for those Protestant churches that are affiliated to the World Council of Churches, that is, for an overwhelming majority. For most Christians there are also various post-patristic formulations and confessions which are also normative. On the other hand, none of these doctrinal confessions were formulated by the biblical writers, nor (in all likelihood) even envisaged by them. Although the biblical writers provide a content for which the Fathers and others have sought to provide appropriate means of articulation and appropriation, such formulations are always technically anachronistic with regard to any particular biblical text in its likely original context.

It is common knowledge that modern biblical criticism only became a recognizable discipline through the process of explicit severing of the Bible from classic theological formulations. The basis for this was the belief that only so could the Bible be respected and heard in its own right, untrammelled by preconceptions which supposed that the answers were already known even before the questions were asked, or by anachronistic impositions of the conceptualities and assumptions of subsequent ages. The fruitfulness of the severance, in terms of a clearer sense of practical and conceptual differences both within the Bible and between the Bible and post-biblical formulations, is well known. Moreover, the approach has been justified theologically, at least by Protestants, in terms of the need for the authentic voice of scripture to critique the always provisional formulations of post-biblical theology.

*[margin note: denial of the church's role in revelation]*

This has led to a curious situation. To be a Christian means, at least in part, the acceptance and appropriation of certain theological doctrines and patterns of living. Yet the task of reading the Bible 'critically' has regularly been defined precisely in terms of the exclusion of these doctrines and patterns of living from the interpretative process.

*[margin note: summary of the tension]*

To be sure, it can easily be shown that many biblical scholars have been less than entirely consistent in their actual practice of interpretation. This is clear, for example, if one considers the frequency with which outstanding German scholars have brought an understanding of faith rooted in Luther and Lutheran confessions to bear upon the interpretation of the biblical text; neither Baur and Wellhausen in the nineteenth century, nor Bultmann and von Rad in the twentieth century, can be understood apart from this context (amidst many other influences upon them). Yet too often formal questions about the relationship of faith and interpretation have been neglected, or conducted in the light of a debilitating polarization between faith as practical piety, or existential authenticity, and faith as theological dogma. Defining Christian doctrines, such as Trinity and Incarnation, and their relationship to faith and interpretation, are rarely on the agenda, except to show the tenuousness of their rootage in the biblical text or the distance of their supposedly abstract conceptualities from concrete biblical faith.

*[margin note: good pt.]*

From the perspective of a history of religious thought, it may be as readily conceded that the New Testament writers did not think in terms of the trinitarian categories of the fourth century, as that the writers of Israel's scriptures did not think in terms of Jesus Christ. But the crucial issue in the present argument is not the history of ideas – did the earlier writers think in terms of subsequent perspectives, and how did the subsequent perspectives develop? – but the problem of theological hermeneutics – do certain subsequent perspectives genuinely enable the reader to penetrate more deeply into the meaning and significance of what the earlier writers said? To this hermeneutical question the answer is much less simple or straightforward. If it be acknowledged that appeals to Trinity and Incarnation may in practice sometimes function as anachronistic impositions which distort true historical understanding, it does not follow that this is their sole function. May they not be insights of an ultimate kind into the nature of God and humanity, focussed in Jesus Christ, whose role is to enable understanding of God and humanity in any context, not least within the Bible – insights, however, whose content is not fully given in advance but rather is clarified and deepened only in and through the continuing quest to discern the reality of God within human life? More generally the basic issue is the adequacy of the interpreter's categories of understanding as regards the substantive moral and theological content of the Bible, and hence the inadequacy of the assumption that if only biblical interpreters are well trained in appropriate languages, biblical history, and history of religious thought, they are well placed to understand what the Bible says.

Finally, under this heading, it should be remembered that the hermeneutical dialectic of biblical text and post-biblical faith is not peculiar to Christians and Jews. In general terms, whenever there are structures, communities, and patterns of life whose identity is in some fundamental way defined by a particular textual corpus, there should always be a healthy two-way interaction between text and community. The community seeks to develop its own life and to understand its text better through exploring the text's various possible implications and developments, and there is constant discussion as to whether particular developments are, or are not, good and valid in relation to the original text. This pattern, in one form or another, pertains not only to Judaism, Christianity, and Islam in relation to their scriptures – it can be seen in some of its elements in the historic responses to major thinkers from, say, Plato and Aristotle to Marx and Freud. Or it can be seen in more specific form in America's continuing interpretation of its Constitution. When such interaction flags in vitality then it is a sign that the tradition of thought and life is in perilous condition; if the interaction cannot be revived, the tradition is moribund and its end is at hand, and differently structured patterns of thought and life will be adopted (for better or worse).

In broadest terms, one can suggest that one of the central issues facing contemporary Western culture in general, and Christian and Jewish communities of faith in particular, is whether or not they can continue to engage positively with those texts and traditions which historically have been formative, and whether serious engagement with the changing conditions of the present will energize or marginalize creative appropriation of the wisdom of the past.

### (4) Speech about God

One basic issue which is raised by the Bible in conjunction with the faiths rooted in it concerns the nature of God. It is axiomatic (in Jewish and Christian, also Muslim, contexts) that God is not a 'being' or 'person' or 'object' like any other being or person or object in the world with which one might be familiar; in theological parlance the Creator is distinct from the creation. This raises the problem of what it means – if indeed it is meaningful at all – to speak about God or to make claims to knowledge of God. If someone speaks about God, how can we know that they know what they are talking about?

Classic Christian theology developed an extensive set of protocols of an intellectual, moral, and spiritual nature for responsible engagement with this issue. However, in the development of early modern Western culture, in which knowledge and method in relation to the empirical and mathematical natural sciences became the norm of epistemology, fundamental conceptual shifts took place. Since God could not be studied scientifically, as this had come to be understood, the focus of theology became increasingly uncertain, with some tendency to swing between metaphysical abstractions and pietism; and, with the rise of the social sciences, there has been a tendency for theology in one way or another to focus on the human dimension which could be scientifically studied – human language, thoughts, and feelings about God could all be analysed and classified with a sense of scientific rigour. The subject of theology thus shifts from God to the history and conceptuality of belief in God.

Such factors, among many others, have tended to leave biblical interpreters in a difficult position. They have often wanted to talk about God, and make truth claims in relation to God, on the basis of the biblical text. Yet in practice their work has often consisted predominantly in the analysis and classification of human beliefs and practices in relation to belief in

God as attested in the Bible. The status of such human beliefs and practices in relation to contemporary truth claims about God has usually been highly problematic. Some scholars have, of course, tackled the problems. Perhaps most famously in the twentieth century Bultmann combined meticulous philological and historical work with a consistent engagement with fundamental issues of philosophy and theology, precisely so that the truth status of the Pauline and Johannine accounts of God and humanity could be clarified and proclaimed. But the wide scope of Bultmann has been more of an exception than a rule among biblical scholars, and in any case his particular way of construing the issues as a whole has generally ceased to persuade either believers or non-believers. The question of God in relation to the Bible is thus easily either left in abeyance, or it becomes a matter of assumption or affirmation whose intellectual depth and seriousness may be open to doubt.

Into such an ocean one can throw no more than a pebble. Nonetheless the purpose of this book is to suggest ways in which one might make some progress.

These preliminary reflections will, I hope, give the reader some sense of the general drift of the argument I wish to make. We will now turn to more specific discussion. First I will consider one essay from an Old Testament scholar, James Barr, and one from a New Testament scholar, C. K. Barrett. Although the essays were written a few years ago now (Barr, 1977; Barrett, 1981), each essay is a model of lucidity and insight, which distils priorities and concerns evident in the wider work of each scholar. Both scholars have a high international reputation within the world of biblical study, and their work is characteristic of the kinds of approach to the Bible which, until recently, constituted a widespread scholarly consensus. Although this consensus may be diminished now, it is probably still much more widespread than might be realized solely by attending to those who reject it in part or in whole.

### James Barr, 'Does Biblical Study Still Belong to Theology?'[2]

#### (1) Exposition

James Barr's essay was written as his Inaugural Lecture in the Oriel Chair of the Interpretation of Holy Scripture in Oxford University. It was delivered on 26 May 1977.

Barr begins by briefly describing the contemporary academic context

2. Barr 1980.

in which, as a matter of fact, study of the Bible is increasingly detached from the study of Christian theology (specifically, the training of ministers for ordination). He notes that theology is 'a constellation of different fields and subjects held together by the fact that they are studied as they relate to God, to the church, its work and its tradition, and to the Bible' (1980: 19). Given that such a constellation is intrinsically difficult to accommodate within a three-year curriculum, it seems inexorably likely that the more theology concentrates on present-day issues the less prominent will the study of the Bible become, since the learning of the biblical languages, 'the foundation of serious study of the church's own scriptures' (p. 20), both takes a lot of time and lacks immediate relevance or applicability. This general dilemma that Barr sketches is painfully familiar to all who work in the field.

Barr's specific interest lies in the inner philosophy of biblical scholarship: 'How far must [the biblical scholar] think and work, and how far does he think and work, in terms that are really theological?' (p. 21). This question requires definition of the term 'theology', and Barr distinguishes two basic senses (p. 22). On the one hand, confessing[3] statements such as ' "God is X", or, in other words, "We believe that God is X" ', which are 'statement[s] of personal faith, or a statement of the church's faith', and which constitute theology 'in the stricter sense'; on the other hand, descriptive statements, ' "This or that biblical writer said, or thought, that God is X." ' The essential difference between these kinds of statement is explicated in terms of their relationship to evidence. The former 'is a statement which, however closely related to evidence, is not merely an interpretation of evidence: its logic is not exhaustively explained by stating the evidence to which it may relate itself'. The latter 'is an interpretation of given evidence'. Biblical study, as generally practised, predominantly takes the form of the latter. This enables the question to be reformulated. If a scholar is to make descriptive statements about the content of the Bible 'in an adequate and comprehensive way', does the scholar also 'have to make' confessing statements? To this the answer is negative, as a simple consideration of the realities of contemporary scholarship reveals. Although confessing biblical study is important for some, it is not for others, and the work of differing scholars is not necessarily distinguishable on this basis. 'Theology in the strict sense is optional rather than necessary' (p. 23).

---

3. Barr does not use the term 'confessing', but I think the term accurately depicts his meaning.

Having thus established the independence of biblical study from theology, Barr goes on to show what this does, and does not, entail. First, he does not wish to deny the propriety of linking theology (in the strict, confessing sense) with biblical study, or to maintain that theology is necessarily distorting on the grounds that it lacks 'objectivity'. On the contrary:

> Though theology can distort and damage objectivity, as theologians themselves continually admit, strong theological conviction can coexist with and rejoice in a very high degree of objectivity. It is true that complete objectivity is not attainable, but a high degree of objectivity is attainable, and a high degree of it is very much better than a low degree. (p. 24)

Those who do not espouse a confessing theological position may themselves hold 'some secular or pseudo-theological ideology which is equally destructive of objectivity' (p. 25). What matters is a quality of openness on the part of both theological and non-theological biblical study.

Barr further recognizes the value of theological approaches to the Bible in its asking of certain questions which otherwise might not be on the agenda:

> Experience suggests that certain levels and dimensions of scripture are not explored except when scholars are prepared, even if only as a hypothesis for the sake of argument, to think theologically, to ask the question, how would it be if this were really true of God? Or, to take a simple illustration from another sphere, from philosophy, how much would the study of an ancient thinker like Plato have been impoverished if throughout the ages scholars had confined themselves to expounding the text and its internal semantic linkages and had rigorously excluded from their minds the question 'Is Plato right?' (p. 25)

Barr then briskly dispatches two arguments that would insist that study of the Bible must be theological. First, the argument about the need for empathy with the matter under study. This applies equally to any subject, and empathy should not be confused with acceptance. In any case, scholars regularly express judgments about religious and philosophical positions which they themselves do not hold. Secondly, discussion about presuppositions has its place, but the validity of scholarly biblical work is determined by how well it accounts for the evidence.

Thus Barr concludes that biblical study and theology should coexist in a relationship of 'lively dialogue'. To exclude theology would leave biblical study the poorer, but theology must recognize its situation as one interpretative option among many.

## (2) Preliminary critique

Much in Barr's discussion is admirable. He has a clear sense of the way things are. And his robust comments about theology, ideology, and objectivity disperse a fog that all too easily gathers in the minds of students. There are few specific points, as such, on which I disagree with him. Nonetheless, there are certain features of Barr's account which I would like to probe on the grounds that he assumes certain things which are in fact open to dispute.[4] One is to do with the definition and public placement of study of theology and the Bible. The other is to do with criteria for the recognition and affirmation of religious truth. The latter will be postponed until after a preliminary discussion of the essay by Barrett. However, as will be seen, these two issues merge into each other. Although my discussion is structured around Barr's essay, for the most part my remarks apply to a wider tradition of scholarship which I take Barr to represent and so regularly move beyond the specifics of Barr's essay.

Barr considers theology (in the stricter, confessing sense) in relation to biblical study only as it affects any individual scholars, in terms of their objectivity, empathy, and presuppositions. He has little to say about such theology, but nonetheless works with a model of it which appears distinctly individualistic. It is probably because of this tacit individualism that he does not discuss theology as a corporate, public activity, nor does he consider theology in relation to the public definition and location of the study of the Bible.

Barr's brief allusion to confessing theology, and his depiction of it as optional within biblical study which can thus flourish without it, could leave his reader wholly innocent of the fact that the Bible is itself a confessing construct. His language that '[theology] is a constellation of different fields and subjects held together by the fact that they are studied as they relate to God, to the church . . . and to the Bible' (p. 19) seems to presuppose that there is a Bible quite independent of the Church. But how far is this really so? Of course there are particular texts. But in what way do they constitute a Bible, a particular *collection* of texts with given contours, apart from reference to those Jews and Christians who collected and shaped them for religious purposes? For the Bible which Barr assumes is

---

4. It would, of course, be improper to suppose that Barr should have included things which the constraints of an inaugural lecture precluded. My concern is to highlight assumptions which can be found in the lecture, and which are characteristic and representative of his work elsewhere – I can find no significant differences in his recent extensive discussion of these same issues (Barr 1999).

the Christian Bible with Old Testament and New Testament,[5] which, as a total collection, is a product of the Christian Church of (arguably) the fourth century.[6] It is a collection whose coherence depends on the assumption that the texts relating to Jesus of Nazareth appropriately belong with, and interpret, the antecedent scriptures of Israel.

The basic point that the Bible is a confessing construct is well spelt out by Robert Jenson (1996: 89–90):

> The volume we call the Bible is a collection of documents. The *single book* exists because the church in her specific mission assembled a certain collection of documents from the very ancient Near East and from first-century Mediterranean antiquity.
>
> Saying this, I mean something commonsensical, that should not ignite theological argument. Protestantism emphasizes that these precise documents *impose* themselves on the church; Catholicism East and West emphasizes that it is the *church* that recognizes the exigency. I mean only to make the simple point presupposed by and included in both emphases: the collection comes together in and for the church. Where the church's calling to speak the gospel is not shared, the binding of these particular documents between one cover becomes a historical accident of no hermeneutical significance.

The supposition that there is a book called 'The Bible' which can self-evidently stand on its own is, I suggest, something analogous to an optical illusion. Although, for example, there has been extensive debate in recent years about the appropriateness of the terms 'Old Testament' and 'New Testament' for the two major divisions of the Bible, this debate has usually ignored the underlying, prior issue of why one should continue to group these particular texts together in the first place (in each testament respectively, as well as the testaments together) when they could be redistributed and redescribed within the regular categories of the humanities and social sciences (from philology and archaeology, via literature, ancient history and philosophy, to sociology of religion and psychology). To suppose that the name of the collection of texts is an issue quite inde-

---

5. The intriguing, yet generally complex and obscure, questions of the history of the formation of the Christian canon of scripture, and the particular problems posed for the Old Testament by the more extensive documents of the LXX as opposed to the MT, need not detain us here. Likewise the fact that differing Christian churches show some disagreements as to the precise extent of the canon should not obscure the consensus both that there is a canon and that the majority of texts within it are not disputed.
6. Barr is, of course, well aware of this fact, which introduces his discussion in Barr 1983. But although he uses it to make various criticisms of certain classic Protestant accounts of a doctrine of scripture, he offers no positive alternative account in which the possible implications for biblical study are explored.

pendent of the validity and significance of the collection *qua* collection is to misunderstand the nature of what one is discussing.

It is likely that the taking for granted of the Bible as Bible is significantly dependent upon the publishing convention whereby for the most part the texts which constitute the Bible are only available as the Bible or as explicit extracts from it. The oddity of the situation becomes clear when one reflects on regular scholarly practice. That is, it is commonplace for biblical scholars to treat the biblical text as a source for ancient history (poetics, ideology, etc.) which is on a par with other non-biblical sources, and to refuse as inappropriate (in principle) any privileging of the biblical text in such work – for not only may the biblical text be historically inaccurate, but also the views it promotes may have been quite unrepresentative of their period.[7] What would be the publishing practice that would accurately reflect these working assumptions? It would be to disperse the particular collection which is the Bible and to relocate and rearrange the material.

For example, once the canon is dispensed with, why not print the 'canonical' gospels in conjunction with the Gospel of Thomas, and perhaps some or all of the other 'apocryphal' gospels?[8] If (as is often supposed) proximity to 'the Jesus of history' is a prime criterion for the worth of a gospel, why privilege the gospel of John over that of Thomas? Once the strongly evaluative terms 'canonical' and 'apocryphal' have been disposed of, why not publish a collection of 'Ancient sources for the life of Jesus'?[9] Instead of *Ancient Near Eastern Texts Relating to the Old Testament* (Pritchard 1969), why not publish *Ancient Near Eastern Texts* which includes Israelite texts presently in the Old Testament in the same way as other texts? That would certainly show independence from a privileging (i.e. Christian or Jewish) assessment of the value of these texts; though whether so many people would still be interested in the resulting volumes seems doubtful. There is thus a nice irony in the fact that the recurrent rhetoric on the part of biblical scholars about freeing the Bible from ecclesiastical

---

7. J. S. Kloppenborg, for example, observes: 'What Paul held to be the heart of his theology, and what in the canonical gospels achieves prominence through the sheer bulk of the passion narratives seems not to have been widely celebrated outside the literary elites responsible for the production and transmission of these documents. We might ask whether the very forcefulness with which Paul asserts a *theologia crucis* has misled generations of scholars into thinking that this rhetoric was successful in promoting his vision and that this vision was representative of the various Christianities in the Mediterranean basin' (Kloppenborg 1992: 119).

8. This is characteristic of the work of the 'Jesus Seminar'. See Funk and Hoover 1993.

9. See e.g. Robinson and Koester 1971 and Koester 1990.

and dogmatic presuppositions, so that it can speak for itself, tends to coexist largely uncomplainingly with the preservation of that ecclesiastical and dogmatic construct, the Bible itself.

A further point, of which Barr is fully aware but which he considers needs no mention, is that 'the Bible' is not only a confessing construct, but also a contested confessing construct. For there is an alternative confessing definition of 'Bible' held within Judaism. Here there is no New Testament, and the Hebrew scriptures are therefore by definition not 'Old Testament'; they are Miqra' or Tanakh, and their content is the Law, the Prophets, and the Writings. This poses the question of which Bible – Jewish or Christian? – should be the object of 'biblical studies'.

For example, much of the most interesting work in recent literary study (poetics) of Hebrew scripture has been done by Jewish scholars. One wonders whether the deep roots of Jewish tradition in Midrash do not make this a particularly congenial and fruitful perspective for at least some Jewish scholars. Be that as it may, many Jewish scholars in this new wave of study make no allusion to their religious affiliations and do not adopt any confessing position.[10] But when they use the term 'Bible' it is consistently the Jewish, not the Christian, understanding of that term which is presupposed, for their roots are Jewish.[11]

When Barr refers to strictly theological (i.e. confessing) study of the Bible, he says that that kind of study 'must be done in the context of the church and with a personal involvement related to that context' (1980: 26). That it might be done in the context of the synagogue, and that the wider theological context might be shaped around Talmud, Midrash, and Jewish tradition, is entirely ignored. Although Barr clearly does not intend to be discourteous to, or unappreciative of, Jewish scholarship (he refers positively to contributions from 'Jewish studies', p. 20), his unexamined usage of 'the Bible' as somehow a self-evident term in fact privileges a Christian position at the expense of a Jewish one. 'Bible' is not a neutral term.[12]

10. This was not true of such scholars of a previous generation as Martin Buber or Franz Rosenzweig. There is an interesting comparison between the generations by Fox in Buber and Rosenzweig 1994: xxiv-xxvi.
11. See, for example, Alter 1981; Berlin 1983; Sternberg 1985; Bar-Efrat 1989.
12. This is not parallel to the recent shift from inclusive to gender specific uses of 'man' and 'he'. In earlier ages the inclusive sense of 'man' (*homo, anthropos, 'adam*) was unquestioned both in principle and practice, and the widespread rejection of this inclusive sense is a novel development. But the Christian understanding of 'Bible' as Old and New Testament together has always coexisted with an alternative Jewish account. What is novel is for Christians (other than in exceptional cases) to take the alternative account with full seriousness.

Another point is that Barr appears to take for granted that the existence of 'the Bible' implies *expectations brought to the text*. In general cultural terms, there is an expectation that the biblical text (or at least parts of it) says something important and profound, deserving of serious study. In specific religious terms, there is an expectation that what the biblical text says is, or at least might be, a definitive truth about God and human life. These are both perfectly reasonable assumptions to make, and have been (and still are, though to a much lesser extent) widely made within Western civilization. They are assumptions which are made when the biblical text is read as a canonical collection in conjunction with its history of reception by Christians and Jews. Yet today there is a renewed questioning with regard to the Bible: why study these particular texts, and not others?[13] On the one hand, the sacred texts of many other religions are better known, and their adherents more socially visible. Why privilege Christian scripture rather than other scriptures, when these other scriptures also offer comprehensive accounts of human life and destiny? Why should any interpreters of the Bible suppose that they have arrived at 'the truth about God and human life' once they have got to the heart of the biblical text, in a way that they would not also suppose if they were studying, say, the Qur'an or the Bhagavad-Gita? On the other hand, why privilege *any* scriptures? Why not adopt a thoroughgoing secularist view that all scriptures are interesting texts of historic religious ideology, which have had a remarkable afterlife which still lingers today, but which intrinsically have no more merit than any other claim to truth? In the present cultural context, the question of why one should continue to attach special expectations to the study of the Bible needs to be specified rather than taken for granted.[14]

It is, of course, perfectly possible to formulate pragmatic and non-theological justifications for 'biblical studies'. One might, for example, straightforwardly accept a greatly diminished role for the discipline, within departments of ancient history, oriental studies, classics (or any other configuration of the study of ancient texts), where study of the language, history, and religion of ancient Israel and early Christianity takes its place alongside the study of other ancient cultures, with as much, or as little, assumption of continuing significance as characterizes the study of ancient Egypt, Mesopotamia, Greece, or Rome. Such texts, and related

13. Barr certainly raises the issue of 'Why the Bible?' in relation to contemporary cultural relativism (1973: 35–52), but generally tends not to give much space to the question.
14. I am indebted to the illuminating and incisive discussion of Levenson 1993b.

cultural artefacts, can be studied because they are there and because they are interesting.

But a more common move is to appeal to the notion of the Bible as a classic of Western culture, a collection whose meaning and significance can be considered in its own right, independently of the communities of faith which shaped it and constituted it as canonical and still regard it as such. Nonetheless, although there is an obvious sense in which the Bible can and does often function as such a classic of Western culture, a justification of its study on such terms may create its own problems in various ways. First, in a contemporary context the nature and status of all classics and 'literary canons' is a matter of debate because of a diminishing sense of common cultural identity and purpose; the Bible as classic, even as *the* classic of Western culture, is not exempt. Secondly, one obvious way of studying the Bible as classic is to study the history of its interpretation and usage – a kind of study which is indeed on the increase. But such a study would marginalize the kinds of questions which have in fact dominated modern biblical study, which have generally been to do with what the biblical texts 'really' mean, when read in their original languages and ancient context (before 'the Bible' as such ever existed). Study of the Bible as cultural classic would be quite different from study of the Bible as hitherto generally practised. That is not an argument against it, but an observation with more than marginal implications for the guild of biblical scholars as generally constituted at present.[15] Thirdly, if the Bible is studied as a religious classic (to try to do justice to its obvious central concern with God), how is this study to be carried out? That is, if readers become excited about the intrinsic depth and significance of these particular texts, what frameworks or discourses would there be to explore and render such significance in publicly meaningful terms? The obvious answer is – those of the Jewish and Christian faiths, which, in one sense, exist for this purpose. But if the point of reading the Bible as a classic is precisely to sever its links with the specific contexts of Jewish and Christian faiths, the exercise would become self-contradictory (or at least in need of major rethinking).

One likely move, therefore, (which anticipates our discussion of *The Postmodern Bible*) is to cease primarily to try to understand the content of the Bible in categories that enable its own voices to be heard, and instead to read it in terms of modern categories such as class, race,

---

15. For a nicely provocative essay along these lines, see Clines 1997.

gender.[16] But then it is unlikely that the Bible would appear other than as sadly deficient in comparison with prevalent and fashionable norms.[17] The idea that we the readers might be the deficient ones, and that we could learn and be changed through encounter with the truth about God and humanity within the Bible would no longer be on the agenda.[18] The Bible thus studied would be a simulacrum of the Bible which actually mattered to people. Or, in other words, 'the Bible' as classic is, in fact, not the same as 'the Bible' as holy scripture, for the assumptions that are brought to its study change the nature of the exercise.

If the study of the Bible is an issue, there are certain basic questions which must be addressed. Should one devote time, money, and energy to the Bible rather than some other sacred, classic, or significant text? If so, which Bible, and what kind of resources for what kind of study? And on what basis should all these be decided? These are not just issues in the continuing debate between secular academy and confessing institution.[19] They are issues within confessing institutions, where questions

16. The point of the argument is not to encourage a simplistic 'either-or', as though those who attend to categories important to the biblical writers should not also attend to categories of contemporary thought. It is in the engagement between differing perspectives that much interesting biblical interpretation arises. My concern is to try to articulate the logic of proposals and the likely direction in which they lead.

17. Clines 1993 is a striking programmatic essay along these lines.

18. This seems to be the general tenor of Clines 1995. Clines speaks of the importance of 'critique', or evaluation, of the biblical text as an ethical imperative. He says: ' "Critique" does not of course imply *negative* evaluation, but it does imply evaluation of the texts by a standard of reference outside themselves – which usually means, for practical purposes, by the standards to which we ourselves are committed . . . To evaluate the text according to our own best values, we have to read it as the people we are' (p. 20).

This interesting programme is in certain important respects a secularized counterpart to the programme I am proposing. But despite the disclaimer that critique is necessarily negative, negative critique is in fact the predominant thrust of Clines' essays, and religious language is only construed in literary and functionalist categories. I find it also striking that Clines takes 'our own best values' as (apparently) uncontroversial, needing neither analysis nor critique, at any rate not from the Bible. The possibility of transformation through the Bible is effectively ruled out of court.

19. Barr refers elsewhere to the fact that universities have often regarded biblical studies as more scientifically objective than theology. Theology has often been considered sectarian because churches insist on denominational theology (Anglican, Baptist, Catholic). Since the university could not be expected to judge between these, for 'it had no criteria for doing so', it followed that theology 'seemed to people to be non-scientific'. Critical biblical study, by contrast, was comparatively free from this weakness (1983: 113). This is fair comment. But once it is recognized that study of the Bible *qua* Bible is not a 'neutral' undertaking, the question of the criteria by which the discipline is constituted and recognized returns to the agenda.

Perhaps biblical and theological studies should seek to be regarded as disciplines like economics, where rival and sometimes irreconcilable schools of thought, contested implications for human priorities, failed predictions about the future, and extensive links with interested parties beyond the academy are not considered as disqualifying academic engagement with the subject.

about the role of the Bible are usually an integral element of larger debates about the nature of religious vocation and mission in the modern world. The fact that Barr can speak of the study of the Bible with only minimal reference to such issues is, among other things, suggestive of an individualistic understanding of the study of the Bible and theology; an individualism which can only flourish when certain corporate assumptions and structural decisions are so securely in place that the individual may be mistaken as to the real nature of the freedom which he, or she, enjoys.

In concluding this discussion of Barr, it may be instructive to note not dissimilar assumptions in the inaugural lecture of James Barr's successor but one, John Barton (1993). Barton reflects on the growing fragmentation of biblical study and considers that proposals 'for Old Testament study to be reunited with theology proper, reorientated towards religious faith and theological truth' (p. 6) may be likely to become an increasingly prevalent response to such fragmentation. This is not, however, something he applauds, even though his own self-understanding is as a theologian (p. 6). The basic reason for this is the principle of intellectual freedom which must be unconstrained by authority, so that it is free to ask whatever questions it likes and go wherever the evidence leads – which Barton expounds in terms characteristic of nineteenth-century debate (pp. 8–19).

Early in the lecture, in the context of various acknowledgements, Barton notes that

> the difficult times in which we live might well have resulted in a long vacancy in the Chair, had it not been for the generosity of Sir Kirby Laing. Many will know, from the news of other benefactions to Theology in Edinburgh and Aberdeen, that Sir Kirby is not among those who consider the study of theology, or of the Bible, a waste of time. . . . My own gratitude, as the first Oriel *and Laing* Professor, can hardly be disinterested, but it is certainly heartfelt. (p. 3)

It is revealing that Barton draws no links between the benefaction and his vision of the discipline. Sir Kirby Laing was a successful businessman of strong Christian (Methodist) conviction, who secured the endowment of the Oriel Chair because he saw it as a contribution to Christian faith and theology. Anyone can study the biblical texts as they will. But one cannot expect institutional space, time, and money to be devoted to such study unless it is funded and is considered appropriate (not 'a waste of time'). In this instance the Chair is still there because Sir Kirby Laing affirmed the traditional Christian understanding of the Old Testament as integral to Christian faith and theology, and Oxford university was happy to recognize this affirmation (some others might not). Barton expounds a curiously individualistic account of intellectual freedom which ignores both its public embodiment (in this particular case, in terms of continuing recognition of the institutional shape of Christian theology) and its responsibilities (in terms of contributing to the study of the Old Testament specifically as part of Christian theology).

We have argued thus far that Barr's discussion of the Bible and theology takes for granted assumptions and structures which are in fact open to contest, and contested, and that explicit recognition would change the nature of the debate. We turn now to the essay by Barrett.

### C. K. Barrett, 'What is New Testament theology?'[20]

#### (1) Exposition

After a brief personal note, mentioning his life-long fascination with New Testament theology and the fact that he lectured on it for many years, Barrett says that it is only recently that he has come to ask the question 'what New Testament theology is'.[21] His concern is to reflect on the nature of the discipline as it actually exists and as he knows and practises it, rather than to ask more fundamental questions about the justification of such a discipline in the first place.[22] Nonetheless his account may not improperly be considered from an angle different to that with which he wrote.

A brief historical sketch yields three possible conceptions of New Testament theology (1995a: 243). First, there is a classic patristic, medieval, and Reformation understanding of the New Testament as a basis for Christian theology as a whole ('New Testament theology is the foundation of dogmatics'), through reformulation of its content in whatever way is most appropriate. Secondly, there is an Enlightenment discontent with the cobwebs of dogma which sought freedom and purity in 'back to Jesus' and 'back to the theology of the Bible'; New Testament theology is thus an escape from Christian dogma, though forms of Christian faith may still be presupposed. Thirdly, there is an Enlightenment historical awareness which made possible New Testament theology as an independent historical discipline, with no necessary links with what followed after, where

---

20. Barrett 1995a.
21. Barrett describes his essay as 'no more than a preliminary attempt to answer the question at the head of the paper' (p. 253).
22. Prof. Barrett particularly emphasized this in conversation with me.

Christian faith and dogma may simply be ignored. Barrett then comments, 'I see no reason why any of these propositions should be taken to represent the whole truth to the exclusion of the other two' (p. 244). This sets the context for all that follows.

Barrett sees New Testament theology as 'generated internally' by the very act of rigorous study of the New Testament. In expounding Hoskyns and Davey, but apparently also expressing his own view, he says:

> The core of the New Testament is not a religious experience but a historical event; but this event is such that the critical study of it generates theology. The historian begins by asserting the crown rights of his own subject: history is and must be independent, and the historian serves but one mistress. Yet precisely in practising his own trade as a historian he finds that he becomes, whether he will or no, a theologian. (p. 244)

Barrett is aware of the problem, classically expressed by Wrede, that once New Testament theology is conceived as an independent historical discipline, then questions of Christian faith and theology (dogmatics and systematics) may become simply irrelevant. But the problem does not greatly concern him because he is convinced that, even though 'it is of primary importance that New Testament theology should retain full independence as a critical historical process' (p. 244) the relationship with Christian theology may be retained through the intrinsic nature of the subject matter.

Barrett develops his main observations about New Testament theology through reflecting on facets of the notion of 'process', based on the historical span of events within the New Testament. On the one hand the relationship between Jesus and the primitive church is seen in terms of continuity through change (Last Supper and Lord's Supper; the gospel message of Jesus in the light of the resurrection) in such a way as to suggest that 'the task of New Testament theology is . . . to relate all parts of the New Testament to its [the New Testament's] centre, and to interpret them in the light of that centre', that centre being 'justification by faith (*sola fide*), and Jesus crucified and risen (*solus Christus*)', which 'are if not identical at least so closely related as to be indivisible' (p. 250). On the other hand the conflicts within the primitive church show theology to be a 'critical' enterprise in which patterns of thought are subjected to examination and sometimes rejection, while the diversity of thought contained within the books of the New Testament show that theology can be neither static nor monochrome.

In sum, 'the New Testament theologian traces the development of Christian thought from its origins – or presuppositions – in the ministry of Jesus through a variety of religious and intellectual contexts' (which means that in a book on New Testament theology a historically developmental account is 'correct', while a topical arrangement is 'wrong', p. 253). The purpose underlying all this is 'to liberate the contents of the New Testament from their original setting that they may be made intelligible and thus applied in a new one – or rather in an indefinite number of new ones' (p. 247).

### (2) Critique

There is much in Barrett's account with which I would not disagree. And rather than focussing on particular points of difference, I wish again to focus rather on what Barrett does not say, what he takes for granted. Much of what was said above about Barr's question-begging use of 'the Bible' could apply equally to Barrett's use of 'the New Testament', but a different tack may offer more progress.

This may be approached through Barr's distinction between two senses of the term 'theology': between confessing statements about God – statements which are truth claiming – and descriptive statements about what the biblical writers said about God – statements which may be indifferent (or positive, or hostile) to the truth of what they describe. Barrett offers no such distinction, and does not see 'theology' as in itself a problematic term needing definition; for in practice he moves freely between descriptive and confessing senses (in line with much historic Christian practice).

That 'truth' (not just about the facts of ancient history and the beliefs of ancient people, but about God and humanity both then and now) is what the New Testament gives is not in doubt for Barrett. Although he recognizes it as a contestable position – the death and resurrection of Jesus 'is the great watershed which, *on the Christian view*, divides all history in two' (p. 247, my italics) – his general stance is clear, and sometimes emerges in particular wording. For example, '[Paul] was constantly at work establishing truth over against what he took to be error' (p. 251) – not the strictly descriptive 'what he took to be truth' but the confessing 'truth'. That is, Barrett comes to the New Testament as a Christian. He comes with the expectation of finding truth, and that expectation is not disappointed (although he is of course at pains to stress that the process is more complicated than sometimes supposed).

It is interesting, therefore, that nowhere in Barrett's account is anything said about Christian faith as a prerequisite for doing New Testament theology. Even at the point where one might most expect it, there is silence. Barrett distinguishes himself from Wrede's *religionsgeschichtlich* approach (i.e. descriptive religious history) solely by appeal to the content of the New Testament as intrinsically theological ('a historian finds that he becomes, whether he will or no, a theologian'). But would Wrede (or perhaps, more recently, Räisänen (1990)) be persuaded? Might he not respond that there is indeed great diversity, complexity, development, and so on, in the religious thought of these particular texts, and that to understand them the scholar must therefore have familiarity and empathy with such religious material – but that what that shows is that one must be a good religious historian, and that *Religionsgeschichte* is a demanding task?

To put it differently, Barrett surely equivocates about the meaning of 'theology' at the key point, introducing unjustifiably (in terms of his argument) two confessing notions: both the placement of the New Testament documents as a canonical collection within the wider context of Christian theology, and assent to the truth-claims of the text. He assumes that it is the task of New Testament theology to describe and analyse the content of the New Testament *in order that* it may be 'liberated' and transferred to new contexts (i.e. related to the continuing life of the Christian Church). But why should one make that assumption, or analyse the text with that purpose, unless one is a Christian? Barrett clearly does not think that study of the New Testament necessarily entails assent to what the New Testament says (though of course it may lead to such assent), yet he defines the academic discipline of New Testament theology in such a way that only someone who does assent to the New Testament is likely to practise it. Christian faith is thus integral to the discipline as defined, yet is nowhere included within the definition.

Is there not here, in a way similar to in Barr, an implicit and confusing individualism with regard to the meaning both of 'faith' and of 'theology'? That is, it appears that 'faith' is seen primarily as a possible, indeed desirable, attribute of an individual scholar, such as Barrett himself; but it is not seen as a necessary attribute, for the discipline of New Testament study is defined as 'history', whose study is open to anyone. That 'faith' might also be a matter of the public assumptions and structures which enable particular texts to be construed as New Testament, and which enable study of the New Testament as 'theology' to be undertaken at all, is nowhere in view, even though this is what Barrett's account in fact entails.

There are thus important similarities between Barr and Barrett amidst their differences. Barr sees the Church and theology as possible and legitimate, yet optional, contexts for the study of the Bible; the Bible can be studied perfectly well on its own. Barrett sees theology and the life of the Church as intrinsic to the study of New Testament theology, yet offers no satisfactory account as to why this should be so. For his definition of the discipline invokes nothing beyond the New Testament text and seems to suppose that biblical study stands on its own feet; and the fact of the compilation of the documents within the New Testament as a canonical collection, with the particular expectations this generates, is entirely taken for granted and not deemed a necessary subject of reflection. Neither Barr nor Barrett makes explicit that his subject of study – the Bible as Old and New Testaments together or solely the New Testament – is a confessing construct; and so they do not reflect upon what that might entail for their disciplines.

### The question of religious truth within the accounts of Barr and Barrett

The question of truth about God and human life, which in general terms is raised as an expectation by the status of the biblical texts as holy scripture (and is part of the common connotations of 'Bible'), deserves further reflection. Both Barr and Barrett recognize that Christian theology is concerned with questions of truth, and that Christian accounts of truth are inseparable from the Bible. But neither of them engages with the extraordinarily difficult question of what is necessary for truth in religious language to be a meaningful and valid concept. (This conceptual issue is of course distinct from apologetics, although the two may easily merge.) Their silence here is again, I think, revealing.

Barr sees that theology (in its strict, i.e. confessing, sense) 'is not merely an interpretation of evidence: its logic is not exhaustively explained by stating the evidence to which it may relate itself' and that it 'makes assertions about the divine' (1980: 22). But beyond observing that concern with theology may bring into the agenda of biblical study 'even if only as a hypothesis' the question 'how would it be if this were really true of God?' (p. 25) he says nothing whatever (except implicitly in terms of an individual's empathy and presuppositions, whose role he downplays) about the kind of criteria and conditions that might be necessary for such a question to receive a responsible affirmative answer.

It is then revealing that at the end of his essay the one example he cites to illustrate lively dialogue between theological and non-theological interpretation of the Bible – 'the question of the integration of scripture as a theological whole, the problem of how it can be understood to hang together as a meaningful totality' (pp. 28–9) – is used solely to reiterate the point that the 'viability' of theological proposals 'never rests upon theological considerations alone, but rests on the data of the [linguistic and historical] levels where it is subject to non-theological control'. Thus traditional models for understanding scripture as a whole 'are not validated by the fact that they come out of [the church's] tradition: they are validated by the degree to which they make sense of the evidence that exists, evidence which has already been classified and to some degree interpreted on other levels of the total process of study' (p. 29). Not only, as already noted, does Barr simply assume that it is the Christian canon of Old and New Testaments together that poses the problem, he also regards the decisive factor, the 'control', as 'the interpretation of given evidence', that is, that which he has defined in terms of descriptive, non-confessing, statements.

Thus it would appear that questions of truth are questions of scientific study of language and history, upon which foundation, if properly laid, confessing theology may advance its own proposals. According to Barr, the intrinsically confessing issue – the coherence of Old and New Testaments as Christian scripture, which presupposes the key role in some way of Jesus Christ in the understanding of God and of human nature and destiny – is indeed 'not merely an interpretation of evidence'. But in so far as the question of the truth of the confession is raised, it is evidence of a linguistic and historical kind which must apparently be decisive; the alternative to this – 'rest[ing] upon theological considerations alone' – is left unexplained (but what does it really mean, and does anyone in fact advocate it?). Neither decisions concerning the constituting of texts as scripture, nor questions about the adequacy of the interpreter's categories of understanding, are apparently considered comparably significant.

Barrett differs from Barr in his interest explicitly to make the New Testament text available for Christian theologians to restate and apply it. Yet, for reasons already given, it is unclear how far his construal of the relationship between Bible and theology differs from that of Barr. His rhetoric about the discipline of New Testament theology as being first and foremost a 'critical historical process' which should retain 'full independence' (1995a: 244) is presumably directed against the skewing prejudices of confessing theology as that from which history should be independent.

Barrett does not discuss 'truth' as such, but we have already seen that this is what he finds in the New Testament. In so far as he specifies the content of this truth, it is found in his discussion of the centre of the New Testament, to which all the parts must be related by the New Testament theologian: that is 'justification by faith (*sola fide*), and Jesus crucified and risen (*solus Christus*)', which 'are if not identical at least so closely related as to be indivisible' (p. 250). Even if one accepts that it is the case that these two notions (if that is the right term) are indeed central to what the New Testament says – though a theological shorthand about the New Testament which does not mention God at all is surely too short – the further question arises: how can one know that what the New Testament says is true? What is necessary so that *sola fide* and *solus Christus* might represent a truth about God and humanity valid for today? A question about the conditions necessary for the affirmation of religious truth does not need (apparently) to concern the New Testament theologian.[23]

It becomes clear, therefore, that the kind of agenda which Barr and Barrett take for granted has striking omissions.[24] Barr recognizes the question of truth in relation to God as a genuine issue, but then either marginalizes it or offers an account in terms of language and history which seriously diminishes its scope.[25] Barrett does not doubt that truth is at stake, and that this includes human responsiveness in terms of the obedience of faith; but his depiction of the discipline of New Testament theology as essentially 'historical', and his account of the centre of the New Testament which does not even mention God, fails to provide those

---

23. Although Barrett nowhere explicitly addresses this question, some elements of a possible account are scattered through the essay, and through another related essay (Barrett 1995b).

24. Another recent example, unusual perhaps for its candour, is the observation of Rex Mason about the task of scholarly interpretation of the Old Testament (offered in the context of a discussion of Amos and prophecy): 'Strictly speaking, it is the Old Testament scholar's brief to try to explain as well as he or she can just what he thinks the biblical author is saying . . . If we go on to ask, "Does what the biblical writer is saying here make any sense?", or "Is there any way it can possibly be relevant or even 'true' for later times?", the scholar is no more equipped than anyone else to answer' (1997: 107–8).

25. In his recent study (Barr 1999), Barr argues that questions of religious truth are the responsibility of the doctrinal, rather than biblical, theologian. How doctrinal theologians might rightly carry out that task is not discussed.

elements which would enable coherent discussion as to how the religious history within the New Testament may, or may not, offer truth in relation to God. The classic protocols for speech about God have so thoroughly disappeared from view that their absence is no longer noticed.

### The 'Introduction' to *The Postmodern Bible* by The Bible and Culture Collective[26]

#### (1) Exposition

Before proceeding further it will be valuable to consider a new paradigm for biblical study and to ask how far a 'postmodern' approach to the Bible and theology constructively addresses some of the problems we have thus far encountered.

The volume *The Postmodern Bible* offers a guide to, and appraisal of, the various methods, theories and practices of biblical criticism which have flourished in recent years and which qualify for the label 'postmodern'.[27] The stance of the writers themselves is postmodern, in that, while they often take issue with the work they report, they nonetheless identify with, and consistently promote, the general tenor of postmodern ideology. Although none of the writers are yet of the stature of Barr or Barrett, their opening chapter, which introduces the volume and sets out their concerns in general terms, is one of the most succinct statements of a wide-ranging postmodern ideological perspective in relation to biblical interpretation of which I am aware.

The Collective describe their basic concern as being 'to understand the influence of the Bible on Western culture' (1995: 1), and they write for people in both academic and non-academic contexts who are 'interested in the compelling and contentious effects of the Bible on culture' (p. 8), with a view to the question: 'What might an engaged reader need to know in order to make sense of the Bible in relation to contemporary culture?' (p. 8). They are thus critical of 'the dominant methodologies of historical criticism' on the grounds that they sever study of the Bible from this contemporary context: 'The pervasive modern emphasis on the objective

---

26. Bible and Culture Collective 1995. The members of the Collective who jointly wrote the book are: George Aichele, Fred W. Burnett, Elizabeth A. Castelli (editor), Robert M. Fowler, David Jobling, Stephen D. Moore (editor), Gary A. Phillips (editor), Tina Pippin, Regina M. Schwartz (editor), Wilhelm Wuellner.

27. The seven chapter headings are: Reader-Response Criticism, Structuralist and Narratological Criticism, Poststructuralist Criticism, Rhetorical Criticism, Psychoanalytic Criticism, Feminist and Womanist Criticism, Ideological Criticism.

recovery of the ancient context in which biblical texts were produced has had the double effect of obscuring the significance of the Bible in contemporary Western culture and of turning the Bible into an historical relic, an antiquarian artifact' (p. 2).

Corresponding to this, biblical scholarship has 'left unexamined its own critical and theoretical assumptions as well as the cultural conditions that produced, sustained, and validated them' (p. 2). It is these two conditions that the Collective wish to change, in a process of *aggiornamento* that would bring biblical study back into vital engagement with the issues of the contemporary world. Thus:

> We are arguing for a *transformed* biblical criticism, one that would recognize that our cultural context is marked by aesthetics, epistemologies, and politics quite different from those reigning in eighteenth- and nineteenth-century Europe where traditional biblical scholarship is so thoroughly rooted. We are also arguing for a *transforming* biblical criticism, one that undertakes to understand the ongoing impact of the Bible on culture and one that, therefore, benefits from the rich resources of contemporary thought on language, epistemology, method, rhetoric, power, reading, as well as the pressing and often contentious political questions of 'difference' – gender, race, class, sexuality and, indeed, religion – which have come to occupy center stage in discourses both public and academic. In short, we hope in this volume to contribute to the process of bringing biblical scholarship into meaningful and ongoing engagement with the political, cultural, and epistemological critiques that have emerged 'in modernity's wake' (Phillipson) and that have proved so fruitful in other literary studies and cultural criticism. (p. 2)

Such postmodernity is not a rejection of modernity. Rather it presupposes modernity and so develops it as to make the insights of modernity self-aware and self-reflexive in a way they have not been before. It is 'a direct consequence of the intensification of those very aspects of critical self-consciousness that were prominent in the birth of modern scientific study of the Bible', with the consequence that 'both the postmodern and the modern share common cause in reaction to the grip of an uncritical premodern tradition' (p. 13). Postmodernity is 'modernity coming of age' (p. 3). What does this coming of age entail? It is a loss of innocence – not of an actual innocence, but a supposed innocence, a false assumption that either the Bible or its study (or anything else) could be exempted from questions of power. Since power tries to disguise itself, some iconoclasm is necessary in order to demonstrate what is really going on:

> The various critical stances brought together here under the sign
> 'postmodernism', for all their differences, *share a suspicion of the claim to
> mastery* that characterizes traditional readings of texts, including
> modern biblical scholarship. This suspicion is at once epistemological
> and political. That is, by sweeping away secure notions of meaning, by
> radically calling into question the apparently stable foundations of
> meaning on which traditional interpretation is situated, by raising
> doubts about the capacity to achieve ultimate clarity about the
> meaning of a text, *postmodern readings lay bare the contingent and
> constructed character of meaning itself.* Moreover, by challenging
> traditional interpretations that claim universality, completeness, and
> supremacy over other interpretations, *postmodern readings demonstrate
> that traditional interpretations are themselves enactments of domination or, in
> simpler terms, power plays.* (p. 3; my italics)

Such an agenda is in no way politically, socially, or ethically neutral. Quite
the contrary: it represents an engagement with the Bible and the contemporary world that has definite goals in view. In general terms, these goals
are the promotion of 'self-reflexivity, heterogeneity, contingency and difference' (p. 12). More specifically, the Collective envisage 'the radical
recasting of the premises and practices of biblical interpretation' which
have shown 'complicity in the establishment and maintenance of the
Bible's cultural power' (p. 4), and this for one basic reason:

> To read the Bible in the traditional, scholarly manner has all too often
> meant reading it, whether deliberately or not, in ways that reify and
> ratify the status quo – providing warrant for the subjugation of
> women (whether in the church, the academy, or society at large),
> justifying colonialism and enslavement, rationalizing homophobia, or
> otherwise legitimating the power of hegemonic classes of people. (p. 4)

To sum up, traditional biblical criticism has been characterized by ideological conservatism, with regard both to the Bible and to the contexts of
its study: 'So far, with few exceptions, the vast majority of biblical critics
have been slow to read against the grain of the biblical texts and the institution of traditional biblical scholarship, and they have generally been
content to re-enact the ideologies inscribed in their respective narratives
and meta-narratives' (p. 15). By contrast, 'We are certain that the future of
biblical criticism hinges squarely on its ability and willingness to make
gender, race, ideology, and institutional power substantive concerns –
which means a change in institutional structures, discourses and practices' (p. 15). It is thus in reaction to unself-reflexive and exclusive ideological stances that *The Postmodern Bible* has been written:

We wrote out of concern about systems of power – institutional, ecclesiastical, cultural – that authorize or block what can be said or written about the Bible. We wrote out of concern about the politics of inclusion and exclusion that determine whose reading of the Bible counts, whose does not, and why. We wrote eager to see explicit acknowledgments of ethical stances, ideological positionings, self-critical and self-reflexive consciousness, and affirmations of the positive values of difference and multiplicity. Most important, we wrote out of a concern to make sense of the Bible in a cultural context for which there can be no detailed, comprehensive, or fully accurate road map (p. 15).

The introduction ends with an account of how valuable it was for the different writers to work together as a group – to discover unity in diversity, to generate trust and friendships, to discover ways of working which were so much more fruitful than the 'isolationist' and 'individualistic' models of scholarship that they had inherited (p. 18). Thus their own experiences in writing the book were a preliminary embodiment of the fresh approach to scholarship which they advocate.

### (2) Critique

The Collective offer a striking vision of biblical study which, when set alongside the essays of Barr and Barrett, shows clearly the changing and diversifying nature of contemporary scholarship. In so far as study of the Bible does engage with prevalent agendas of the early twenty-first century, the Collective no doubt give a good idea of the shape of many things to come. Moreover some of their key terms – contemporary context, transforming criticism, engaged reader – are those which are important for my own argument. However, as noted above, although the self-reflexive move in contemporary hermeneutics helps create space for the recovery of a more robust and integrated account of the Bible in relation to Christian faith and theology, it has agendas of its own which may move in more or less different directions from those of Christian faith.

Although the Collective present their argument with the kind of confidence of those who are doing something self-evidently correct (with a certain sense, no doubt not unjustified, of 'the tide of history is with us'), it is important to probe a little as to what their own account and vision of the discipline really entails.

First, how accurate is the picture of 'traditional biblical scholarship' against which they react? The idea that mainstream scholarship may reduce the Bible to 'an historical relic, an antiquarian artifact' has in fact

been a recurrent concern more or less since the inception of modern critical historiography on the part of many of its practitioners. To be sure, a
perusal of the tables of contents in some of the leading scholarly journals
could well give an antiquarian impression. But it is not an impression one
gets from any of the giants of the discipline, from a Bultmann or a von
Rad (who are unrecognizable in the Collective's picture), nor from such
distinguished contemporary scholars as Barr or Barrett. These scholars
may have unresolved problems and oversights in their work but a sharp
isolation of the biblical text from contemporary concerns is not characteristic of any of them (in their different ways).

Or consider the words with which Harnack prefaces his *History of
Dogma*, words which he would have applied equally to the study of the
Bible:

> In taking up a theological book we are in the habit of enquiring first of
> all as to the 'stand-point' of the Author. In a historical work there is no
> room for such enquiry. The question here is, whether the Author is in
> sympathy with the subject about which he writes, whether he can
> distinguish original elements from those that are derived, whether he
> has a thorough acquaintance with his material, whether he is
> conscious of the limits of historical knowledge, and whether he is
> truthful. These requirements constitute the categorical imperative for
> the historian: but they can only be fulfilled by an unwearied self-
> discipline. Hence every historical study is an ethical task. The historian
> ought to be faithful in every sense of the word; whether he has been so
> or not is the question on which his readers have to decide. (1905: vii-
> viii)

Harnack's words surely qualify as a prime example of that supposed, but
unreal, innocence which so much recent hermeneutical work has made
problematic and against which the Collective inveigh. But anyone familiar with Barth's critique of Harnack will know that perception of the
problematic nature of Harnack's stance is not a recent perception[28]
(which usefully reminds us that Barth's sense of the shortcomings of
much modern criticism anticipated important aspects of 'postmodern'
concern, though Barth receives no mention whatever in *The Postmodern
Bible*).[29] Moreover, whatever criticisms may properly be made of Harnack,

---

28. See conveniently Rumscheidt 1972.
29. As Robert Jenson (1997: 22) puts it: 'Indeed, if there is such a thing as "postmodernism",
Barth is its only major theological representative so far, for his work is an attempt not only
to transcend the Enlightenment but to transcend nineteenth-century Protestantism's way
of doing the same.'

one can hardly fail to respect his sense of the highly demanding nature of the historical study of ancient texts as a truth-requiring and truth-seeking activity. Rhetorical dismissal of this on suspicious grounds, that it is essentially 'enactment of domination' or 'power play', simply invites an equally suspicious rejoinder that those who speak thus have themselves never mastered the disciplines necessary for reading ancient texts with accuracy and insight.

The fact, therefore, that the Collective take 'traditional biblical scholarship' as something homogeneous and undifferentiated, whose defects are so obvious that they have only to be asserted, needing neither argument nor analysis in detail, does not command confidence. Likewise, it is regrettable that the Collective continue to propagate one of the more questionable aspects of modern biblical criticism's own conventional self-understanding, that they, like it, 'share common cause in reaction to the grip of an uncritical premodern tradition'. When people say things like that, one wonders how much premodern biblical interpretation they have actually read.[30] Premodern interpretation was as critical, or uncritical (depending on whom you read), as modern or postmodern interpretation. The difference is constituted by the issues that people were critically interested in, and the criteria of critical evaluation that they employed. Those who have actually studied biblical commentators such as Rashi or Calvin may find many things with which to take issue, but their being 'uncritical' is unlikely to be one of them. Failure to recognize this suggests that the Collective are not well grounded in the history of biblical interpretation and that their poorly founded assertions about it do not display those qualities such as heterogeneity and difference which they advocate. As so many before them, in order to gain space for themselves, they misrepresent what they disagree with.

Secondly, the Collective, no less than Barr, take 'the Bible' as something self-evident. Neither in the introduction, nor anywhere else in the book, do they ever refer to the fact of the Church's (or Synagogue's) decision to constitute the various documents of the Bible as one book, or the contested nature of this decision,[31] despite the fact that engagement with

---

30. One might compare C. H. Dodd's famous and influential depiction of traditional, premodern parable interpretation as allegorical in the mode of Augustine's interpretation of the parable of the Good Samaritan (1935: 1–2). This must be one of the most inaccurate and irresponsible things Dodd ever wrote, and it reveals only his own failure to study the history of parable interpretation.

31. There is a passing reference (1995: 240) to the question of the Bible in relation to Jewish and Christian identity, but nothing more.

such issues would seem an obvious element in a more self-aware, self-reflexive engagement with the Bible which attends to 'the constructed character of meaning'.[32] The reason for this appears to lie in the nature of their interest in the significance of the Bible within contemporary culture. Their interest appears to be solely with the Bible as a cultural fact (in terms of my earlier discussion, a 'classic'), where the issue is not, as for Christian (or Jewish) scholars, to understand and promote the Bible's significance in responsible ways and seek to correct its misuse; rather, the issue is to understand that significance as an exercise of power play on the part of some at the expense of others, so that one can appropriately combat and diminish it. What the Bible actually is as a canon of religious texts, and what its moral and religious meaning might really be, does not appear to matter so much any more (and even to express matters in this way may be seen as part of the problem).[33] What matters is understanding contemporary culture and participating in the contemporary cultural struggle, in which the Bible has continuing and problematic significance and where postmodern perspectives offer the best way of diminishing the Bible's baneful effects.

In this context it is worth looking again at one of the passages cited above, where traditional scholarship was castigated for reifying and ratifying the status quo and 'providing warrant for the subjugation of women ... justifying colonialism and enslavement, rationalizing homophobia, or otherwise legitimating the power of hegemonic classes of people' (1995: 4). To uphold the status quo is, apparently, problematic. It is notable that, elsewhere in the book, to call a position 'conservative' is deemed thereby to demonstrate its inadequacy.[34] Why should this be so? Because of four consequences of such conservatism: two of these are readily recognizable as major contemporary social issues, the position of women, and the recognition of gays and lesbians; the other two categories

32. The Collective say: 'Those of us who teach biblical literature are perhaps a step removed from the academic "canon wars" that have been raging in institutions of higher learning. We are not called upon to defend *what* we teach – the most canonical of Western literature – but the question of *how* we teach it has become a highly contentious one' (1995: 268). It is remarkable that they think it possible neatly to separate the what and the how in this way.
33. Mieke Bal is introduced as 'paradigmatic for postmodern biblical criticism' (1995: 255). In her own words, she is not at all interested in 'attribut[ing] moral, religious, or political authority to these [sc. biblical] texts'. Rather, 'it is the cultural function of one of the most influential mythical and literary documents of our culture that I discuss, as a strong representative instance of what language and literature can do to a culture, specifically to its articulation of gender' (p. 255, citing Bal 1987: 1).
34. See the criticisms of Daniel Patte, 1995: 113–15, and the introduction to the section on p. 110.

seem to me mere rhetoric, unless they are codes which I do not recognize. For who, at the present time, is justifying colonialism and enslavement, and using the Bible to promote such justification? There have been such debates in the past, with the Bible used on both sides; but at least in the case of slavery, the biblical argument against slavery was considered stronger than the argument for its retention, and this was a factor in abolition (see Swartley 1983: ch. 1). As for 'legitimating the power of hegemonic classes of people', I simply do not know to whom this refers, or why such a sweeping generalization, which marginalizes the question of whether or not people have exercised power responsibly and in the service of others, should be taken seriously.

All the language about 'transformation' and 'engagement' therefore apparently means engagement in a socio-political struggle to bring about a transformation of those elements in society (particularly affecting women and those sexually attracted to others of the same sex) which the writers consider problematic. Since traditional interpretation of the Bible does not promote this struggle, it needs to be replaced by interpretative stances that 'read against the grain' and do promote it. The question of what the Bible really implies in these areas is greatly exercising many Jews and Christians at present, as they seek to discern the implications of God's self-revelation in social contexts different to any encountered previously in history, where discernment of the strengths and weaknesses of those changing social circumstances is itself a demanding task.[35] The Collective's construal of the issues in terms of a rhetoric of suspicion and change in which conservatism is a mistake – as though it were somehow self-evident that there is no wisdom to be gained from the past, no practice of life or institution worth conserving – is a narrowly one-sided contribution to difficult debates. This is not to deny that there are hard contemporary social issues, in which the role of the Bible may be problematic, and in which Jews and Christians may need to relearn their own vocation not least through attending to criticism from those who do not share their faith. But it is to question both whether the shape of desirable

---

35. For example, the changing role of women, many of whose benefits are not to be gainsaid, has been accompanied by a profound problematizing of the nature and role of the family and of the upbringing and formation of children. Likewise contemporary problems of gender identity and sexual practices are probably inseparable from an atomizing of personal identity in fluid social contexts. If the churches are often slow to embrace these changes, it is not simply because of being instinctively reactionary (though no doubt this is often an element), but because of a sense that some social changes may diminish human life and that particular changes need to be evaluated in a less individualistic way than is sometimes proposed.

change is as self-evident as the Collective imply and whether the role of
the Bible in all this is necessarily negative unless it is systematically construed 'against the grain'.

Thirdly, it is remarkable (though consistent with the above) that the
question of God features nowhere in the introduction, nor in the rest of
the book; and, correspondingly, the question of human response to God –
'faith' – is nowhere discussed. If, of course, one knows in advance that all
human religion and biblical interpretation is nothing more than power
plays, sometimes in elaborate disguise, then such an exclusion might perhaps be justifiable. But how do the Collective know? In particular, they do
not even mention, let alone discuss, a classic Christian (or Jewish) understanding – that the Bible gives access to the mind of God, and that to
engage with the Bible and God responsibly requires radical transformation and reorientation of human life towards (in convenient shorthand)
faith, hope, and love, and that this is a process in which critical confrontation with human tendencies to manipulative self-will is a constant and
central element. If they wholly ignore all this, how can their readers know
that they know what they are (not) talking about?

One can approach this general issue differently by observing that,
while the Collective say much about suspicion and power, they say nothing about truth. Why such an omission? If their claim is to have discov-
ered that 'truth' does not really exist, and that whatever people hold to be
true they hold only because their notions of coherence and rationality are
dictated by people in power (and that therefore notions of truth only
change as those in power change), then the claim is both false (for notions
of true and false are intrinsic to human thought and language) and useless (for if it applies to everything without exception – which must
include also the claim that this is the case – then it is no help in the urgent
practical task of distinguishing those who are more trustworthy and cred-
ible from those who are less so). If their position is that questions of truth
cannot be separated from considerations as to how that truth is used, and
that use of truth is not only something public and political but also regularly manipulative, then it makes some sense. But then it invites engagement with the characteristic biblical insight that truth is moral as well as
intellectual, and that self-serving attitudes can turn even that which in
itself might be true into something that is false.[36] For Christians have

36. A classic example is Jeremiah 7:4 within the context of 7:1–15. Although there was an
obvious sense in which it was perfectly true that the building in question was the temple of
YHWH, Jeremiah does not hesitate to designate the people's words as *sheqer* – 'false',
'deceptive' – because of the morally complacent and self-serving way in which they were
being used.

generally supposed the Bible to be significant precisely because it enables engagement with a truth about God and humanity that can transform human life from the deceptions of self-will and manipulation into what it should be. That this may be a demanding process, which is easily derailed, does not mean that it is not a genuine process or that the substantial body of life and thought which has accumulated over the centuries in relation to this process need not be taken seriously in the changing situations of today.

In this regard, it is interesting that the one place where some of the traditional language of faith appears is in the section on the experiences of the writers in coming together as the 'Bible and Culture Collective' (pp. 15–19). It is an account with many of the elements that characterize the testimonies of religious groups (albeit here secularized) – mutuality and support, acceptance, trust, confession, conversion, belief, new identity in a supportive group, liberation rather than suppression in corporate identity, the inadequacy of previous patterns of life, the lack of understanding among others who have not shared the experience. The human value of this cannot be gainsaid. But it is revealing that, although it takes place in the context of the study of the Bible, it takes place with no reference to the content of the Bible, or engagement with God through that. Nor do those who shared the experience show recognition that theirs is the kind of experience that characterizes many who come to study the Bible within the context of Christian faith and theology, and who, not least because of such experience, are reluctant to suppose that the Bible is primarily a tool of oppression (however often it may be used thus).

Although the Collective say they seek to overcome exclusions, it appears that in practice their ignoring of the concerns of Christian and Jewish faith performs precisely the function of marginalizing such concerns in favour of a wholly secularized agenda. Theirs is an exercise in persuasive definition, which replicates the kind of exclusion it castigates. I see no reason why modernity's becoming appropriately self-reflexive should solely take place within the categories that the Collective use (even though, of course, they are important categories and are characteristic of much debate), for those categories may beg the question as to what matters most. If one learns to take God seriously things may look different. A move towards postmodernity looks rather different if, for example, Kierkegaard or Dostoyevsky or Barth (who are not even mentioned, let alone discussed),[37] are sources of insight; or if the work of

---

37. The one qualification to this is that there is a passing reference to Dostoyevsky on p. 94, but one without significance for the discussion.

other contemporary thinkers who are seeking constructive alternatives to modernity, such as Alasdair MacIntyre (unmentioned) or Paul Ricoeur (mentioned three times in passing, but entirely undiscussed), features on the agenda. Likewise, a postmodernity that is determined still to engage with and learn from the best in both modernity and premodernity will look different from one that supposes that the concerns of the present time constitute sufficient subject matter.

I agree with the Collective that it is vital to relate the study of the Bible to contemporary concerns. But, pressing as are the many seemingly intractable problems of our world, it remains important to address issues whose immediate 'relevance' may be less obvious, but which nonetheless underlie regular life. Such issues are in essence to do with the nature and meaning of human life – what does it mean to be a human being, and what counts as living life well? In the Bible, and in Jewish and Christian faiths, this kind of question cannot be addressed without reference to God, for it is fundamental that human beings are 'in the image of God'. One of the consequences of people generally ceasing to believe in God (as classically understood by Jews and Christians, also Muslims) is that their understanding of what it means to be human inexorably changes also. The question of what it means to be human cannot solely be resolved by a religious perspective. Yet one should at least be aware what such a perspective might have to contribute.

For example, it is well known that from the perspective of Christian faith sin is an inescapable part of the human condition, and that realistic attempts to improve human life need to take sin seriously. Yet what concern for sin might mean, other than an individual morality and piety (which can easily turn in upon itself to become individualistic moralism and pietism) which addresses none of the bigger concerns of justice, peace, and the environment, is often far from obvious. It is interesting, therefore, in this context, that there is a renewed interest among some theologians in the ancient biblical category of idolatry. What idolatry might mean, as a particular focussing of sin, is well set out by Nicholas Lash, from whose recent extensive discussion I take two brief excerpts:

> It is taken for granted, in sophisticated circles, that no one worships God these days except the reactionary and the simple-minded. This innocent self-satisfaction tells us little more, however, than that those exhibiting it do not name as 'God' the gods they worship.
> (1996: 49)

And, a little more fully:

> All human beings have their hearts set somewhere, hold something sacred, worship at some shrine. We are spontaneously idolatrous – where, by 'idolatry', I mean the worship of some creature, the setting of the heart on some particular thing (usually oneself). For most of us there is no single creature that is the object of our faith. Our hearts are torn, dispersed, distracted. We are (to use the seventeenth-century term) polytheists. And none of us is so self-transparent as to know quite where, in fact, our hearts are set.
>
> Against this background, the great religious traditions can be seen as contexts in which human beings may learn, however slowly, partially, imperfectly, some freedom from the destructive bondage which the worship of the creature brings. (1996: 21–2)

Whatever precisely one makes of this, it is a good example of the kind of difference which interpreting the Bible in relation to the question of God and faith might make in our contemporary context, where the issue is no less than a re-envisioning of the nature and meaning of human life within the world.

### The Bible and the question of God

Thus far we have argued that the concerns expressed by Barr and Barrett, while valid as far as they go, take for granted in a potentially question-begging way basic issues about the Bible as a canonical compilation of Old and New Testaments. And their way of conceptualizing issues of theology in relation to the Bible too easily transposes the question of God into questions about the history of religious ideas and practices. Although any proper contextualizing of their work within a modern history of thought lies beyond our present scope, I do not think it is too much to suggest that their way of formulating issues represents variations on a theme which can be traced back to the beginnings of modern biblical study as a distinct *wissenschaftlich* discipline: they stand within a trajectory which can be traced back to such a formative (at least in retrospect) work as Gabler's inaugural lecture of 1787, 'On the Proper Distinction Between Biblical and Dogmatic Theology and the Specific Objectives of Each',[38] or perhaps even Spinoza's *Tractatus Theologico-Politicus* of 1670.

Our concern to articulate a broader, in certain ways more structural, understanding of theology and faith, with a corresponding concern to engage with fundamental issues of contemporary human life, leads

---

**38.** A convenient translation is Sandys-Wunsch and Eldredge 1980.

naturally to characteristic priorities of postmodern thought. The representative essay considered, however, was disappointing. Although the Collective realize some of the defects and omissions in the kind of approach represented by Barr and Barrett, their own concerns to escape individualism and to engage with structural issues of the public exercise of power show a complete failure to engage with the critical content of the Bible and of the Jewish and Christian faiths rooted in it.

Our argument is that the question of what may count as truth in relation to God requires a searching rethinking of the nature of biblical and theological study. This is not to argue that only theologians or believers may properly study the Bible. Nor is it to deny that there are many questions other than the question of God which may fruitfully be studied within the Bible. Nor is it to suppose that the question of God could be studied without indispensable reference to much of the not-very-overtly theological content within the Bible (this rootedness of the reality of God within the realities of human life being one of the significant points at issue in the much used and abused assertion that Christianity is inescapably an historical religion). The point is rather that if the question of religious truth is seen to be foundational to the study of the Bible as Bible (however much other questions may also properly be addressed), then criteria for articulating, clarifying, disputing, and appropriating such truth are not matters for optional afterthought but should be integral to scholarly engagement.

How then might we proceed? In broadest terms I wish to advocate the kind of strategy which was famously expressed in the twentieth century by Karl Barth (1960) when he appealed to Anselm as a model of theological method; that is, to reach behind Enlightenment conceptions of truth and method (while still learning from them) to classic (not just Reformation) Christian conceptions of biblical and theological study with corresponding protocols for speech about God; to recognize that the last two centuries have been times not only of gain but also of loss, and to try to recover some of that loss without forfeiting the important gains. I conclude, therefore, with an outline of some basic elements of historic Christian hermeneutics, all of which I have sought (with what degree of success the reader must judge) to exemplify in the textually based discussions in the rest of this book.

The basic premise is that the question of God, around which the content of the Bible, and of Jewish and Christian faiths, revolves, is always simultaneously a question about humanity.[39] This is not to concede to the suspicion that talk about God is, at heart, only a coded projection of talk about humanity. It is rather to affirm that an understanding of God, as the Bible depicts God, and a self-understanding of humanity, with corresponding implications for how people live, are necessarily interrelated dimensions of a complex reality. From this much follows.

### Interpreting the Bible in relation to the question of God: some hermeneutical presuppositions

First, biblical interpretation becomes inseparable from the question of how people live. That is, no matter how elaborate and sophisticated the technical skills which are brought to the task, and no matter how rigorous the use of these skills must be, the interpretation of the Bible is not detached from basic human questions of allegiance and priorities, of spirituality and ethics – 'How should we, how should I, live? What should we, what should I, live for?' Such questions are not only about individuals and their possible choices, but raise also corporate and structural concerns to do with the configurations of life which shape people and provide the working assumptions, constraints, and possibilities which people consciously and unconsciously absorb.

In classic theological parlance, such an understanding of biblical interpretation is 'faith seeking understanding'. One characteristic way in which this was expressed by the Fathers is found in the dictum of Evagrius, 'If you are a theologian, you will pray truly, and if you pray truly, you are a theologian.'[40] This concisely articulates the understanding that theology requires personal engagement with that reality of which one speaks. This is itself rooted in the Bible's own presentation of the matter. The classic Old Testament formulation is 'The fear of YHWH is (the beginning of) wisdom'[41] on which von Rad (1972b: 67) succinctly comments:

> There is no knowledge which does not, before long, throw the one who seeks the knowledge back upon the question of his self-knowledge and his self-understanding. . . . The thesis that all human knowledge comes back to the question about commitment to God is a statement of

---

39. This biblical and patristic understanding was, not surprisingly, foundational also for Bultmann, who recast it in an existentialist way (1969).
40. *On Prayer: 153 Texts*, §61.    41. Proverbs 1:7; 9:10; 15:33; Psalm 111:10; Job 28:28.

penetrating perspicacity. It has, of course, been so worn by centuries of Christian teaching that it has to be seen anew in all its provocative pungency. . . . It contains in a nutshell the whole Israelite theory of knowledge.

Within the New Testament the classic formulation is the words of Jesus in John 7:16–17: 'My teaching is not my own but his who sent me. If anyone is willing to do his will, then he will know about the teaching – whether it is from God or whether I am speaking solely from myself' (my translation). Down the ages this text has been basic to an understanding of Christian theology as 'faith seeking understanding'.[42] It is not necessary to engage with the many uses to which the text has been put in order to observe that it directly addresses the key question of the relationship between historical, descriptive religious statements (Jesus, according to the evangelist, says such and such) and theology as 'dogmatic', as confessing affirmation (what Jesus says truly reveals God). Jesus' words enunciate what may reasonably be seen as a general principle, that a certain kind of knowledge (whether particular human words truly derive from, and refer to, God) is not attainable apart from an engagement of the person which is more than just an intellectual or rational exercise. What this might mean, especially when 'faith' is not construed in an unduly narrowed sense, is one of the prime concerns of the present discussion.[43] It is not surprising, however, that a significant discussion of biblical hermeneutics should stress that 'there is . . . a sense in which the articulation of what the text might "mean" today, is a necessary condition of hearing what the text "originally meant"' (Lash 1986: 81); or that some recent work on the nature of theology reintegrates theology with spirituality (McIntosh 1998); or that some attempts to reformulate the task of biblical interpretation should direct attention to the character of the interpreter and the question of how one develops wisdom (which puts in a moral and theological form some of the valid insights of reader-response theory) (Fowl and Jones 1991; Fowl 1998).

Secondly, there is the issue, already mentioned, of the sheer difficulty of speaking of God, since God is not a 'person' or 'object' accessible to sci-

---

42. So, for example, Augustine comments: 'Understanding is the reward of faith. Therefore do not seek to understand in order to believe, but believe that you may understand. . . . What is "If any man be willing to do his will?" It is the same thing as to believe' (*Homilies on Gospel of John* 29:6).

43. This issue has also, of course, been in one way or another a foundational concern of liberation theology, with its special attention to the social and political dimensions of faith.

entific examination. The Bible, to be sure, regularly depicts God with a host of analogies drawn from known life. Yet at the same time it sees the misdirection of human responses to God, supremely in the form of idolatries of one kind or other, as a fundamental and recurrent problem. The extensive analogies for God do not, therefore, make genuine encounter with God in any way easy or straightforward. A sense of the problematic nature of religious language as such is not often made explicit within the Bible.[44] In this the Bible differs from much subsequent theology, which regularly emphasizes the inadequacy of human understanding with regard to God and stresses the need for apophatic denial to complement the affirmative use of analogy.[45] But this should not lead one to overlook that this issue is constantly implicit within the Bible. Recent renewed appreciation of the role of metaphor and symbolism within religious language has made significant contributions to biblical study, not least in the work of Paul Ricoeur (see, for example, Ricoeur 1978). Much of the burgeoning narrative theology in biblical study is, in essence, a rediscovery of something about religious language and discourse which was almost wholly obscured when it was too readily assumed that certain kinds of critical historiography provided the norms for understanding and assessing the biblical writers' depiction of their history. In a complementary way, the Bible regularly assumes the problematic nature of the actual use of language about God. On the one hand, people who speak for God may fail to do so truly (the so-called problem of false prophecy), while on the other hand those who hear words which do truly speak of God may fail to understand that this is the case, or to respond appropriately (the problem, in biblical idiom, of a hardened heart and/or a stiffened neck, of eyes that see without seeing and ears that hear without hearing). We shall see, in the next chapter, that a form of this problem is basic to a *locus classicus* for biblical interpretation, that is the story of the road to Emmaus.

44. For a study of a possible exception, see Moberly 1998. Other relevant biblical passages would range from the sweeping poetic vision of the incomparability of God in Isaiah 40:12–31 to Jesus' blunt response to James and John that, in asking for seats of honour beside Jesus in his kingdom/glory, 'You do not know what you are asking' (Matt. 20:22//Mk 10:38).

45. Donald MacKinnon (1987: 12) observes, 'In . . . the schools, it became a commonplace that in speech about God, we continually swing between an anthropomorphism that ultimately reduces the divine to the status of a magnified human worldly reality, and an agnosticism which continually insists that where God is concerned, we may only confidently affirm that we do not know what we mean when we speak of him; nor indeed do we know how the concepts we apply to him latch onto his being, borrowed or developed as they are from the familiar world of our experience. Always agnosticism was judged less perilous than anthropomorphism.'

A third presupposition, which follows from that just mentioned, is that of 'mystery'.[46] Here the sense of mystery is not that of a puzzle which ceases to be a puzzle as soon as enough information becomes available (which is the nature of many philological and historical problems), but rather that of something whose intrinsic depth cannot be exhausted – simply expressed, the more you know, the more you know you do not know. Many famous and central biblical passages have regularly been understood to come in this category – such as 'I AM WHO I AM', 'YHWH is one', 'the word became flesh', 'God is love', and the double commandment to love God with heart, soul, mind, and strength and one's neighbour as oneself; and much more besides could also be considered in this light. The use of 'mystery' in this context should not function prematurely to pre-empt or close down discussion ('that is a mystery – we must not question it too closely').[47] Rather it should open up interpretation that moves beyond the possible position and meaning of such texts within a history of religious thought (which is often the primary concern of biblical commentators) to an engagement with the meaning and truth of the content which may draw on many disciplines and may be explored through a wide range of media (poetry, picture, music, imaginative story, drama), and not least in prayer and the living of life (for it is the faithful lover who best understands the meaning of love).

Finally (though my sequence is not in order of priority), there is the 'rule of faith'. It was very early recognized that study and scrutiny of the biblical texts need not lead to God, or might lead to a defective understanding of God. The rule of faith was formulated in the early Church concurrently with the process of canonical recognition and compilation. The purpose of the rule of faith, which was in due course summarized in the creeds, is to guide readers so that they may discern that truth of God in Christ to which the Church, through its scripture, bears witness.[48] In an historic Christian understanding, formation of canon, rule of faith, and

46. See e.g. Louth 1983: 66–71, 144–7; Kasper 1989: 19–31.
47. It must however be recognized that this is a not uncommon perception of how it does function. See, for example, Oden 1987. Oden comments upon appeal to 'the mysterious' that 'within the theological tradition – at least as this bears upon and shapes biblical study – explanation by reference to the inexplicable is hardly unusual. Outside this tradition, that which is apparently inexplicable is rather that which cries out for explanation' (p. viii); and 'the apparently inexplicable presents a challenge and not a solution' (p. 160). He offers a discussion of the Jacob narrative as a case in point, where premature appeal by theologians to the mystery of divine election has mystified aspects of the story which can be explained by social anthropology. One may readily concede that theologians sometimes appeal to mystery when the real issue is either laziness or incomprehension. But, as ever, abuse does not remove right use.    48. A valuable recent account is Blowers 1997.

creeds are mutually related and integral to the quest of recognizing truth about God. In general terms, guidelines such as a rule of faith embodies are obviously integral to the health of the never-ending dialectic between an authoritative text and a community which seeks to conduct itself in the light of that text.

The notion of a rule of faith, of course, regularly excites suspicion and hostility among professional biblical scholars, as being a tool for prejudgment, manipulation or coercion, and just plain bad scholarship – to say what texts 'must' mean on the grounds of post-biblical dogmas, and to attempt to marginalize or silence those who have the courage to show that biblical texts do not necessarily mean what later tradition has thought them to mean. There are, sadly, so many examples of a rule of faith being used thus that an attempt to gain a fresh hearing for it is not an easy task.[49]

How then might a rule of faith be understood? It sets the biblical text within the context of the continuing life of the Christian Church where the one God and humanity are definitively understood in relation to Jesus Christ. In this context there is a constant interplay between the biblical text and those doctrinal, ethical, and spiritual formulations which seek to spell out its implications. The concerns in this are at least twofold. On the one hand, the initial concern is not so much to explain the Bible at all (in senses familiar to philologist or historian) as to preserve its reality as authoritative and canonical for subsequent generations, so that engagement with the God of whom it speaks, and the transformations of human life which it envisages, remain enduring possibilities; that is, to say 'God is here'. On the other hand, the interest is not so much the history of ideas and religious practices (though this remains an important critical control) as the necessities of hermeneutics and theology proper, that is, the question of what is necessary to enable succeeding generations of faithful, or would-be faithful, readers to penetrate and grasp the meaning and significance of the biblical text; that is, to say 'God is here' in such a way that the words can be rightly understood without lapse into idolatry, literalism, bad history, manipulation, or the numerous other pitfalls into which faith may stumble. It is when the Christian community fails sufficiently to grasp the implications of its own foundational text that a rule of faith changes role from guide to inquisitor.

49. For some of the issues concerning a trinitarian rule of faith see Heron 1991, Webster 1998, and the collection of essays in Miller 1997.

In sum, the presuppositions just mentioned set a context for the exercise of the appropriate technical skills (linguistic, historical) and the engagement with substantive existential issues (ideological, moral, theological) which directs them to a particular goal – using the biblical text to engage with the question of God, with a view to the transformation of human life through engagement with God in Christ, understood not as some kind of optional or sectarian religious exercise, but as engagement with the deepest accessible truth about human existence.

# 2

# Christ as the key to scripture: the journey to Emmaus

In the previous chapter we have discussed in general terms some of the considerations applicable to the Christian desire to address the question of God in and through scripture. On the one hand, it was argued that the Christian Bible, as a particular collection of texts, primarily has meaning and coherence in relation to the Christian Church, which affirms that the one God, revealed in Israel's scripture, is known definitively in Jesus Christ. On the other hand, it was argued that without taking that context seriously one lacks the resources for fruitfully engaging with the question of God in and through the biblical text.

It is necessary now to turn to the biblical text itself to give focus to these wider concerns, to try to indicate how they relate to the biblical text. What then might be the basis within the New Testament for interpretation of scripture in the light of the one God as known in Jesus Christ? I will consider only one passage: the encounter of two disciples with the risen Jesus on the road to Emmaus (Lk. 24:13–35). Although many other passages would need to be looked at in any comprehensive study of biblical hermeneutics, and they would qualify and extend the present discussion in significant ways, the exclusive focus here upon this story is deliberate. The Lucan text explicitly raises the issue of the interpretation of scripture (vv. 25–7), and it does so in relation to Christ in such a way that it has been a *locus classicus* for Christians down the ages. If the evangelist portrays the risen Christ himself expounding scripture to his disciples, it is imaginatively as weighty a story about biblical interpretation and Christ as one could hope to find.

[45]

## The concern of the text

One of the most difficult tasks in understanding this, as all other, resurrection stories is to know what the nature and purpose of the text is.[1] It might perhaps be thought, as indeed Bultmann (1963: 288) said explicitly, that the 'dominant motif' of the story is that of 'proving the Resurrection by the appearance of the risen Lord'. Yet the text says nothing about proving anything. More to the point is H. D. Betz's observation that the story 'reflects theologically and programmatically upon the problem of how Christian faith is made possible and what elements constitute its nature' (1969: 33). Yet even this may allow the particular hermeneutical thrust of the story to become secondary. I propose, therefore, that the story is best understood as an exposition of the hermeneutical issue of discernment, focussing specifically on the question, 'How does one discern the risen Christ?'

The encounter of the two disciples with the risen Christ is framed by the references to their recognition (*epiginosko*) of him being withheld (v. 16) and given (v. 31). The verb *epiginosko* is consistently used in Luke–Acts for an act of identification, when there is an encounter with someone previously known whose present identity might not be immediately obvious.[2] This is the basic issue in this resurrection narrative: the Jesus who is present is the Jesus the disciples had known previously, yet there is something different about him now – which makes recognition not a mere formality but rather a demanding engagement.

If one tries to imagine the scene within the story, it is difficult to know how to specify precisely what it is that the disciples do not see so that they do not recognize. It is in no way implied that Jesus is invisible or that his presence as a fellow-walker on the road is unreal or imaginary. He is there

---

1. In addition to standard commentaries, there is also extensive material in three monographs I am aware of: Wanke 1973; Dillon 1978; Guillaume 1979. But these are primarily concerned with questions of source, form, tradition-history, and redaction, and only engage in a limited way with the hermeneutic logic of the received text. There is also useful material, especially with regard to the significance of meals and table fellowship within Lukan theology, in Just 1993.

2. Rhoda recognizes the familiar voice of Peter, even though she cannot see him because he is on the other side of a door and it is a time when Peter was thought to be in prison; with a result, reminiscent of resurrection narratives, that her testimony is disbelieved by the disciples, who are astounded (*existemi*, cf. Lk. 24:22) when they learn the truth (Ac. 12:13–16). The crowd of people in the temple precincts recognize the man who is now walking and praising God as the one who had been a crippled beggar (Ac. 3:9–10). The religious authorities in Jerusalem are surprised at the bold and eloquent speech of the professionally unqualified Peter and John, yet recognize them as having been with Jesus (Ac. 4:13–14).

and can be seen – yet recognition is not straightforward. This problem of recognition is of course characteristic of other resurrection stories, especially in John's Gospel; Mary sees the risen Jesus but is unable to identify him as Jesus until he calls her by her name (Jn 20:14–16); the disciples who have made an astonishing catch of fish know the identity of the one who speaks to them, and yet this knowledge is compatible with their not daring to, and so somehow implicitly needing to, ask him his identity (Jn 21:1–14, esp. 7, 12).

Problems of recognition are, of course, a known literary topos, and were already expounded at length by Aristotle in his discussion of *anagnorisis* in Greek drama.[3] Although Luke's story resonates with this topos, its primary affiliations are rather with a particular biblical concern. The underlying issue, particularly focussed in several resurrection stories, yet regularly implicit in both Old and New Testament, is that of the nature of spiritual reality in relation to the mundane world. How, in essence, can one depict and evoke God and encounter with God with the language and categories of daily life? How can created beings find within the created order appropriate ways of expressing their and its relationship with the transcendent creator?

There is, moreover, a significant analogy between the problem envisaged within the story and our problem of biblical interpretation. Just as the relationship between the human and the divine in Jesus has often been understood as in some ways analogous to the relationship between human and divine in scripture, so too with discernment. The recognition of the risen Jesus in an earthly presence, which is not described as abnormal in any respect other than in the difficulty of recognition, is analogous to the problem of scriptural interpretation, that is the recognition of the living God (through Jesus, in the Spirit) in a book whose language and content can be described and explained in the familiar categories of the humanities and social sciences.

This issue of recognition is expressed in the Emmaus story by means of the recurrent biblical idiom of eyes which do not see, and which do see (which is parallel to ears which do not hear, and which do hear). Although these idioms of seeing and hearing are often used separately, the biblical *locus classicus* for the problematic nature of discernment, Isaiah 6:9–10, conjoins the two, and it is unlikely that there is significant difference between them (however much it may be possible to construct arguments

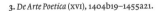

---

3. *De Arte Poetica* (XVI), 1404b19–1455a21.

about the differences between those religious systems founded on hearing and those founded on seeing). When Isaiah 6:9–10 is cited in the Synoptic Gospels with regard to Jesus' speaking in parables and in John's Gospel with regard to Jesus' public ministry of signs,[4] no difference between seeing and hearing is implied. The point of the language is to take the two human senses which are most used in human recognition and communication and to apply them to recognition of, and communication with, God.

It is striking that the eyes of the disciples are passive recipients of action done to them: their eyes are kept from recognizing (v. 16) and they are opened (v. 31). Commentators regularly note that these are passives implying divine action, and this is certainly correct.[5] Yet enquiry too often proceeds no further; or the issue is transposed into purely literary terms – 'This comment of the evangelist [sc. v. 16] . . . is part of the dramatic concealment used by Luke to build up suspense' (Fitzmyer 1985: 1563).

One might reasonably ask why God does this: why withhold and give recognition? And, if the question posed in this form might perhaps be unanswerable – on the grounds that it depends upon the sovereign and inscrutable will of God – one may still ask whether the divine action is conceived to be essentially arbitrary, or whether there is some human corollary or counterpart to it; that is, although it remains within God's initiative to withhold or give sight, God's withholding or giving nonetheless may be in some ways correlated with certain human actions and attitudes. It is precisely this interrelationship between divine gift and a human context for the receiving of that gift that is probed in our story.

### Narrative and metaphor

The greater part of the story focusses upon the conversation between Jesus and the disciples. Before looking at this conversation, it is worth noting the circumstantial language used to set the scene; for, as with so many biblical (and other) stories, the language is intrinsically open to metaphorical significance,[6] and it can be genuinely difficult to know on what level one should read the text. One can, for example, note the language of 'going' (vv. 13, 15), and being 'on the road' (*en te hodo*, vv. 32, 35); this might be connected with Luke's theological geography in which Jeru-

---

4. Matt. 13:10–17; Mk 4:10–12; Lk. 8:9–10; Jn 12:37–43.
5. Cf. Deuteronomy 29:3, where YHWH is said to have withheld understanding, sight, and hearing from Israel.    6. See e.g. Alter 1992: 85–106.

salem is the city of destiny and so is the locale within which the resurrection appearances take place (Fitzmyer 1981: 164–71; 1985: 1557–8, 1562); and/or the language may be a metaphor for discipleship, the Christian life as a whole being depicted in travelling terms as the 'Way' (*hodos*, cf. Ac. 9:2; 19:9; 19:23; 22:4; 24:14, 22). This latter sense might be supported by the reference to the disciples conversing and discussing with each other (vv. 14, 15) 'about all these things that had happened', that is about the death and resurrection of Jesus which Luke has just recounted. Unlike the references to the journey, without which the story could not be what it is, this introductory description, at least in v. 15a, is somewhat pleonastic, for the following dialogue could be more briefly introduced. There may therefore be metaphorical significance in the setting in which discussion of the story of Jesus becomes the context for Jesus, albeit unrecognized, coming alongside; that is, active interest in the stories of the death and resurrection of Jesus, an interest perhaps involving impassioned disagreement (if one combines the possible implications of *suzeteo, antiballo, skuthropos*, vv. 16, 17)[7] may be a preliminary to understanding.

### The preliminary conversation (24:17–24)

The conversation is opened by Jesus with a question whose purpose is presumably not to express genuine ignorance but rather to introduce himself into a discussion whose content he knows full well, so that in dialogue with him it can be given a new direction (v. 17). The initial exchange (vv. 18–19a) which sets the scene for the disciples to speak is gently ironical; for their assumption that they know what has happened while their new companion does not is about to be turned upside down.

In the words that Cleopas and his companion then speak (vv. 19–24) the irony becomes much more acute. For they accurately summarize the Christian story (as Luke has told it) and yet entirely fail to perceive its significance. The crucial question thus becomes, 'How can accurate knowledge of information become genuine understanding?'

The disciples begin with a concise description of Jesus in terms of the prime Jewish category for depicting such a remarkable figure, that is as a prophet; Moses and Samuel could equally be depicted as 'powerful in

---

7. *Suzeteo* often denotes a discussion between parties who disagree (e.g. Lk. 22:23; Ac. 9:29); *antiballo*, despite its neutral use as 'consider' in its sole occurrence in the LXX (2 Macc. 11:13), can have its literal, adversative sense in classical usage; and *skuthropos* readily suggests that a person is deeply upset; cf. Evans 1990: 904; Hickling 1994: 30, n. 3.

action and speech before God and all the people'. Although the gospels already contain other categories for understanding Jesus, and it is in categories other than prophet that Christian theology develops its understandings of Jesus, there is an obvious appropriateness in context in the use of the resonant and hallowed term 'prophet'.[8]

They continue with a statement of the responsibility of the Jewish ('our') religious authorities for having Jesus put to death (v. 20). It is interesting that in this concise account no reason is given for such a hostile action by the authorities, and such a silence is perhaps characteristic of the Christian story. For, to anticipate later discussion, it has always been a problem to explain why Jesus died; why, in Christian terms, he had to die. It is not that one cannot find particular conflicts and accusations within the gospels which enable some kind of account to be given; but such accounts as can be given of Jesus' conflict with the authorities tend to leave unanswered the more fundamental theological and moral issues of why Jesus should see death as integral to his vocation. The mystery of the reason for Jesus' death is perhaps implicit in the stark juxtaposition between his prophetic power and his execution.

The men then speak of their hopes that had attached to Jesus (v. 21a) – that he would be the one who was to rescue/redeem (*lutrousthai*) Israel. Whatever the precise nature of Jewish messianic hopes of the period, for the first disciples those hopes were fixed on Jesus. The irony, of course, from a Christian perspective is that Jesus has fulfilled those hopes, and it is precisely through his death and his resurrection on the third day that he has done so (cf. Lk. 9:18–36; 24:5–7). The men even emphasize that this is the third day since his death (v. 21b), and such a time reference is not needed to introduce the account of the women's testimony, which could follow on directly from mention of Jesus' death and their disappointed hopes; nor does it in fact introduce the account of the women, since that begins with an adversative 'but even' (*alla kai*, v. 23a) rather than a conjunctive 'and' (*kai*). So the point of the time reference is its own intrinsic significance, through its resonance with what Jesus had said would happen on the third day. Thus far, all the disciples have said is contained within the story of the earthly ministry of Jesus as Luke has presented it – yet to them its meaning and significance is still hidden.

The men then speak of the new events of Easter day – the early visit of the women to the tomb, their not finding the body of Jesus, and their

---

8. Cf. the use made of 'prophet' as the prime category for Jesus' ministry in Wright 1996: pt. II.

report that they had even had a vision of angels who said Jesus was alive (vv. 22–3). Here we have the basic elements of the Easter story – the negative evidence of the absence of the body, which in itself could be understood in many ways, combined with the positive testimony that Jesus is alive. However, the fact that this testimony comes from angels means that the primary witness to the risen Christ comes from precisely that spiritual realm which risks being so opaque to human perception. It is presumably for this reason that when some of the men act to verify the women's testimony (v. 24), they are able only to verify their testimony to the extent that they too do not find the body of Jesus. This absence does not signify to them that Jesus is risen.

### Jesus interprets scripture (24:25–7)

Jesus responds in a surprising way. For he does not, as one might perhaps expect, speak of his own ministry, death, and resurrection and re-explain their significance. Nor does he, like an Enoch, make new and astonishing pronouncements about the nature of a world beyond this one or about arcane puzzles within this world. Rather, he appeals to the Jewish scriptures. This has at least two primary implications. First, the point is that there is no knowledge available from a realm beyond this life which is more significant or helpful for understanding Jesus and life with God than the moral and spiritual content already accessible in Israel's existing scripture. Secondly, the implication is not that the story of Jesus does not have intrinsic significance, but that it needs to be set in a context beyond itself for that significance to be understood; that is, existing scripture provides the necessary context for understanding Jesus.

But even this is not straightforward. For the disciples of Jesus are Jews and as such would already possess an extensive familiarity with the content of their scripture. The clear implication is that the story of Israel in Hebrew scripture is no different from the story of Jesus – it is possible to know the material without understanding it (v. 25). The key is provided by a particular perspective, one which is indeed rooted in the actual content of the scripture, but which is only realized, and so made accessible, through the passion and resurrection of Jesus (v. 26). So, as Jesus cannot be understood apart from Jewish scripture, Jewish scripture cannot be understood apart from Jesus; what is needed is an interpretation which relates the two – and it is this that Jesus provides (v. 27).

These words of the risen Jesus accord with those of his earlier ministry.

The mind of Jesus at the beginning of his ministry is interpreted by the story of the testing in the wilderness (Lk. 4:1–13). In response to each test Jesus discerns the will of God for himself in the words of Israel's scriptures. And Luke has so arranged the material that the culminating challenge is not just set in Jerusalem but also involves the very issue of biblical interpretation. The satan[9] cites verses from Psalm 91 in what looks to be their plain sense – the protection of God is promised to the believer, in language which suggests that angels lift up and carry one who is falling. The fact that Jesus will not claim such a scriptural promise suggests that the protection and deliverance of God will take on a far-from-straightforward meaning in his life and ministry.

Jesus' public ministry begins with a reading from scripture about one who is anointed by the Spirit of the Lord (Lk. 4:18–30); Jesus claims that this scripture is 'fulfilled today' (v. 21), implicitly in his own person and ministry. Yet his ensuing exposition of scripture arouses such public anger that an attempt is made to put him to death.

Jesus speaks to his disciples of his future destiny (Lk. 9:18–27), reinterpreting what it means for him to be 'the Christ of God' in terms of death and resurrection, both for himself (v. 22) and for others (vv. 23–7). Following this, Jesus at prayer is seen speaking with Moses and Elijah; and the very fact that the coming deliverance which Jesus will bring about is spoken of by Moses and Elijah (Lk. 9:28–36, esp. 30–1) shows that its substance is rooted in Israel's scripture; and when the divine voice says of Jesus 'listen to him', at the same time as Jesus appears on his own again, it is clear that Jesus is the one who will have to expound the content of what Moses and Elijah have said – it is Jesus, and, by implication, those who listen to him and follow him in the way he went, who have understanding of the meaning and significance of Moses and the prophets.[10]

There is thus strong continuity between the content of Jesus' ministry and message before and after Easter. As C. Hickling (1994: 26) puts it, 'Just as the risen Jesus is one and the same person as the teacher of the Galilee days, so those who preach his gospel after his ascension proclaim the same message that had been a principal part of his own teaching, reinforced on

9. I choose this form, in continuity with Old Testament usage, in preference to the more familiar 'Satan' as a proper name, to retain something of the ambiguity in context about the nature of the figure thus designated; cf. Wright 1996: 451 and n. 33.

10. The precise significance of Moses and Elijah is, of course, a moot point. My general categorization of 'Moses and the prophets' (cf. Fitzmyer: 1981: 799–800) may need to be made more specific in terms of Jewish traditions about the eschatological significance of Moses and Elijah.

the day of his resurrection.' In this regard we may note that the Lukan portrayal of Jesus is very similar to that of Matthew, where also the continuity of the post-Easter proclamation with the pre-Easter ministry is affirmed by the final commissioning containing the injunction to teach people to 'observe all that I commanded you' (Matt. 28:16–20, esp. 20) (cf. Bornkamm 1971: 203–29; Childs 1984: 64–9).

The possible wider implications of this construal of scripture is an issue to which we will return. For present purposes, we must look more closely at the content of Jesus' words in Luke 24:25–7 to see what they do, and do not, mean.

Jesus begins with a rebuke to the disciples for their failure to understand (v. 25) on the basis of[11] 'the prophets', that is on the basis of Israel's scriptures as a whole, understood as prophetic witness to the will of God (cf. v. 27). No doubt this wording, like that of the general exposition of scripture in verse 27, to some extent looks beyond the context of the story to address the readers of the gospel more generally. However, it still retains its own logic within the story. Earlier in the gospel the disciples have been uncomprehending in response to Jesus speaking of his coming passion (Lk. 9:43b-45; 18:31–3), and this has been set in the context of concealment (*parakekalummenon*, 9:45; *kekrummenon*, 18:34), implicitly by God, as at the outset of the Emmaus journey (24:16). In those contexts there was no rebuke, presumably because at that stage what Jesus was saying could not yet make sense within the disciples' frame of reference; the key to understanding – present within the scriptures and already in some way held by Jesus – was not yet given to them. On Easter day, however, that which had been missing, that which would make sense of everything else, was given in the resurrection of Jesus. Now the disciples could in principle understand what Jesus was about. But as yet they do not.

The rebuke also serves rhetorically to introduce the key words whereby Jesus provides the interpretative key to understanding scripture and himself – 'Were not these things necessary – that the Christ should suffer and enter his glory?'[12] This is the heart of the matter.

---

11. There is a small translation problem. Although *pasin* is commonly taken as the object of *pisteuein epi*, that is, 'to believe all [that the prophets said]', I am inclined to follow Evans (1990: 910) who comments: 'The construction which follows – *pisteuein* followed by *epi* and the dative – is not used elsewhere by Luke for "to believe in". The verb may then be taken absolutely, and the meaning be – "slow to become believers (i.e. to see the facts aright) on the basis of (*epi*), or with the assistance of, all that the prophets had said".'

12. I think it is preferable to see *tauta* as the subject of *edei*. But the difference in sense from the more common 'Was it not necessary that the Christ should suffer these things . . . ?' is small.

The sense lies in a paradox – the linking of suffering with glory. This is amplified in two ways. First, it is not any suffering that is correlated with glory, but the suffering of the Christ; the very person who is the agent of God's deliverance of Israel must suffer to enter glory. Secondly, there is the note of necessity; the suffering of the Christ was not one possible way among others, but was *the way*, the one and only way within the purposes of God, for his work to be fulfilled. How is this to be understood?

It is obviously necessary to probe the meaning of the key terms. First, 'glory' (*doxa*): if one reads the Emmaus story in close conjunction with the following resurrection appearance of Christ (Lk. 24:36–49), where the suffering of Christ is linked with his resurrection (24:46), one may be inclined to identify 'glory' with 'resurrection'. Yet although the two terms are clearly linked, it would be a mistake to identify them, for glory is the more biblically resonant term.

In the Hebrew scriptures, 'glory' (*kabod*, regularly *doxa* in LXX) is used in many ways but is supremely a mysterious splendour which represents the presence of YHWH, especially in places that are holy to him, in so far as this presence is accessible to human perception. YHWH's glory resides[13] on Sinai where Moses is summoned to the divine presence (Exod. 24:16); the glory fills the tabernacle, which is to be the vehicle of divine presence as Israel leaves Sinai (Exod. 40:34–8); and the glory fills the temple in Jerusalem (1 Kgs. 8:10–11; more fully in 2 Chron. 5:13–14; 7:1–3). If one tries to imagine what the glory looks like, one is faced with a problem. The glory is consistently associated with a cloud. Yet Exodus 24:17 offers an explicit description – 'the appearance of the glory of YHWH was like a devouring fire on top of the mountain in the sight of the Israelites'. How does that whose presence is depicted by a cloud appear like a fire?[14] One senses the attempt to express the presence of God to human perception in ways that resist easy rendering into mundane categories.

It is this 'glory' which is used by Luke, in continuity with scriptural usage, to express the realm of God when it becomes humanly visible. The

13. Heb. *sakan*; LXX interprets with *katabaino*, descend.
14. The problem is in no way resolved by an appeal to possible distinct traditions and layers within the text, not least because there has been a consistent consensus that Exod. 24:15b-18a is all P.

Elsewhere the OT distinguishes between 'a pillar of cloud by day and a pillar of fire by night' that led Israel in the wilderness (Exod. 13:21–2). It is presumably one pillar, whose appearance varies according to its context of visibility, that is, at night it has to appear as fire in order to be seen.

key passage is the story of the transfiguration (Lk. 9:28–36).[15] Here Jesus prays, and the transformed state of his face reflects something of his inner being as his prayer brings access to God and the spiritual realm (see Reid 1994: 44–5), which is the context in which Moses and Elijah are 'seen in glory' (v. 31). Peter and the other disciples are rewarded for fighting off sleep[16] (and, presumably, persisting in prayer)[17] by being able to see the glory of Christ; there is a strong implication that the disciples would not have been able to perceive the glory had they not fought off their natural desire for sleep. When Jesus overtly has the visible characteristic of the divine realm in the form of a transformative light, it may still be possible to miss seeing it. Thus the 'glory', the divine realm into which Jesus has entered in his prayer, is something accessible to human perception, but not straightforwardly so.[18]

Luke conveys the visual aspect of Jesus' 'glory' by using the image of clear light similar to lightning (v. 29; cf. Lk. 2:9). This suggests both the brightness of the light, and its dynamic, mobile quality. It is thus similar to the imagery of YHWH's glory on Sinai; for likeness to a 'devouring fire' (Exod. 24:17) draws attention to the vitality of a fire, suggesting both the brightness of its flames and their restless, mobile quality. It is imagery that readily suggests a realm beyond human control, that of divine transcendence.

It is the more remarkable, therefore, that Luke does not depict the re-surrected Jesus in these terms. The imagery of lightning-like brightness

---

15. One may note that the use of *doxa* to depict the transfigured Jesus is peculiar to Luke's account of the transfiguration. Luke does not use the verb 'transfigure' (*metamorphoo*), and his narrative might well be termed 'the glorification of Jesus'.

16. It is possible that 'weighed down with sleep' means that the disciples actually slept, and that *diagregoresantes* means that they awoke. But the preposition *dia* attached to *gregoreo* should in itself have the intensifying sense of 'continue to stay awake', and there is nothing in context against this. Commentators sometimes waver between these two meanings, but the overall preference seems to be for depicting the disciples as sleeping and then waking; see e.g. Ramsey 1949: 112, 121; Brown 1994: 193, 206 n. 7.

Further, the use of the aorist participle need not indicate that the disciples had become fully as opposed to partially awake as a process of coming out of sleep (so Evans 1990: 418, 415). Rather, although 'weighed down with sleep' in the sense that their tiredness and desire for sleep was almost overwhelming, the disciples consistently fought to stay awake, and it is as a result of having done this that they saw Christ's glory.

17. Although the verb used of the disciples' staying awake, *diagregoreo*, occurs only here, the related (and weaker) form *gregoreo* is used in Luke 12:37 in the context of a parable (12:36–8) which explicitly emphasizes the rewards of staying awake. Despite the absence of any explicit terminological links, it is natural to see the disciples' perseverance at the transfiguration as a counterpoise to their failure in Gethsemane.

18. The basic thought of this passage about the accessibility of divine light is common to many religious traditions. It is particularly characteristic of Eastern Orthodox theology, where the notion of the divine light transforming human life plays a central role.

is indeed used with regard to the appearance of the angels at the tomb (Lk. 24:4; cf. 24:23) where it evokes in the women the reverential awe which regularly characterizes human encounters with the divine (cf. Exod. 3:6; Josh. 5:14). But the risen Jesus is not so depicted – neither before nor at the moment of recognition (24:31), nor in the subsequent appearance to the disciples as a group (24:36–49). A natural implication would be that the risen Jesus, now participating in the divine realm in such a way that it is fully his own – Christ enters *his* glory (*ten doxan autou*), not God's glory (*ten doxan tou theou*) – gives access to the divine realm precisely in human categories; although he could shine in splendour and awe, he retains his familiar human form, and it is thus that his disciples need to be able to see him.

The second key term is 'suffer' (*pathein*, aorist infinitive of *paschein*). For to enter his glory the Christ must 'suffer'. The primary meaning of the word is well spelt out by C. F. Evans (1990: 407):

> The verb *paschein* acted in Greek as the passive of the verb *poiein* = 'to do'. Its basic meaning was not, as in the modern use of 'suffer', the endurance of physical or mental pain, but 'to be done to', to be the 'patient' or object and recipient of the actions of others, almost always in a bad sense.

The possible significance of this can hardly be separated from the fact that it is 'the Christ' who must suffer thus. Whatever the varieties of Jewish messianic expectations of the first century, all alike shared the assumption that the Messiah would be an active agent on God's behalf, whose actions would bring about God's deliverance of Israel. For such a person to be fundamentally acted upon by others, as succinctly expressed in Luke 9:44,[19] would be, quite simply, incomprehensible. To add further that this is 'necessary', that it is the outworking of the will of God, whose nature and will has already been definitively given in Israel's scriptures, compounds the problem. For it is those scriptures which regularly depict God's will to deliver Israel in terms which involve Israel's triumph over her enemies.

What then is the relationship between the 'necessity that the Christ should suffer' and his 'entering into his glory'? It is easy to assume that

---

19. Luke 9:44 refers to the son of man rather than the Christ. In Luke's presentation, Jesus does not refer to himself as the Christ until after his resurrection (24:26, 46), and during his earthly ministry his preferred term 'the son of man' is the term which he uses to express his messiahship (9:20–2).

the relationship is one of temporal sequence, in which the former precedes the latter. Certainly this is explicit in 1 Peter, which speaks of 'the
Spirit of Christ in the prophets witnessing in advance to the sufferings for
Christ and the glories after these things' (1:11) and closely links resurrection and glory through reference to 'God who raised Jesus from the dead
and gave him glory' (1:21). This may then be contrasted with the characteristic Johannine emphasis on the cross itself as the moment of glory (Jn
12:23–33). Does suffering precede glory? Or is glory integral within suffering? Or both? Although there is an undoubted difference of emphasis
between Luke and John, there may also be important continuities.

On the one hand, there is no explicit temporal sequence in Luke 24:26.
The text does not say that 'the Christ should suffer and after this (*meta
touto*) enter into his glory'. Of course, since the glory of the divine realm is
closely associated with Christ's state on the third day after his death, that
is, with his resurrection, the temporal sequence makes appropriate sense.
Yet, as already noted, glory is a broader term than resurrection, since it
refers to that divine realm in its human perception which was already
apparent to Israel in the Old Testament and was also revealed at the transfiguration. Although God's glory fully belongs to Jesus after his resurrection, this need not preclude the possibility that glory might also be visible
prior to the resurrection, within and during the suffering of the Christ.

On the other hand, one must consider Luke's portrayal of Jesus during
his suffering, that is especially in his final days of earthly life in Jerusalem
(Lk. 22–3). If the suffering of Jesus is first and foremost a matter of giving
himself into the power of others, it does not thereby exclude physical or
mental pain; yet within this context the behaviour and demeanour of
Jesus is consistent, and Luke draws no attention to either the physical
or the mental pain of Jesus. Rather, the consistent emphasis is on Jesus'
concern for others within the context of enduring trust in his Father.

At the Last Supper Jesus shows concern for his disciples, reassuring
them about their future place within the purposes of God (22:28–30).
Even though the disciples are to face a searing time of trial, mysterious
words of reassurance are offered (22:31–2), though Peter does not grasp
what is being said (22:33–4). Further symbolic words of warning about
the imminent overturning of their lives are completely misunderstood,
yet the rebuke is mild (22:35–8). In Gethsemane Jesus prays, without the
anguish of Mark's account (Mk 14:34–5), yet with an intensity of struggle
to appropriate the Father's will such that a close-up view reveals sweat

drops of great size (Lk. 22:41–4).[20] At his arrest he heals the ear of the high priest's slave (22:51), and when held at the high priest's house he is mindful of Peter (22:61). At the crucifixion Jesus speaks four times, showing concern for the women of Jerusalem (23:28–31), compassion for his executioners (23:34), mercy and assurance to a thief (23:43), and trust in God his Father (23:46). Jesus shows unswerving compassion for other people and unwavering trust in God in the face of incomprehension, desertion, injustice, cruelty, and death. May not such a portrayal of good overcoming evil in undiminished relating to God and others be a major dimension of what glory means? The glory of God, into which Jesus enters fully in his resurrection, is already evident within the suffering of the Christ.[21]

The significance of Luke's passion narrative for the nature of the relationship between the suffering of the Christ and glory should especially be noted in the light of the tendencies of recent theology to marginalize Luke's account. Two major theologies of the death and resurrection of Christ that have been written since the Second World War are Jürgen Moltmann's *The Crucified God* and Hans Urs von Balthasar's *Mysterium Paschale*. Despite the differing provenance and outlook of the two writers, both agree in according prime significance to Jesus' cry of dereliction recorded in Matthew and Mark.

Moltmann (1974: 149) concentrates entirely upon 'an interpretation of the words of Ps. 22.2 as Jesus spoke them. We shall take into account the fact that the church attempted to interpret Jesus' dying cry in these words, but shall regard this interpretation as the most accurate'. By contrast with the Markan narrative, 'this terrible cry of the dying Jesus was gradually weakened in the passion narratives and replaced by words of comfort and triumph' (p. 146), a development which Moltmann considers retrograde: 'Luke omits these words [sc. Ps. 22:2] completely and replaces them by the confident utterance of the Jewish evening prayer from Ps. 31.6 ... In his view Jesus did not die "forsaken by God", but as an exemplary

---

**20.** There is, of course, a difficult text-critical problem about the status of 22:43–4, as there is also with Jesus' prayer for forgiveness in 23:34a. Nonetheless, even if the verses were not part of the original Lukan text, they have generally been seen as consonant with, and furthering, its portrayal of Jesus, such that they may appropriately be seen by Christians as part of the received version of Luke's Gospel. For a discussion of the role of textual criticism within a scriptural context, see Childs 1984: 518–30.

**21.** Compare the conclusion of Michael Ramsey's study of *doxa* within Luke (1949: 40): 'Thus the Lord approaches the Passion; and, although Saint Luke never applies the word glory directly to it in the Johannine manner, he sets it in a frame of glory. . . . Saint Luke is not far from the final Johannine interpretation of the life of Christ as a manifestation of glory from first to last.'

martyr' (p. 147). Luke's presentation of the cross should, in Moltmann's view, be discarded by Christian theology as a seductive error:

> Thus in the context of his [sc. Jesus'] life, his abandonment on the cross, which he expressed in his last cry, should not be interpreted as the ultimate test of a deeply religious man in temptation and suffering, on the pattern of the martyr christology which ever since Luke has repeatedly presented Jesus as the archetype or example of faith under temptation. (p. 148)

Von Balthasar is in many ways more nuanced than Moltmann, but nonetheless is in complete agreement about the centrality of the cry of dereliction. He says that: 'Christ's cross . . . must not be rendered innocuous as though the Crucified, in undisturbed union with God, had prayed the Psalms and died in the peace of God' (1990: 122). His wording captures precisely the sense of Luke's portrayal, with the exception that 'undisturbed' diminishes the sense of struggle necessary in Gethsemane for the union with, and peace of, God to be maintained to the last; but he does not reflect on the fact that Luke hardly sees the cross as 'rendered innocuous' by such an account.

With regard to the various sayings ascribed to Jesus on the cross, von Balthasar says that 'primacy must go to the cry of abandonment' and that 'besides this fundamental word, the other words from the Cross could, without any essential narrowing of their bearing, be understood as interpretations of that actual situation of judgment (both objective and subjective) which the events render distinct enough' (p. 125). He then proceeds to offer an account of the words from the cross in which no attention is given to the Lucan portrayal, an account whose contours are drawn from Matthew and John.

It is not the present purpose to offer a systematic understanding of the death of Christ, nor to overlook the many factors in our contemporary, fragmenting, post-Holocaust context which may make appropriate a focus upon the possible implications of the cry of dereliction. Rather, the purpose is to understand the words of Jesus in Luke 24:26, which must be done in the first instance by considering the meaning of the words in their Lukan context; a task which is rendered more difficult by a pronounced contemporary tendency to take only the cry of dereliction in Matthew and Mark with full imaginative and theological seriousness (a tendency which in effect restricts and inhibits the full canonical witness to the death and resurrection of Jesus). Two points in particular need emphasis.

First, one should not so romanticize the process of moral and spiritual struggle that the Lukan depiction of Jesus as one who maintains apparent serenity and trust amidst suffering is downgraded; as though an anguished and in some ways vacillating struggle for faith is intrinsically superior to a steadily trusting faith; or as though a steadily trusting faith did not involve its own kind of moral and spiritual struggle.[22] Secondly, the too ready categorization of Luke's Jesus as 'martyr' may overlook one crucial point of difference from martyrs generally. Martyrs, in so far as they truly are martyrs and not just the tragic victims of cruelty and abuse of power, die for a cause which can always in principle be identified. It is this which is so elusive in Luke's account of Jesus,[23] since it depicts the death of Jesus primarily in terms of obedience to the will of God, with no particular issue at stake, other than Jesus' own integrity as messiah.[24] The question 'Why did Jesus die?' cannot be answered in the same way as 'Why did the Maccabean martyrs or Rabbi Akiba die?'[25]

In the light of all these factors, we must attempt to summarize the meaning of Luke 24:26. If this is the key that unlocks the meaning of scripture, what sort of key is it? The short answer is that there is no short

22. As Paul Gooch (1996: 137–8) puts it: 'And as for the submissive praying of Jesus in Luke: we must not be deceived by Luke's omission of the cry of dereliction from the cross, or by his stress on Jesus' willingness to do the Father's will, into thinking that the discontinuity between his praying and ours removes him entirely from our condition. The bloodlike sweat in Luke is unmistakably proof. Just as blushing is a sign of self-consciousness beyond the control of the agent, so sweating externalizes that internal struggle of protest against death that is part of our biology. . . . The difference in the praying of Jesus that reflects his special relation to God does not lie in his having been provided with a will that is automatically identical to the will of the Father.'

23. There is a slightly different emphasis in Matthew and Mark on account of their statement about the purpose of the coming of the son of man (Matt. 20:28//Mk 10:45), a statement without parallel in Luke (despite some resonances in Lk. 22:27). It is unclear, however, whether this statement can bear the weight of interpretation it sometimes is made to carry. It makes clear that the death of Jesus is for the benefit of others in terms of enacting God's anticipated deliverance of his people. But that is also evident from elsewhere in the gospels.

24. Gooch (1996: ch. 2) offers an unusually interesting account of martyrdom and its relation to the death of Jesus.

25. Wright (1996: esp. pt. III) discusses the death of Jesus in relation to Jesus' own purposes. Wright plausibly reconstructs Jesus' self-understanding in his ministry as messiah, and indicates certain key biblical texts which are likely to have informed Jesus' outlook: Daniel, esp. ch. 7; Zechariah 9–14; certain Psalms; Isaiah 40–55, esp. 52:13–53:12. But even if Wright's argument be granted in its entirety, at least two caveats remain necessary. First, it is arguable how much of Jesus' outlook was shared by Luke as he wrote his gospel, so the one cannot be used *tout court* to interpret the other. Secondly, Wright himself concludes that 'Jesus' personal reading of Isaiah belongs not so much in the history of ideas, as in the history of vocation, agenda, action and ultimately passion' (1996: 604). If I understand this correctly, Wright's characterization of Jesus' interpretation of scripture as 'vocational' means that his construal was peculiar to himself, with no particular issue at stake that would have been publicly recognizable as such at the time, whatever the overtones of Jesus' temple-action.

answer, for its substance is that of the life, ministry, death, and resurrection of Jesus as a whole. It is Jesus as portrayed by Luke (and, in a Christian context, by the other evangelists and by the rest of the New Testament) who is the key to interpreting scripture. A permanent hermeneutical dialectic between Israel's scripture and Jesus is established. A prime point of continuity with Israel's existing understanding is the faithfulness of Jesus to the will of God, trusting God even in the face of undeserved death. A prime point of discontinuity is the discernment of the will of God within Israel's scripture, with the resulting question whether Jesus' discernment and enactment of that will, and so entering glory through suffering, provides the focal point of reference for future discernment and enactment. Loving obedience to the will of God is already an established category within Israel's scripture. Jesus extends and transforms it in such a way that Christians find in him a redefinition of the very nature of God and God's action in the world.

To put things in this way goes beyond the text of Luke 24:26. Yet it seeks to do justice to its key concerns in such a way that their significance can be understood: the necessity for God and humanity that Jesus as Israel's deliverer should go the way of the cross ('was it not necessary that the Christ should suffer . . . ?'), and the fresh disclosure of the divine reality in the person of Jesus, disclosed in his life and passion and definitively constituted by the resurrection ('should suffer and enter into his glory').

Such is Jesus' exposition of scripture within the story. It becomes all the more significant, therefore, that this does *not* have the effect of opening the eyes of the disciples. We might expect the tension of the story, the lack of recognition of the risen Jesus, to be appropriately resolved at this point – the risen Jesus himself expounds scripture! – but it is not. Certainly, the disciples refer later to the way in which their hearts burned within them while Jesus spoke (v. 32; a suggestive metaphor for the excitement of engagement with a new and living reality within the core of their being); but however deeply they are moved, the crucial element of the opening of their eyes to recognize the risen Jesus is still withheld. There is yet more to the story, there is still another necessary stage in the journey of the disciples.

## The meal at Emmaus (24:28–35)

The story continues by reverting to the context of the journey, again using language appropriate to the story but also readily suggestive of metaphorical meaning. The disciples arrive near to the village they were going to (they have almost, but not quite, reached their destination – a destination which will mean seeing the risen Christ), and Jesus behaves as though[26] he has to go on separately from them (he deliberately acts in a mysterious and elusive way to draw out a further response). The disciples use force on Jesus (*parebiasanto*) to get him to come with them, a force to be envisaged primarily in the words that follow when they say to Jesus 'stay with us' (a basic prayer); to which Jesus accedes.

The scene now shifts to a meal. Although food was not mentioned in the previous verse, the conventions of hospitality would naturally include it and take it for granted. More surprising is that Jesus the guest assumes the role of the host in blessing the bread and distributing it. Perhaps within the logic of the story the person who has given such an authoritative exposition of scripture is instinctively deferred to. In any case the meal is briefly described in terms of what Jesus does with the bread; and at this point the eyes of the disciples are opened and they recognize Jesus; and Jesus then can no longer be seen at all. The nature of Jesus' disappearance is unclear. The language may be designed to suggest not that the risen Christ goes away, but that the spiritual reality to which the disciples' eyes were opened is such that full seeing can only be momentary. Yet the text clearly implies that the momentariness of the vision does not matter, since the grasp of its content may be enduring; for the disciples' immediate response is to link their recognition of the risen Jesus with their earlier response to the exposition of the scriptures. They then return to Jerusalem to find the other disciples, to whom they do not need to say that the Lord is risen, for the other disciples, especially Peter, already know this. Rather, they tell their story in its two parts: first, 'the things on the road', the story of Jesus and his interpretation of scripture, and secondly the fact that the moment of recognition was in the breaking of bread.

How is this recognition in the breaking of bread to be understood? For a Christian reader a symbolically significant meal naturally suggests a eucharist. Yet even if Luke himself meant the meal to be associated with those early Christian breakings of bread which feature in his continuing account (Ac. 2:42, 46; 20:7, 11) – meals which appear to be an early form of Christian eucharist, though the historical developments are not straight-

---

26. There is no reason why *prospoioumai* should not have its usual meaning of 'pretend'. The point is that the implicit proposal to continue along the road is a means to the end of eliciting an invitation from the disciples.

forward – the action of Jesus within the framework of the story can hardly have that significance for the disciples. Moreover the language chosen is not distinctive. Although there are obvious similarities to the account of the Last Supper in Luke 22:19 (taking bread, thanking/blessing, breaking, giving), there are at least equal similarities to the feeding of the five thousand in Luke 9:16 (taking bread, blessing, breaking, giving); and in both cases the language is essentially that of grace before meals within Jewish households (Jeremias 1966: 109, 174–5). This presumably signifies that in important respects the meal at Emmaus is to be seen in continuity as much with the practice of Jesus in his earthly ministry as with the Last Supper; and that, if there are overtones of the Christian eucharist, then the eucharist is to be seen in that same continuity.

Why then are the eyes of the disciples opened now? It is because the breaking of bread is an action, and a particular kind of action – sharing the basic necessity of life (bread), in continuity with the earthly practice of Jesus. Although the disciples' hearts burn at the expounding of scripture it is only when words are complemented by action, the action of sharing that which is necessary for daily life in the manner of Jesus, that the recognition of the risen Jesus comes.

The story, then, is about discernment of the risen Jesus. The recognition takes place in the context of the exposition of scripture and the sharing of a meal. One way of summarizing this might be as recognition through Scripture and Eucharist, Word and Sacrament. Yet such a summary has the danger that it may allow the sharp implications of the biblical story to be obscured. On the one hand, the disciples know both the story of Jesus and the scriptures, yet fail to understand either until they are given a particular way of understanding (v. 26). Familiarity with the content of scripture is no guarantee of encountering the risen Christ through it; and even when Christian understanding is given, this does not of itself suffice to open the disciples' eyes; more, in the form of prayer to Jesus and a meal, is necessary. On the other hand, the breaking of bread opens eyes precisely because it is an act of sharing continuous with that of Jesus in his earthly ministry; and if the Christian eucharist is to enable genuine encounter with the risen Christ, its symbolism must represent and express action that shares with, and meets the needs of, others in a way characteristic of Jesus.

The Emmaus story thus relates the seeing of the risen Christ to particular human contexts. The divine initiative is not thereby diminished, but it is shown not to be arbitrary, in the sense that a certain combination of factors – in traditional terms, 'means of grace' – appropriately enables it to achieve its purpose.

## The enduring significance of the story

When the logic and meaning of the story has been grasped, we have to ask what the contemporary reader is to make of it (although it will be apparent that the way in which I have set out the exposition already implies a certain kind of answer to this question). This can be approached by way of two possible objections to drawing out continuing implications of the story for Christian faith today.

The first objection is that of critical historiography. However comprehensible such a story and such a theology may be in the context of the first-century Christian church, it makes assumptions which are no longer possible for those who have learned to think historically and to read texts accordingly. Put simply, we know (through extensive philological and historical study) that the Hebrew scriptures often do not mean what New Testament texts say they mean. As Fitzmyer (1985: 1565) succinctly puts it, when commenting on Luke 24:26, 'the notion of a suffering Messiah is not found in the OT or in any texts of pre-Christian Judaism'. To be sure, certain texts, in particular the account of the servant in Isaiah 52:13–53:12 came to be understood in this way, by Jews as well as by Christians (p. 1566). But such an understanding belongs to the history of interpretation which, from the perspective of the historian of religious thought, may regularly be a history of misinterpretation.[27] What may have been intelligible for Luke in his context is no longer an option for anyone now, as a matter of intellectual honesty. To propose it can only mean to resubject the text to blinkered ecclesiastical control, emancipation from which has been a chief purpose of historically oriented biblical criticism over the last couple of centuries.

27. For a rousing restatement of such a position by an (apparent) cultured despiser of religion, see Lane Fox 1991. He describes ancient Jewish and Christian biblical interpretations as 'ha[ving] nothing to do with truth' and as constituting sheer 'rape' of the Hebrew text (1991: 341–3). For similar criticism of the related phenomenon of scripture and canon, see Carroll 1997. According to Carroll, it is of the nature of canonical scripture in its effects on people that 'it bypasses the critical faculty', that 'the notion of canon is a serious deformation of the Bible as text', and that 'canons wrench texts from their original integrity and reassign them values in the canonizers' system of thought'. In short, 'canons subdue writings and make them conform to hermeneutic principles other than the ones under which the texts were originally produced. Canons reflect the powerful ideologies of the canonizers. . . . Canonization is about power and empowerment' which entail political issues which are 'notoriously absent from all such discussions'. 'Proper academic study' can ignore questions of canon altogether (1997: 312, 317–19).

The second objection is of a moral nature, a kind of ideological critique. Does not the very notion of a unique and authoritative interpretation of sacred texts open the way for endless self-deception on the part of those who claim to carry it out, together with manipulation and abuse of others, either to make them agree or to persecute them if they do not agree? Can the Christian Church be trusted with a claim to exclusive insight into the true meaning of its scriptures? The history of Christian attitudes to Jews, as the prime historical exemplar of those who generally resisted the Church's claims in this matter, suggests not. If the Church no longer considers Jews to be fleshly, blind, broken, and wandering, and is seeking new ways of understanding and relating to the Jewish people and Jewish faith, is this not at least in part because the Church has been forced to abandon delusive and dehumanizing claims of privileged understanding?

These are both serious objections, to which no glib answers are possible. Nonetheless, one purpose of this book is to try to indicate one way forward in which we can learn from such difficulties without being paralyzed or debilitated by them; for it may be that Christians need to relearn what the scriptural foundations of their faith do, and do not, mean. I hope it will already be clear from the preceding exposition that the particular ways in which the objections are formulated depend upon a rather narrow construal of the possible implications of the Emmaus story. Although I have tried to formulate the objections in the way they are commonly encountered, the way they express things tends, in my judgment, to beg the question. Rather than trying simply to rebut the objections – which would be improper as well as futile – the crucial matter is to rethink the nature of the problems at stake.

To take the second objection first. We should take with full seriousness the Emmaus story's linkage of scriptural understanding with the breaking of bread. As already noted, even if this indicates a classic Christian understanding of encounter with the risen Christ through Word and Sacrament, the story does not envisage this in any merely formulaic way but rather expresses the demanding and surprising nature of the process. As already noted, the meal is symbolically suggestive of the kind of action through which Jesus, the Christ, welcomed people and mediated God's kingdom to them.[28] If this is the context for seeing the risen Lord, it

---

28. In Luke's context, the feeding of the five thousand seems to be understood primarily in christological terms as a sign of Jesus' messiahship, coming as it does between the questions of 9:9, 18–20.

means that a Christian understanding is inseparable from a certain kind of 'eucharistic' lifestyle and practice. It is to those who are willing to live and act as Jesus did that the way Jesus understood God and scripture is most likely to make sense.

Thus we return to the thesis that the understanding of scripture is inseparable from appropriate contexts of faith and life as a whole. This does not mean that the Bible cannot be studied from perspectives other than those of Christian faith. Quite the contrary: one can study questions of language, poetics, history, ideology, and so on, with little or no reference to the question of God. But in so far as people try to engage with the bigger questions of what it is that the Bible as a whole, or at least significant parts of it, says and means, what they make of it will always relate to their wider understanding of what life is about. Whenever people are willing to listen and learn, there can always be fruitful dialogue. But for the Christian, good interpretation will be indebted not only to the mastery of the necessary intellectual disciplines and to continuing dialogues with other interpreters but also to a 'eucharistic' practice of life (whose implications can be as broad as eucharistic theologies usually are) which continues the way of Jesus. To appeal to the privileged position of the Church as witness to Christ as a basis for ignoring, or persecuting, those who interpret the Bible differently will entail forfeiting that serendipitous sense that true understanding, like life and faith, is a gift—a recognition which is essential to the Church's *raison d'être* in the first place.

What then with regard to the first objection? The fact that the risen Jesus points his disciples back to the existing scriptures of Israel deserves further reflection in two ways. First, it is commonly supposed that what is at issue is a Lucan theology of 'proof-from-prophecy',[29] that is, the appeal to a particular selection of texts which might be interpreted as messianic prophecies. And if one asks which texts these might be, then one looks in the first instance to those texts cited within Luke–Acts. As A. Loisy put it, 'the evangelist envisages all the passages of the OT wherein primitive Christianity thought it recognized messianic prophecies, chiefly the texts cited by himself in this book and in Acts'.[30] Yet this neglects the fact that Luke gives one story explicitly about Jesus' vocation and mission and the

---

29. 'Luke has been at pains from the very beginning of his gospel to develop his theology of "proof-from-prophecy", of which chapter 24, recording the resurrection of Jesus as the Lord, is but the literary, historical and theological climax' (Schubert 1957: 178).
30. Loisy 1924: 579, cited in Fitzmyer 1985: 1567. Or, even more restrictively, 'When Jesus is said to have expounded "the things about himself" in the Pentateuch (24.27), the text which Luke will principally have in mind is Deut. 18 (with *anastesei* in v. 15 doubtless construed as an allusion to Jesus' Resurrection)' (Robinson 1984: 482).

use of scripture as formative within that vocation – the testing in the desert (4:1–13), following the baptism and preceding the Galilean ministry; here, the Deuteronomic texts which Jesus uses to define the meaning of his sonship are none of them, by any reckoning, ancient or other, either Jewish or Christian, messianic prophecies. On the one hand, this directs our primary attention within the Old Testament to passages which speak of obedience and trust in relation to God as the likely primary reference of the risen Jesus' words in 24:26–7. On the other hand, this suggests that we should allow that Luke was well able to distinguish between that use of scripture which he ascribes to Jesus in the gospel, that use of scripture which he ascribes to the early church in Acts, that use of scripture which he practises himself in both books, that use of scripture which he may anticipate on the part of his readers, and that use of scripture on the part of his readers which he may not anticipate and which yet may be appropriate, and not conflate the five as Loisy and others do.[31]

Secondly, there is, if one reflects on the scenario, an enormous temptation at the moment that the risen Jesus speaks – to explain his life, death, and resurrection by appeal to Israel's scripture – to make him say something else. For here is the critical moment when the silence of the grave is decisively broken. Here is the moment when, from 'the undiscover'd country from whose bourn no traveller returns', someone *has* returned; and that someone is not just anyone, but Jesus the Messiah. Here, therefore, is the opportunity to reveal mysteries about God, the world, and the life to come which a saviour who had been to, but returned from, the realm of the dead might be supposed to be supremely well qualified to speak about.

That such temptation could prove overwhelming is exemplified by some of the gnostic texts whose content proved enticing to many at a time when the identity and self-understanding of the Church was still relatively loose and unformed. For example, Bentley Layton, in introducing *The Secret Book According to John*, 'one of the most classic narrations of the gnostic myth', observes that: 'the narration of the gnostic myth in BJn is encapsulated within a frame story which seems to imply that the content of the work is a post-resurrection teaching of Jesus. This would agree with the gnostic belief that after his resurrection Jesus remained on earth for

31. So also Conzelmann: 'In his own way Luke has given a foreshadowing in the life of Jesus of the function of Scripture in the Church. During his lifetime Jesus employs the proof from Scripture – Luke xxiv, 44 provides evidence of this – and also after his Resurrection (Luke xxiv, 27). These passages set out the principle of exegesis which is later frequently employed in the Acts of the Apostles' (1960: 157).

eighteen months and taught "the plain truth" ' (1987: 23–4). The decision of the Church to exclude and oppose gnostic tendencies represents, among other things, a profound understanding of the implications of Luke's portrayal of the risen Christ.

The basic issue, in general terms, is simple – where does the truth about human life lie? The answer of Israel's scripture, as focussed in the book of Deuteronomy which is explicitly foundational for Jesus (Lk. 4:1–13), is in terms of the moral and relational character of human life under God, which is given particular content in God's election of, and covenant with, Israel. Here some of the key categories are such as fear of God (*yir'at 'elohim*), repenting (*shuv*), obeying (*shamaʿ*), loving (*'ahav*), and embodying justice (*mishpat*), steadfast love (*ḥesed*), faithfulness (*'emunah*), and holiness (*qodesh*). These may be hard to embody in life, and numerous alternatives may seem more attractive. But the key question is whether these represent the truth about human life, in such a way that once they are known and their practice made possible then alternatives either fail to add to them or distract from them.

This, we may observe, is precisely the issue in another passage in Luke, the parable of the rich man and Lazarus, especially in its conclusion, where Abraham declines to send someone from the dead to move the rich man's brothers to repentance on the grounds that 'If they do not heed Moses and the prophets, they will not be persuaded even if someone should rise from the dead' (Lk. 16:27–31). The point of the text is easily missed. Bultmann, for example, relates it to his concern for the relationship between faith and evidence: the point is that it is not right 'to ask God for a miracle as a confirmation of his will' (1963: 203). Yet the point is that anything that someone, who returned from the dead, could say could neither replace, nor make somehow more palatable, the moral and spiritual challenge already present in Israel's scripture. And that, as the Emmaus story makes clear, includes even the return of Jesus from the dead. To suppose that there must be something somewhere which would somehow make true life easier than the demanding, transformative, moral, and spiritual categories of Israel's scripture is, according to Luke's Gospel, a delusion.

If this discussion is at all on the right lines, it instantly raises the question: 'Why then the New Testament?' Does it not add to Israel's scripture in the kind of way that has just been ruled out? To which the answer is both 'No' and 'Yes'. The answer is 'No', in the sense that the New Testament has the same kind of moral and spiritual concerns as

Israel's scripture, thus continuing them. The answer is 'Yes', in that the New Testament fundamentally reconstrues the content of Israel's scripture in relation to the person of Jesus. But in Jesus the reconstrual takes place not in relation to something arbitrary or esoteric, but precisely in the unreserved living of human life in relation to God which is the purpose of Israel's scripture. In the classic terms of Matthew 5:17, Jesus does not abolish but fulfils the scripture.

To be sure, Jews and Christians have substantial disagreements (both between each other and among themselves) as to the appropriate content of 'unreserved living of human life in relation to God', such that one knows what to do to achieve it, or how to recognize it when one sees it. But for Christians a foundational premise of faith is that Jesus, as portrayed by the gospels, did live thus, so that in Jesus the glory of God is found as nowhere else. A major part of the gospel testimony is that Jesus lived thus through his discernment and appropriation of the will of God as his father in Israel's scripture; and Luke portrays others' grasp of what this means as only becoming possible in the light of Jesus' resurrection from the dead. This indicates not only that Israel's scripture is indispensable to the discernment of the will of God, but that the discernment practised by Jesus was, and is, far from self-evident. Thus, as already noted, to suppose that what is at stake is essentially the appeal to a particular selection of texts which might be interpreted as messianic prophecies is largely to miss the point. For that could leave people still in the position of the puzzled disciples on the road, knowing the story – even including Easter! – and yet failing to grasp, or be grasped by, it. Rather, the question is what it means to discern and encounter God through Israel's scriptures, a process which requires engagement with those scriptures as a whole within the context of obedient openness to the God of whom they speak; and which, for Christians, is shaped and motivated by the pattern of Jesus in his life, death, and resurrection.

### Conclusion

To read the scriptures in the light of Christ constitutes the heart of a continuing Christian claim to read Israel's scriptures as the Old Testament. It does not deny that the material may be read otherwise, with differing hermeneutic assumptions and priorities, by Jews in genuine engagement with the will of God, or by philologists or historians concerned to understand the meaning of the text in its ancient contexts, or by artists or novelists or filmmakers who imaginatively interpret the text. Nor does it deny that Christians can profitably learn from, and be corrected by, these other interpreters (a process one hopes will always be mutual). Rather it affirms that once Israel's scripture has been interpreted by Jesus Christ, then it can most fruitfully be read and appropriated as a whole in ways and with priorities which might otherwise not have been evident to its readers (most of whom, without this particular context of understanding, would never bother to become its readers in the first place).

Thus the Christian appellation of Israel's scriptures as Old Testament is not just an unfortunate derogatory term which can be replaced without significant loss by some other term such as 'Hebrew Bible'.[32] It represents an assessment of Israel's scripture as the indispensable account of the one God who is known in Jesus Christ – in which, nevertheless, God is not yet known in Christ as he comes to be known through Christ's life, death, and resurrection as portrayed by the New Testament. Israel's scriptures not only prepare the way for Christ, not least by presenting an understanding of God and humanity in which Jesus' life, death, and resurrection become possible and intelligible in the form they take. There is also a retrospective movement from Jesus back to Israel's scriptures whereby they are recognized to be what they would not otherwise be recognized to be, that is Old Testament alongside the witness to God in Jesus Christ in the New Testament.

In sum, therefore, an understanding of the difference Jesus makes to the interpretation of Israel's scriptures as the Old Testament is always as much a goal still to achieve as a task already accomplished. To try to reduce the issue to a few familiar formulae and the rehearsal of well-known interpretations of well-known texts would lose the hermeneutical challenge of the Emmaus story, in effect making the burning of the heart and a eucharistic context into dispensable options. This is not to deny that certain formulae can have a real pedagogic role, but rather to insist that their function is to introduce and enable, rather than substitute for, genuine engagement with the substantive issues of scripture. In every generation, the challenge to discern the living God in Christ through scripture remains.

---

32. See also Moberly 1992: esp. ch. 5.

# 3

# Abraham and God in Genesis 22

In the light of our preceding discussion of Christ as the key to scripture, how best should we proceed in actual engagement with Israel's scripture? I propose, for several interrelated reasons, to consider only one story – but that one story is the story of Abraham and Isaac in Genesis 22:1–19,[1] one of the most memorable and resonant of all biblical stories (often conveniently referred to by its Jewish name, the *Akedah*).[2]

For both Jews and Christians in their differing contexts (and differently again for Muslims, through the Qur'an), Genesis 22 has been one of those highpoints in scripture where the nature and meaning of the Bible as a whole is illuminated with unusual clarity. The story has served as an interpretative key to other parts of scripture, and has interacted with continuing post-biblical patterns of faith and life. It has an enormous history of reception, rooted in its intrinsic meaning.[3] I wish to stand within that broad tradition.

Genesis 22 is also one of those stories within scripture which is regularly used as a focus for discussion of fundamental and wide-ranging issues of a theological and moral nature. Probably the most famous example of this is Kierkegaard's *Fear and Trembling*, but there is no shortage of

---

1. For convenience I will refer to Genesis 22:1–19 as Genesis 22. In doing so I do not, however, wish to overlook the significance of Genesis 22:20–4, where the genealogy introduces the name of Rebekah, who is to be the wife of Isaac, and so the human channel through whom the renewed promise of 22:17–18 is to be fulfilled. Although Genesis 22:1–19 can be read on its own, there are numerous linkages between it and the material that both precedes and follows it.

2. *Akedah* is a noun meaning 'binding', taken from the Hebrew verb in Genesis 22:9.

3. Standard histories of Jewish and Christian interpretation respectively are Spiegel 1979 and Lerch 1950. There has been a remarkable outpouring of literature on Genesis 22 in recent years, but this is not the context in which to document it. A more general account of the history of reception of the figure of Abraham, and its possible implications for today, is Kuschel 1995.

other such discussions both before Kierkegaard and subsequently. This seems to me a thoroughly appropriate use of the text, to which I hope this present study may contribute in a small way.

Moreover, Genesis 22 features in recent scholarly work as a recurrent paradigmatic example for theories of interpretation, not least for Christian interpretations of the Old Testament. Gerhard von Rad (1971) wrote a small book on the story, while Brevard Childs (1992: 325–36) used it as his prime example within the Old Testament of his wider thesis about Biblical Theology. It is not, of course, necessary that all Christian interpretation of the Old Testament should follow patterns of interpretation suggested for Genesis 22. But one must start somewhere. And since many scholars, both within and outside communities of faith, are more or less doubtful about the whole enterprise of God-related interpretation as already outlined, one might as well start with a text whose significance, both intrinsically and in terms of its reception, is not in doubt. If we cannot make progress here, we are unlikely to make progress anywhere else.

### The canonical significance of Genesis 22

The modern interpreter comes to the biblical text with interests and expectations aroused by the historic impact of the text within the history of Jewish and Christian thought and practice. However, it is not difficult to show that this historic role develops Abraham's and the story's own intrinsic and canonical significance.[4]

Genesis 22 is a story of Abraham, who stands at the outset of Israel's story. He is the ancestor of Israel in that he is the grandfather of Jacob who was renamed Israel and whose twelve sons are the eponymous ancestors of the twelve tribes of Israel. He is also the one who responds with obedience to the call of YHWH and who is the recipient of a covenant which looks to YHWH's enduring relationship with his descendants. Within the Genesis portrayal of Abraham's life and his relationship with God, Genesis 22 is the climactic moment. It is not the final story of Abraham, for there are still two more stories in which he features. Since, however, his purchase of a burial place for Sarah anticipates his own dying and burial (Gen. 23), and in the lengthy story of the acquisition of a wife for Isaac the focus shifts away from Abraham himself to Abraham's faithful servant (Gen. 24), these stories provide a kind of diminuendo and prepare for the storyline to move on from Abraham. Genesis 22 is the story of the last

---

4. Approaches which reject this assumption will be discussed in chapter 5.

encounter and the last dialogue between Abraham and God, and its content focusses on the nature of the relationship between Abraham and God.

Elsewhere in scripture Abraham is remembered not with the familiar honorific titles, 'man of God' or 'servant of YHWH' but with the remarkable title 'friend of God' (Isa. 41:8; 2 Chron. 20:7; Jas. 2:23),[5] which implies a relationship with God of the most desirable kind – a real, and mutual, life-enhancing relationship. To be sure, some of the resonances of 'friend of God' are likely to be due to a contemporary understanding of friendship and also to some traditional uses (not least in Islam, where Abraham is 'The Friend', *Al Khalil*). The Hebrew verb used of Abraham in Isaiah 41:8 and 2 Chronicles 20:7 is *'ahav*,[6] a verb conventionally rendered 'love', which can have a wide range of meaning (as can 'love' in English). But rabbinic tradition is likely to be near the mark when it links Abraham's *ahav* with the Shema, the summary proclamation of Israel's faith (Deut. 6:4–5), where Israel's response to God, which is to be lived out through obedience to *torah*, is depicted as 'love' (*'ahav*). So one way of understanding 'You shall love YHWH' in Deuteronomy 6:5 is 'Be like Abraham.'[7] It is natural to suppose that the climactic episode in the story of Abraham's walk with God illuminates their relationship with particular clarity.

Recognition of a specific kind of likely original meaning for 'friend of God' should not however restrict, but rather guide, the wider resonances that such a term naturally acquires. Moreover, the difficulty in grasping what the Hebrew and rabbinic notion of 'friend of God' means within its own terms requires that it be explored in far more depth than a cross-reference summary permits. Suffice it for the moment to suggest that, although the following discussion will be focussing on Abraham's 'fear' of God, rather than his 'friendship', the two terms may in fact be close in meaning.

## Introduction to Genesis 22

How should a text such as Genesis 22 be approached? Interest in delving behind the text to earlier levels of its putative tradition-history, as in the

---

5. I am indebted in this paragraph to Goshen-Gottstein 1987.
6. The MT in each passage has the active participle and a personal suffix, most naturally construed with Abraham as subject and YHWH as object. However, the LXX in each passage interprets the consonantal text as a passive participle, *'ahuv* rather than *'ohev* (*hon egapesa*, Isa. 41:8; *tô egapemenô sou*, 2 Chron. 20:7). Goshen-Gottstein plausibly suggests that this difference is likely to be reflective of wider interpretative debates about the relationship between divine initiative and human response in the Hebrew and Greek scriptures.     7. *Sifre* 58 on Deut. 6:5; cf. *Sota* 31a; Maimonides, *Teshubha* 10:2.

influential work of Gunkel,[8] has been largely displaced by renewed interest in the narrative dynamics of the story as a story. In modern times the first, and justly the most famous, interpretation in this regard, which anticipated the subsequent recovery of the intrinsic significance of the narrative form of so much of Hebrew scripture, is that of Erich Auerbach (1953). Auerbach argues for the enduring significance for Western imagination of the depiction of reality in Genesis 22. According to Auerbach, Genesis 22 is 'fraught with background', expresses 'the "multilayeredness" of the individual character' and creates a sense of 'overwhelming suspense', a story whose 'claim to truth . . . is tyrannical – it excludes all other claims' (pp. 12, 13, 14).

From the perspective of Christian theology, the best known and most influential narrative interpretation has been that of Gerhard von Rad. Despite von Rad's small book on the story, his work, at least among English speakers, is best known in his Genesis commentary (1972a; no different from that in the small book). Here von Rad, also anticipating later trends, concentrates on the text in its received form, implicitly rejecting the interpretative priorities of Gunkel.[9] The famous climax of von Rad's interpretation (to which we will return) is: 'One can only answer all plaintive scruples about this narrative by saying that it concerns something much more frightful than child sacrifice. It has to do with a road out into Godforsakenness, a road on which Abraham does not know that God is only testing him (1972a: 244).'

Recently, a notable narrative exposition from a Jewish perspective is that of Jon D. Levenson in his *The Death and Resurrection of the Beloved Son*.[10] Levenson makes discerning and constructive use of traditional Jewish commentary and gently polemicizes against the Lutheran assumptions of Kierkegaard and von Rad. Reverential obedience, rather than trust in a promise, is the concern of the story, in which God's trial of the righteous displays the inner logic and vindication of God's election.[11]

In the light of these, it might seem that the obvious thing to do is to offer my own narrative exposition of Genesis 22. We have already seen, in

---

8. 1997. Two subsequent monographs on Genesis 22 still follow the general line of approach exemplified by Gunkel: Reventlow 1968; Kilian 1970.

9. 'It may have become clear that the supposedly oldest version of the narrative was a cult saga of a sanctuary and as such legitimised the redemption of child sacrifice, actually demanded by God, with the sacrifice of an animal. This idea is quite foreign to the present narrative' (1972a: 243).

10. Levenson 1993a: chs. 11, 12. Levenson relates Genesis 22 to his wider concern with changing attitudes in ancient Israel to child sacrifice.

11. 1993a: 138–9. The nature of election is one of the key issues in the book as a whole.

the exposition of the Emmaus story, that the Bible characteristically explores, and indeed regularly defines, the meaning of its central concerns through narrative form. Within the Old Testament, key words and concepts are often elucidated through being presented in a story.[12] What we today might think of as 'conceptual analysis' is regularly present, if we can but learn to recognize it, within the various dimensions of stories which have been harnessed for this purpose.[13] So Claus Westermann (1980: 71–3), for example, characterized certain Genesis narratives, including Genesis 22, as 'theological narratives' to make this point (though in his great Genesis commentary he utilizes the insight less than he might).

Yet I do not propose to offer a narrative exposition so much as a *contextualization* of the story within the Old Testament – though one of the prime insights of narrative theology, that certain things can only be presented and understood within the movement and development of actual  living, remains basic to my account. There are three reasons for this emphasis upon contextualization. First, recent narrative studies of Genesis 22 display not only the variety and vigour of lively debate but also sometimes offer interpretations which are, in my judgment, increasingly arbitrary, not least for the reason that key Hebrew words and concepts are insufficiently related to their ancient Hebrew context of usage and meaning. Secondly, 'narrative' and 'story' are broad terms which should not let one forget that there are many different kinds of narrative/story within the Old Testament, and that unless diversity of genre is taken seriously interpretation may be flat or even misconceived. For example, the story of Job in Job 1:1–2:10 is (as will be seen) a story making a conceptual point, whose meaning lies within itself, while Genesis 22 has a depth dimension in relation to the history of Israel which requires an engagement with that dimension. Thirdly, some commentators are less concerned with conventional scholarly agendas in either historical or literary form, but wish to start with the apparent surface implications of the story and the problematic ways in which it might be used. That is, despite the positive assessment of Genesis 22 in classic Jewish and Christian use, some interpreters find Abraham to be mistaken in his conception of God, an oppressor of his wife and an abuser of his child, and insist that interpretation

---

12. This is not to claim that all, or even a majority, of stories in the Old Testament have this nature and purpose, simply that some do.

13. The characteristic rabbinic practice of exploring and expounding theology through midrash thus stands in significant continuity with the biblical text.

should start from this point. Questions of meaning in relation to context thus become acute.

## Conflicting assessments of Genesis 22

Questions of how to understand the Bible in its own right, of how to understand the Bible in terms of contemporary categories, and of how to relate these perspectives are *the* questions of biblical interpretation. Arguably, they are nowhere sharper than with reference to Genesis 22, especially because it is rare for the almost unanimous positive consensus of Jewish and Christian tradition to be denounced as misguided and immoral (although texts about homosexuality, women, and animals also generate great friction). As such, it becomes the more suitable as a test case for a proposed theological interpretation of scripture.

The basic problem may be set out simply. On the one hand, the positive traditional use of the story is finely expounded by Clemens Thoma:

> The narrative found in Gen 22 had not only a significant religious and spiritual development in late Old Testament times and afterwards, but above all, it affected the history of piety. Many people, finding themselves in difficult situations, were able to sustain themselves on the strength of this account about Abraham who, confidently obeying the God who was 'testing' him (Gen 22,1), was prepared to slaughter his only and beloved son, and about Isaac who was willing to be offered as a sacrifice. This expression of obedience by Abraham and submission by Isaac constitute an example worthy of imitation. The story motivated people to accept obediently and submissively in their lives what seemed incomprehensible, unendurable and contradictory and to reflect upon it . . .
>
> It is generally accepted then that the adherent of Akedah-spirituality imitates Abraham in a special way when he is threatened with the loss or removal by force of something beloved and dear to him. In contrast, when someone finds himself as a sacrifice on the altar, when rejected, ill or close to death, then Isaac comes into the center of focus. Ultimately the person concerned with Akedah-spirituality concentrates his inner sensibilities neither on Abraham nor on Isaac, nor on the two of them together, but on the God of Abraham, Isaac and other great witnesses of faithful obedience and submission. (1981: 213, 215)

On the other hand, John Hargreaves, in a recent, widely used Christian pedagogical introduction to Genesis, finds the assumptions of the story wanting:

The writers seem to have interpreted these words ['God tested Abraham'] in the following way: 'God wanted to see if Abraham had enough faith and obedience to be the leader of His Chosen People. So He pretended that He required a sacrifice. Secondly, God wanted to increase Abraham's faith by making him use it. He did not want him to sacrifice Isaac, but He allowed Abraham to think that He wanted a sacrifice (so that his faith should develop).'

But since the coming of Jesus we can see that God does not treat us like this. We read in James 1.13 that 'God ... tempts no one.' Good parents do not test their young children's trustfulness or develop their courage by pretending that they are telling them to jump into a deep river ... They do not have to set traps or tests or examinations, nor does God have to set special tests for us. (1998: 103)

Further examples, which I take almost at random, abound. Clare Amos, in a recent review of Steven Saltzman's *A Small Glimmer of Light: Reflections on the Book of Genesis*, writes:

I was particularly struck with his comments on the Aqedah – Genesis 22: 'Avraham failed the test. He chose God over his son. He chose being God's servant over being his son's father. He loved God more than he loved his own son, and he made the wrong choice' (p. 56). When I think of the convolutions so many writers, both Christian and Jewish, get up to in their attempts to 'justify' Abraham at this point, I want to give thanks for Saltzman's sanity and say, 'three cheers'. (1997: 243)

Carol Delaney (1989: 29) no doubt speaks for many feminist interpreters when she says, 'I do not see why the willingness to kill a child should be considered a test of piety and the prime example of it.' Other scholars regularly depict God's command to Abraham to sacrifice Isaac in pejorative terms – 'the insane command to slaughter the promised son', 'words of three-fold beastliness ("take ... go ... burn")' (Clines 1990: 50; Lane Fox 1991: 362). This is sometimes combined with an insistence that the deity in the biblical text should only be seen as a literary entity and not confused with any 'real' deity. As Thomas L. Thompson (1987: 205) puts it:

To a degree, I have a personal and quite horrific reaction, and a sense of resentment, toward a god like that in Genesis 22, if we were to mix him up with a God of the real world. Can this be? A God, who 'sees into men's hearts', and then, for a game, would so pitilessly toy with a father's deepest feelings ... I ask those of you who are parents: If this were truly God, would you even want to forgive him if you were Abraham?

Should Abraham be emulated or abhorred? Is the God of Genesis 22 the true God or a doubtful, indeed diabolical, fiction? The choice is stark. To work seriously at the question should take us to the heart of biblical interpretation in a contemporary context.

## The central concerns of Genesis 22

Taking as a starting point the insight that certain Old Testament stories may revolve around the elucidation of important moral and theological concepts, I suggest that a fruitful approach to Genesis 22 is to focus on four key words, which represent concerns around which the story is structured. Although these words come from different voices within the story – the narrator (v. 1), Abraham (v. 8), the angel of YHWH (vv. 12, 17), I do not think that within this particular story the differentiating of voices plays any significant role. Apart from possible uncertainty over determining the force of Abraham's words in verse 8, all the voices are, in narrative terms, equally reliable.

First, the narrator gives an explicit guide to the meaning of the story at the outset. The story is introduced by 'After these things God tested Abraham', the content of the test being given in verse 2, the request[14] to offer Isaac as a sacrifice. Thus the first key word, representing a central concern, is 'test' (*nissah*, v. 1). Secondly, the primary resolution of the tension within the story set up by the testing request of verses 1–2 is provided by the angel's words 'Keep back your hand from the boy . . . for now I know that you fear God . . .'(v. 12). The eliciting of Abraham's fear of God is said to be the explicit purpose and goal of the test. Thus the second key word and concept is 'fear of God' (*yere' 'elohim*, v. 12). A third key word is 'provide/see' (*ra'ah*, vv. 8, 14). In the one conversation between Abraham and Isaac about what is to happen, Abraham answers that 'God will provide for himself (*yir'eh lo*) a sheep for a burnt offering' (v. 8). And then Abraham's subsequent giving of a name to the place where the altar was built, 'YHWH provides/sees' (*yhwh yir'eh*, v. 14a) provides a second resolution to the initial direction to sacrifice. Thus a third concern is that God 'provides/sees'. The fourth word is 'bless' (*barek*, vv. 17, 18). For God's renewed promise that he will bless Abraham, and that all other nations will bless themselves by his descendants, is the consequence of Abraham's obedience and the final resolution to the issues posed by the test.

---

14. It is difficult to capture in English the precise force of the particle *na'* which qualifies the imperative *qaḥ* ('take'), which is a standard term in the vocabulary of sacrifice with respect to the person who actually carries out the sacrifice (e.g. Lev. 9:2). 'Request' may be too weak a description of such an imperative, but 'command' may too readily assimilate the wording to other divine commands which are not modified by *na'*.

Of these four terms, the primary narrative weight falls on the first two, 'test' and 'fear of God'. These belong closely together, for what God initiates with his test is what Abraham resolves with his fear of God. The importance of the fear of God in relation to the divine testing becomes even clearer in the light of the fact that 'fear of God' is *the* primary term within the Old Testament for depicting a true and appropriate human response to God (a Hebrew equivalent to 'faith' in Christian parlance).[15] Moreover, the particular formulation in Genesis 22:12 involves the participle (*yare'*) which is regularly used as a noun in construct with God/YHWH to denote a particular type of person, a 'fearer of God', 'God-fearing person'. So the sense is not just that on this particular occasion Abraham feared God,[16] but that Abraham shows on this occasion that as a person he is appropriately designated by the Old Testament's prime category, 'one who fears God'.

In Genesis 22 we have not only a story which is definitive of the meaning of 'one who fears God'; but, given its position as the climactic story in the life of Abraham, the friend of God, Genesis 22 may appropriately be read as a, arguably the, primary canonical exposition of the meaning of 'one who fears God'. For a contemporary faith and theology which is  rooted in scripture, this is a passage that will inform, and give a critical edge to, debate as to which people may appropriately be recognized as (in Christian parlance) 'believers'/'people of faith'.

We should also note that of the four key verbs in the story, God is the subject of three ('test', 'provide/see', 'bless'),[17] Abraham only of one ('fear'). The human 'fear of God' is set within a context of language about divine action within which that 'fear' is to be understood. This suggests that one of the issues present within the text is the relationship between divine and human action – an issue already seen to be central within the Emmaus story, there with reference to hermeneutics (the divine closing

---

15. There are perhaps three primary indicators of this. First, in two famous summary statements of response to God, 'fear' (*yare'*) is the first thing specified (Deut. 10:12; Eccl. 12:13; although it is not used in Micah 6:8). Secondly, the term serves an obvious summary function for approved human response to God, primarily in poetic texts (e.g. Ps. 103: 11, 13, 17; 112:1; 128:1; Prov. 31:30; Lk. 1:50) but also in prose texts (e.g. Exod. 18:21; Josh. 22:25; 1 Sam. 12:14, 24). Thirdly, 'the fear of YHWH' is linked with wisdom in the repeated phrase 'the fear of YHWH is [the beginning of] wisdom' (Prov. 1:7; 9:10; Ps. 111:10; Job 28:28), a statement which is foundational to Israel's epistemology.

16. It is in this sense that Hezekiah is depicted in Jeremiah 26:19 in terms of his chastened response to the oracle of Micah.

17. 'All the nations of the earth' are the subject of the reflexive 'bless themselves' (v. 18a), but this human action is clearly derivative from the primary divine action of divine blessing (v. 17); it is when God blesses Abraham's descendants that other peoples will use Israel's name as the pattern of blessing to which they themselves aspire.

and opening of eyes in relation to human engagement with scripture and eucharistic practice). Here it relates to the nature of paradigmatic human relationship with God. We will focus initially on the human action, the fear which Abraham demonstrates, and then consider the various ways in which the three divine actions relate to it.

### The 'fear of God': interpreting in canonical context

First, a further point about method. Genesis 22 does not introduce 'fear of God' as something novel and unprecedented,[18] but presumes its familiarity as a prime term of religious vocabulary. On the one hand, the story shows that Abraham fits into an already established category, while on the other hand it also shows something of what that category, 'fear of God', means.

Standard studies of 'fear of God' tend to trace its history of usage, and to argue for distinctive and specific meanings (numinous, cultic, moral) according to particular literary and historical contexts (Becker 1965; Derousseaux 1970). Within such schemas Genesis 22 is usually ascribed to the Elohist and set at a relatively early date within the particular concerns of the Northern Kingdom. While this is not without value, there are at least two major drawbacks. One is that the date and context of composition of many Old Testament texts, and in particular the narrative texts of the Pentateuch, is a matter of great uncertainty. The other is that, whatever 'fear of God' might have meant whenever Genesis 22 was composed, its meaning is not limited to that. 'Fear of God', like 'religion', is a comprehensive and open-ended term, whose meaning can be extended and deepened according to context. The placement of Genesis 22 within the collection of Israel's scriptures sets it in a literary context in which intertextual resonances abound. That is, the present contextual significance of Genesis 22 as a primary canonical exposition of the meaning of 'one who fears God' means that it is natural to interpret its account of 'one who fears God' in relation to other significant accounts of what that term means within Israel's scriptures. Whether or not those other texts and resonances were there when Genesis 22 was composed, they have become part of its context of meaning as it is now read. While the scholar who seeks to discern the developmental history of 'fear of God' may appropriately limit the number of texts relevant to the interpretation of Genesis

18. Within the canonical story, the only previous usage is Genesis 20:11, where the familiarity of the term is already presupposed.

22, the interpreter of the text as Israel's canonical scripture may range more freely (while still, of course, needing to exercise judgment as to which other uses in the Old Testament are good parallels and so interpretatively illuminating).

### Two key passages for interpreting 'fear of God'

#### (1) Exodus 20:20

Our study of significant uses of 'fear of God' within the Old Testament starts with Exodus 20:20. Here, directly after the giving of the Ten Commandments, when the people of Israel are afraid of the awesome phenomena which accompany God's speech, Moses says to the people: 'Do not be afraid, for it is to test (*nissah*) you that God has come, and that his fear (*yir'ah*) may be before you so that you do not sin.'

Within the context of the Old Testament, the linkage between Genesis 22 and Exodus 20:20 is probably the primary resonance of Genesis 22, and is one which can plausibly be argued to be a resonance intended by the writers of the Pentateuch. The linkage is both terminological and conceptual. In Genesis 22, Abraham's fear (*yare'*) is the purpose of God's test (*nissah*). The only other passage in the Old Testament where we find the conjunction of these two terms, and in the same sequence, is Exodus 20:20.[19] Some linkage between the passages was long noted within terms of the Documentary Hypothesis, as both texts were ascribed to the Elohist, but the interpretative possibilities remained largely untapped. One significant exception, however, is H. W. Wolff in his thesis that the 'fear of God' is the distinctive theme of the Elohist. Wolff recognized the links between Genesis 22 and Exodus 20:20 and commented: 'When God began to speak to Israel his will was the same as it was when he declared it to Abraham . . . God's normative word from Mount Sinai to all Israel is directed toward the same goal that he had set for the Patriarchs: fear of God' (1972: 167). This is excellent as far as it goes; but yet more can be said.

We need initially to consider Exodus 20:20 in its own right before the linkage with Genesis 22 can be fully appreciated. The major contribution to an understanding of this verse in modern scholarship has come from Brevard Childs (1974: 340ff., esp. 371–3). Four insights of his are fundamental. First, the sheer importance of the verse. Whereas many Exodus

---

**19.** There is a small difference in that Exodus 20:20 has the nominal form *yir'ah* rather than the verb in participial form. This may perhaps be to distinguish the fear which God's coming promotes from the fear in the sense of fright (*'al tira'u*, v. 20a) which is not necessary.

commentators have passed over it with nothing more than a paraphrase and perhaps listing references to similar terminology elsewhere, Childs (p. 372) has drawn attention to its key significance:

> Moses moves immediately to execute his office. He accepts his position by exercising it: 'Do not fear.' God's intention is not to crush his people with commands, but to enter into a covenant. Moses then picks up the initial themes of 19.3ff. God has a purpose for his people. What has happened at Sinai is directed to this goal. It is on account of this that God has revealed himself. In a real sense, v. 20 provides the narrator's own key to his understanding of chs. 19 and 20. In two parallel clauses, both introduced by the preposition 'on account of' (*ba ʿabur*) Moses explains the meaning of God's revelation on Sinai.

Secondly, Childs has enabled a recognition of the function of the verse within its present context. For many years a strong source-critical consensus saw Exodus 20:18–21 as a direct continuation to the account of the theophany in Exodus 19:16–19[20] – with which the links, in terms of the depiction of God's presence on Sinai, are indeed obvious.[21] This was done in such a way as to interpret 20:18–21 solely with reference to the theophany, and with no reference to the Ten Commandments which directly precede: this was the meaning of the text in its original Elohist context, prior to the insertion of the decalogue. Childs does not dissent from this consensus view, but insists that it does not lessen the need to interpret the text in its present form in which 20:18–21 represents a response to the decalogue. It becomes a good example of the difference which attention to the canonical form of the text may make.

Thirdly, Childs noted that Deuteronomy 'provides the best commentary' on Exodus 20:18–21 in its fuller development of the implications of Sinai. Deuteronomy has its own explicit statement of the purpose of God's revelation: 'Gather the people to me, that I may let them hear my words, so that they may learn to fear me (*leyirʾah ʾoti*) all their days . . .' (4:10). Again, the enabling of the fear of God is the purpose.

Fourthly, Childs (p. 373) draws out the moral dimensions of the fear of God in this context:

---

20. More precisely, the E elements within this text, vv. 16, 17, 19.

21. It is interesting to see how Benno Jacob, no friend to the rearrangements of the pentateuchal text proposed by the documentary hypothesis, feels free to situate 20:18–21 as directly following on from 19:16–19: 'All this [sc. 20:18–21] takes place before y-h-v-h's descent onto Sinai in 19.20, before the presentation of the ten statements, but immediately after the dialogue between God and Moses.' This is primarily on the basis of an argument advanced by Maimonides that only Moses clearly heard the words spoken by God on Sinai (*Guide for the Perplexed* (1956) pt. 2, ch. 33). But he also appeals to the similarities between Exodus 20:18 and 19:16 (Jacob 1992: 576–7).

> The basic point of this verse [sc. Exod. 20:20] is misunderstood when one combines the general concept of fear with the technical biblical term 'fear of God'. Indeed the people have feared before the theophany and are comforted by Moses. But the issue at stake is whether God came in order to evoke such an emotion. Calvin, followed by most modern exegetes, sees the purpose of the theophany to lie here: 'in order to inspire you with the dread of offending him' (Driver, p. 201). However, it is very doubtful whether the passage carries this meaning. The fear of God is not a subjective emotion of terror, but the obedience of God's law. The glory and holiness of God calls forth man's fear (cf. Isa. 6), but the end is not the emotion, rather the deed.

Although it still remains to probe further the meaning of the key terms 'test' and 'fear', the significance of Exodus 20:20 in context is sufficiently clear for the importance of the links with Genesis 22:1, 12 to be appreciated. The one passage is a formal statement of the purpose of YHWH giving the Ten Commandments, the heart of *torah*, to Israel; the other is the supreme story about the nature of Abraham's encounter with God. But before the relationship between the two passages can be formulated, one further general consideration is necessary as to how an appreciation of the likely tradition-history and perspective of composition of the text can illuminate its interpretation. I have discussed this at length elsewhere (Moberly 1992), and so here will state it briefly.

It is highly likely in general terms that the pre-Israelite patriarchal stories of Genesis 12–50 have been told from an Israelite perspective, a point perhaps most clearly visible in the use of the name YHWH in Genesis. Although there is still much evidence within the text to suggest that many of the stories, especially those of Abraham and Jacob, were originally formulated within a non-Yahwistic context with a coherent religious outlook different from that of Mosaic Yahwism, the stories have been preserved by Israel not only because of the historic sense that they are stories of Israel's ancestors but also because they were amenable to varying degrees of moulding and reformulating within the terminology and perspectives of Mosaic Yahwism so that they could function as religiously authoritative within Israel.

The significance of the links between Exodus 20:20 and Genesis 22:1, 12 is therefore that the story of Abraham has been deliberately told in the language of Israel's obedience to *torah* so that Abraham can be seen as a type or model of Israel. If Israel wishes further to understand the dynamics implicit in obedience to the Ten Commandments, then those dynamics are given narrative embodiment by Abraham – that is what the shape of Israel's obedient life should look like. Abraham now serves as the definitive example of the kind of obedient response that God seeks from Israel. Abraham's willingness to relinquish Isaac resonates particularly with the first two commandments, the prohibition of other gods and their images, when these are understood (as Israel came to understand them, whether or not they originally had this significance) as requiring Israel to renounce anything which posed a threat to undivided loyalty to the one God.

To be sure, one can see ways in which Israel's situation, as recipients of *torah*, differs from that of Abraham. The Ten Commandments are permanent, community-forming requirements; and they do not require anything so problematic as the offering of a son. But if the Ten Commandments pose in some ways a different challenge to Israel than that which faced Abraham, they are not thereby rendered in any way less demanding. One may suggest that the parallels between Genesis 22 and Exodus 20 enable Genesis 22 to function in the same kind of way as the words of Jesus in Matthew 5:20–48 – that is, to penetrate the significance of the Commandments in such a way as to evoke a more total response.

Finally, one must still take seriously the narrative sequence in which Abraham precedes Israel and the giving of *torah*. A prime implication of the text read in sequence would be, as Wolff saw, that the summons to fear God characterizes Israel's story from its very beginning in Israel's ancestor, and that what was given to Israel at Sinai was congruous and continuous with what preceded. Some understanding of the typological process embodied within the text not only enriches the reading but helps one avoid inadvertently putting to the text questions which are inappropriate to its genre.

### (2) Job 1:1–2:10

A second parallel to Genesis 22, and the best known, as the conceptual links have been recognized since antiquity (Japhet 1994), is the story of Job (Job 1:1–2:10). It is a story which elucidates the meaning of 'one who fears God' (*yere' 'elohim*) together with the closely related notion of 'integrity' (*tummah*).

Job is introduced by the narrator as a model of right living, in the most positive terms applied to anyone in the whole Old Testament, terms which include the same expression used of Abraham in Genesis 22:12, 'one who fears God' (Job 1:1). Job is also from the land of Uz. Wherever Uz was, Uz was not Israel. That is, Job stands outside the specific context of

God's election of Israel, and so seems to represent something about humanity as such which may be valid independently of God's special revelation to Israel (although it is Israel which recognizes and characterizes it).

After the initial depiction of Job's wealth and piety, the scene shifts directly to a dialogue between God and the satan.[22] After an opening exchange, YHWH speaks words in which he confirms the narrator's initial depiction of Job as a model human being (1:8). However, YHWH's words to the satan are interrogative and so invite a response – implicitly (for the reader) that of emulation.[23] The satan duly responds, but is unimpressed by God's commendation of Job. The satan's speech (Job 1:9–11) introduces the critical issue around which the whole story revolves: 'Does Job fear God for naught?' (v. 9). The point is simple and searching. It is not whether or not Job actually lives a religiously and morally observant life, for that is accepted. It is a point about fundamental motive, whether Job's lifestyle as 'one who fears God' may not at heart be other than it appears to be, in that Job's real concern may be not for God but for himself, his own self-interest. The narrator has spelt out at the very outset the abundance and prosperity that Job enjoys, without specifying in any way the relationship between that abundance (vv. 2–3) and Job's piety (v. 1). Such silence leaves the relationship open to more than one construal, and the satan offers a suspicious construal, the single most damaging obstacle to acceptance of YHWH's invitation to consider Job as a model of what human life should be. The satan suggests that Job does so well out of his fear of God that this is a sufficient explanation for it (v. 10). The way to show this is to remove all that he enjoys and then his lack of genuine reverence for God will become readily apparent (v. 11).

Since YHWH has deliberately opened the way for the satan to offer a suspicious interpretation of Job's fear of God, he naturally accedes to the proposed test (v. 12). However, he sets the limit that only Job's possessions and family, and not his own person, are to be the elements of the test – for it was only family and possessions that were mentioned at the outset of

---

22. 'The satan' (*hassatan*) depicts a title or role, 'the accuser', not a proper name as in later Jewish and Christian thought.

23. The Hebrew 'consider' (*sam leb* [with various prepositions]) is a stronger term than, for example, 'Have you seen/do you know [*hara'ita, hayada'ta*] my servant Job. . . ?' where the point would simply be awareness of Job, sufficient to allow the conversation to continue. Three times *sam leb* is used in contexts where action is implied in the act of 'considering', in a way similar to 'remembering' (*zakar*): in Exodus 9:21, not considering the word of YHWH means not moving servants and livestock when warned that their situation was dangerous; in 1 Samuel 25:25, not considering Nabal means not going to kill him; in 2 Samuel 18:3, not considering the fleeing or dying army means not bothering to pursue or harry it further.

the story, and it was only with reference to these that the satan expressed his suspicion.

A consequent crescendo of disasters, related in stylized fashion (vv. 13–19), leads to the moment of truth for Job. He responds by beginning a conventional mourning ritual (v. 20). But when it comes to the moment for speech he utters not a lament, still less a curse, but rather a blessing where the focus is strongly on YHWH (v. 21). Job seeks not his own self-interest but the glory of God. He has shown the satan's suspicion to be unwarranted, and so has passed the test.

But the pattern repeats itself. YHWH again invites consideration of Job as a model, whose model qualities have shown themselves precisely in the situation where he proved that YHWH's action against him had no more basis in his life than the suspicions of the satan – YHWH's action was 'without cause' (ḥinnam, 2:3), just as Job's fear of God was indeed 'for naught' (ḥinnam, 1:9): Job has shown no quality in which the seed of suspicion might take root (2:1–3). The satan remains unimpressed, however, for a reason which becomes obvious as soon as the initial onslaught on Job was complete. The exemption of Job himself permits continued suspicion, indeed almost encourages a deeper suspicion than previously – that Job was willing to lose his family and possessions precisely to save himself; Job may be not only self-seeking, but also ruthless in his pursuit of it, preserving himself at the expense of others (v. 4). This is hardly a 'fair' construal of Job's situation, but it is the fact that it remains a possible way of construing Job's response that matters. So the terms of a further onslaught define themselves: personal affliction, with the sole limitation that Job must remain alive to be able to respond to it – which is brusquely carried out (vv. 5–8). His wife then voices a natural response to the situation, that the kind of response to God which Job had been maintaining, his integrity (tummah),[24] is simply not worth maintaining – better to be done with it completely (v. 9). At this second moment of truth Job responds as before, though with different words for the different circumstances: fear of God, and its corresponding integrity, means a constancy independent of circumstance. Job will not countenance the reduction of a true relationship with God to that of being a fair weather friend (v. 10). His relationship is indeed 'for better, for worse; for richer, for poorer; in sickness, and in health'.

Three reflections on this story. First, the story is clearly paradigmatic.

---

24. The noun tummah in 2:9 is the same as in 2:3, and is the noun corresponding to the adjective 'blameless' (tam) in 1:1, 8; 2:3.

Job is a model to consider and emulate; and although the nature and implications of Job's response are qualified by its position within the book of Job as a whole, where Job subsequently speaks differently, there is nothing within the story itself to diminish its demanding implications. The story depicts true fear of God as a genuine human possibility. However, the story is also a conceptual elucidation in narrative form which explicates the meaning of 'fear of God' by raising the most damaging possible critique – unrelieved self-interest – and showing that the meaning and significance of the term can be enhanced, rather than diminished, by taking the critique with full seriousness. It would not suffice for God to respond to the satan's suspicion simply by reasserting his initial assessment of Job, for then the viability of the 'fear of God' would be in danger of being reduced to mere assertion and counter-assertion because of the evasion of a genuine difficulty. Of course, the story as a whole is still making an assertion which may not be accepted, but it does so in the light of, and not despite, a rigorous critical scrutiny.

Secondly, the story revolves around the satan's suspicious response to YHWH, a response which poses stark alternatives that are usually muted: *either* God *or* self-interest. Most people most of the time would probably argue that it is a case of 'both-and' instead of 'either-or', rather as most respond to Jesus' stark alternative of 'God *or* Mammon' (Matt. 6:24//Lk. 16:13). Moreover, many biblical characters (perhaps most famously Jacob and Samson) are not <u>such that their motives could ever withstand this</u> kind of scrutiny. <u>Mixed motives are the rule, not the exception</u>. But it is characteristic of scripture to pose sharp alternatives[25] rather as sociologists use ideal types, that is as heuristic tools to enable understanding of what in many empirical contexts presents a rather confusing aspect; though the biblical writers have the further concern of encouraging and enabling change of life in the direction of the more desirable alternative, that is, to refine and purify the mixed motive. Within the story of Job the issue has arisen precisely because it is a matter of holding up Job as a supreme model for emulation, and this necessarily raises the critical question of testing for authenticity more acutely than in many other contexts.

Thirdly, the story makes clear that the issue at stake is not one that can be resolved on a purely theoretical level (any more than can the discernment of the risen Lord, discussed in chapter 2). Questions of integrity and

---

25. For example, righteous and wicked (*tsaddiq, rasha'*; *dikaios, poneros*), wise and foolish (*ḥakam, nabal*; *sophos, moros*), those being saved and those being lost (*hoi sozomenoi, hoi apollumenoi*).

self-seeking can indeed be discussed, but ultimately the only response to suspicion is a *demonstration* of integrity. Access to the court of YHWH cannot of itself resolve a problem which must be resolved within the living of human life.

In all these aspects the story of Job has extensive resonances with that of Abraham in Genesis 22.

### Two problems in understanding 'fear of God'

#### (1) The legacy of Rudolph Otto

The consideration of two Old Testament passages in which 'fear of God' is important has set a context for understanding 'fear of God' in Genesis 22 more fully. On the one hand, fear of God is what is required of Israel as a nation, and Abraham embodies the kind of response God seeks from Israel; Abraham, though an individual person, in some way represents Israel as a nation (as does Jacob in certain stories). On the other hand, fear of God can be a matter of an integrity of relationship with God in which a person trusts and worships God for God's sake. The story of Job is also a valuable pointer to the fact that 'fear of God' may be a richer notion than obedience; for obedience as such is hardly the issue in Job 1–2, but rather integrity and faithfulness of relationship.

Much yet remains to be said, however, about the meaning and significance of 'fear of God/YHWH'. This is a difficult task because, as already noted, 'fear of God/YHWH' is such a fundamental term within the Old Testament that it risks being as difficult to elucidate as terms such as 'religion' or 'morality'; any single or simple definition is likely to be partial and more or less inadequate to the range of textual data. Because one of the most common ways of skewing the meaning of the text is to import questionable and unexamined assumptions, it will be helpful to proceed further by trying to remove two such common assumptions.

First, then, some remarks about the legacy of Rudolph Otto. One of the most famous and influential works in the twentieth century about the nature of religious experience is that by Rudolph Otto (1924). Otto's thesis  is that religious experience is primarily a matter of encounter with that which simultaneously awes a person into shrinking back and attracts them to draw close, a *mysterium tremendum et fascinans*. In time this basic religious experience is developed and rationalized in cultic and moral terms, a process which risks losing the essence of the experience, but which is nonetheless necessary if religion is to be a creative element within human life. It is not my present purpose to criticize Otto as such, but rather to comment on some of the limitations of his thesis in relation to 'fear of God'.

Otto's understanding of the holy has been influential upon many Old Testament scholars' perception of the fear of God (though there have been significant dissenters).[26] Typical is the account by Eichrodt. Eichrodt's primary strategy for preventing misunderstanding of 'fear of God' is an appeal to an apparently self-evident universal phenomenon of religious experience, conceptualized explicitly in Otto's terminology:

> This predominant trait in the personal relationship of Man with God in the Old Testament is given linguistic expression in the habit of describing the whole religious relationship as *the fear of God* or *of Yahweh, yir'at* *ᵉlohim* or *yir'at yhwh*, and likewise, right religious conduct is termed God- or Yahweh-fearing, *yᵉre* *ᵉlohim* (*yhwh*), a usage which persists with remarkable regularity from the earliest to the latest times. There can be no doubt that this shows the sense of the gap between God and Man to be the dominant element in Old Testament piety, and the temptation is never very far distant to take this fact as justifying a depreciatory assessment of such piety as servility and decadent self-surrender. A moment's consideration, however, of *the universal importance of fear in all religions* may be sufficient warning against such a step. Indeed, when this distinctive phenomenon is investigated, it becomes plain that religious fear is not simply a matter of a naked feeling of terror, putting one to flight, but of an *oscillation between repulsion and attraction*, between *mysterium tremendum* and *fascinans* (footnote reference to Otto, *The Idea of the Holy*, Kierkegaard, *The Concept of Dread*). (1967: 268–9)

After discussing the form that this polarity of repulsion and attraction took within Israel, Eichrodt (p. 273) utilizes Otto's categories to describe a process of developmental rationalization within the Old Testament:

> What is happening is clear enough. Because the fear of God is understood as a relationship with the sovereign divine will, the irrational element in that fear, the numinous feeling of terror in face of a divine power which is unknown and which may break forth abruptly

26. Von Rad comments that 'the phrase "fear of God" says almost nothing directly about a special disposition of the soul, a special feeling for God. It must not be considered as a special emotional reaction to the reality of God which is experienced as *mysterium tremendum*' (1972a: 241); and likewise Childs rejects an interpretation of 'fear of God' as 'the mystical sense of the deity described by R. Otto' (1974: 373). Whether it is entirely fair to Otto to depict his notion as 'emotional' or 'mystical' is unclear. It is extremely difficult to disentangle the real significance of such disagreements because they tend to be couched in the categories of other well-known religious controversies.

at any time, is being repressed in favour of an attitude of reverence, learned by human mediation, for divine ordinances which can certainly be known and which remain permanently present. *The fear of God is thus filled with a complex rational content, with the result that predominance is given to the positive element in the God–Man relationship.* Because the will of God is known primarily as something consistent and perspicuously clear, and is accepted into the fabric of life, *quiet confidence in the manifest God* gets the upper hand over terror in the presence of the hidden one.

The value of Eichrodt's overall presentation is less our concern than the way in which such a perspective may skew the interpretation of Genesis 22. At first sight, there may be little problem, for Eichrodt's comment on Genesis 22 is fine as far as it goes: 'This self-commitment, which is ready for the most extreme demands, and which bestows on the true fear of God the character of unconditional trust even in face of his enigmatic and uncomprehended will, is grasped most profoundly in the Elohist's narrative of Abraham's sacrifice of Isaac' (p. 275). Yet when one sets this alongside the comment on Exodus 20:20, which is also conventionally ascribed to the Elohist in the documentary analysis accepted by Eichrodt, and where therefore he might reasonably be expected to look for some similarity of meaning, the problem becomes apparent. Exodus 20:20 is construed entirely in terms of Otto's thesis of repulsion and attraction:

> The intensity with which, in the right sort of fear of God, men are aware of this attracting and binding force in God's self-communication, and feel it as a counterpoise to the sense of sheer terror, is perhaps most strikingly summed up in the words of Moses addressed to the people on Sinai, when they were filled with consuming anxiety: '*Do not fear!* for God has come to prove you, and *that the fear of him may be before your eyes*, that you may not sin.' (1967: 271)

The linkage of *fear* with *prove* within the verse, the linkage of both with the preceding Ten Commandments, and the terminological and conceptual linkage of Exodus 20:20 with Genesis 22:1, 12 are nowhere in view, probably obliterated by the hermeneutical presupposition of Otto's *mysterium*. Moreover, within Eichrodt's discussion the paradigmatic story of Job receives no mention at all.[27] One may at least wonder whether its lack of fit with Otto's categories may have contributed to such an oversight.

27. There is solely a footnote reference to it as illustrative of the regularity of usage from earliest to latest times within the Old Testament (1967: 268).

The enduring appeal of Otto's work for scholars of the Hebrew scriptures thus has three drawbacks, at least with regard to 'fear of God'.[28] First, it encourages a developmental account of the 'fear of God/YHWH' which in fact fits badly even with conventional datings of many of the relevant passages. Secondly, it may lead to a misconstrual of key texts through the imposition of inappropriate categories of interpretation. Thirdly, it tends to a discounting of an important text such as Job 1:1–2:10, because it does not 'fit'.

## (2) Fear of God as fear of unpleasant consequences

A second problematic assumption is that the 'fear of God/YHWH' is to do with anxiety about unwelcome consequences for neglect of particular actions. As Roland Murphy (1992: 176) puts it, 'The moral connotation of fear of the Lord may derive from fear of his actions, especially those of judgment. The fear of sanctions tended to support a given moral conduct.' More specifically, this point of view is developed by Sherryll Mleynek, who discusses Genesis 22 in the light of an Aristotelian theory of tragedy and comments:

> Abraham's *fear* establishes his faith. Yet surely this is fear in the Aristotelian sense: 'Let fear be defined as a painful or troubled feeling caused by the impression of an imminent evil that causes destruction or pain' (Aristotle: 2.5.1.1382a). What other than *fear* of God would have motivated Abraham to sacrifice his son? It has been pointed out to me that the Hebrew *yere*, which in the passage from Genesis quoted above [sc. 22:12] is translated fear, can also mean reverence. However, can we doubt that Abraham's *reverence* was a response to his belief that failing to do God's will would bring about an 'imminent evil that causes destruction or pain'? After all, the history of Genesis argues persuasively that those who disobey God are not lightly dealt with . . .
>
> To summarize, Abraham's fear is generated by his certainty that the consequences of his refusal must be greater than of his assent. Otherwise, why would he comply with God's commandment? For were he merely motivated by faith *without* consideration of the consequences for refusal, one must conclude Abraham would have protected his son, and not felt fear of God in so doing. This is the heart of the dilemma that has so puzzled commentators, for Abraham's motivation can never be seen as pure: fear of God is a contaminated basis for faith. (1994: 114–15)

28. Otto's perspectives remain foundational in recent discussions such as Murphy 1992 and Gowan 1994: 27, 36.

Mleynek's account raises complex issues about the nature of religious and moral rationality. For the present it will suffice to make four brief comments. First, there is no doubt that consequences, particularly in the form of public sanctions of one kind or another, play a large role in the inculcation and preservation of morality. The laws and narratives of the Old Testament (and New Testament) regularly display such a linkage. Indeed, it is not clear how human life might be supposed to be conducted without sanctions of some kind or other. Secondly, it hardly follows from the necessity of sanctions, and fear of consequences, that such things are the best indication as to the real meaning of a moral and religious life – especially when that life is understood as a process of growth and development in which the appropriation and internalization of moral and religious norms makes a difference to how they are practised and understood.

Thirdly, however complex it may be to develop and establish purity of motive, the story of Job, as discussed above, would seem the most unambiguous indication within the Hebrew canon that 'fear of God' should not be understood in the way Mleynek proposes; for the maintenance of Job's fear of God is specifically detached from the good or bad consequences which may or may not flow from it. It would be surprising if Abraham's paradigmatic fear of God should be seen as less pure than Job's in a story which is designed to display what fear of God really is.

Finally, it may be that an underlying weakness in Mleynek's account (beyond the unwarranted, and exegetically false, assumption that the Genesis writer must mean by 'fear' the sort of thing that Aristotle meant) is a failure to take seriously the relational dimension of Hebrew fear of God. It is therefore to a consideration of this that we must now turn.

## The relational significance of 'fear of God/YHWH': three aspects of Old Testament usage

Three interrelated characteristics of wider Hebrew usage of 'fear of God' may be noted. First, it can signify moral restraint out of respect for God, a moral restraint specifically that refuses to take advantage of a weaker party when it would be possible to do so with apparent impunity. A classic statement of this is Leviticus 19:14, 'You shall not curse the deaf or put a stumbling block before the blind, but you shall fear your God: I am the LORD' (RSV), and a closely similar sense of restraint is to characterize the implementation of the jubilee where manipulation of someone else's

misfortune and vulnerability for one's own benefit
25:17, 36, 43). This is not 'a specialized development of ι
of fear of God', peculiar to the Holiness Code (Fuhs 1990: ;
terizes several quite different texts. Abraham's unjust.
about Abimelech and the people of Gerar having 'no fear ι
based on his own unsupported position as a sojourner (*ger*)
community who could be murdered with impunity (Gen. 20:11,
refusal to take advantage of his brothers when he has them entire.
mercy is what gives content to his claim to 'fear God' (Gen. 42:18).   ˎst
strikingly, this sense appears almost as a definition of 'fear of God' in
Deuteronomy's depiction of Amalek as one who 'attacked you on the way,
when you were faint and weary, and cut off at your rear all who lagged
behind you; and he did not fear God' (Deut. 25:18, RSV).[29]

Secondly, this moral restraint is seen as a fundamental element of
being human, one that should characterize those outside Israel as much
as Israel itself. Not only has this been seen in the story of Job as a man from
the land of Uz. The three examples just cited all depict people living outside the context of Israel and Yahwism (even if Joseph stands within the
line of Israel, that is not the case for the people of Gerar or the Amalekites). The depiction of the Amalekites as failing to show fear of God represents a particularly interesting, although problematic, moral construal of
the ban on Amalek.[30] Its logic appears to be that the attack on defenceless
people constitutes such a fundamental denial of God that those who do
such things thereby deny their own humanity and so lay themselves open
to a treatment not otherwise given to other human beings.

Thirdly, the sense that 'fear of God' is a fundamental human requirement, not restricted to Israel, is further conveyed by the regular use of the
generic term 'God' rather than Israel's specific name for God, YHWH, in
passages such as Genesis 20:11; 42:18; Deuteronomy 25:18.[31] It is assumed
that those outside Israel can have some genuine knowledge of the
one God, even though they do not know him as YHWH as do his chosen

29. It is striking not least because Deuteronomy characteristically uses 'fear' in the sense of
worship, to designate religious allegiance, without primary emphasis on ethical content.
Weinfeld comments on Deuteronomy 25:18: 'The meaning of *yir'at 'elohim* here is
conscience, the human quality which deters a man from harming somebody even though
there be no fear of punishment' (1972: 274–5).
30. There are obvious similarities to the account given of why Israel, despite its own
recalcitrance towards YHWH, is given the land of the nations of Canaan (Deut. 9:4–6).
31. The insertion of Israel's name for God in the LXX and Syriac of Deuteronomy 25:18
represents an assimilation to more common deuteronomic terminology which obscures
the logic of MT.

ople Israel. This distinction can lead to subtle variations in terminology. Thus, for example, the astonishing response of Nineveh to Jonah's preaching is a genuine turning to God (*'elohim*, Jon. 3:5, 8, 9, 10), but not a conversion to Yahwism, though such a conversion does happen with the sailors (Jon. 1:4–16, esp. 14, 16). Job, who is not an Israelite but lives in Uz, is a model of humanity in his fear of God (*'elohim*, Job 1:1, 8, 9). In his confession of faith at the moment of truth he recognizes the character of God and blesses God in the language of Israel, to make clear to the reader his sharing of Israel's understanding of God (Job 1:21; cf. Ps. 113:3). But when at the second moment of truth he enunciates a general principle about relating to God, he reverts (in a way characteristic not only of the story but of the book as a whole) to the generic term (Job 2:10). Or, in a not dissimilar way, the prohibition on cursing the deaf and tripping the blind (Lev. 19:14) is a fundamental human requirement, and so is initially worded 'but you shall fear your God'. But since Israel knows God as YHWH, and their obedience is to promote their covenant relationship with YHWH, the fundamental human requirement is brought within the covenant and given a specific context of meaning: 'I am YHWH.'

### Fear of God and fear of YHWH in Genesis 22

It is within the context of this last point that the usage of 'God' (*'elohim*) in Genesis 22:1, 8, 12 may fruitfully be considered, in relation to the uses of YHWH elsewhere in the story (vv. 11, 14, 15, 16). What, if anything, is the significance of first, the general alternation between terms for the deity, and secondly, the usage of *'elohim* rather than *yhwh* in the crucial verses 1, 12?

There have been two main approaches to the possible significance of this usage. On the one hand, a traditional Jewish approach made use of a generalized observation about differences between *'elohim* and *yhwh*:

> The Sages said: Wherever in Scripture *Lord* (YHWH) is used, the reference is to the Mercy Attribute, as it is said (Exod. 34:6), 'The Lord (YHWH)! the Lord! a God compassionate and gracious'; wherever *God* (*Elohim*) is used, the reference is to the Justice Attribute, as it is said (Exod. 22:8), 'The case of both parties shall come before God (*Elohim*).'[32]

This basic model could be utilized in various ways as, for example, in Nachmanides' comment on Genesis 22: 'The view of the Akedah chapter

---

32. *Sifre*, Deut., 27, cited in Spiegel 1979: 121.

is that the one who puts to the test and commands the Akedah is *God* (*Elohim*), and the one who prevents it and makes the (subsequent) promise is the angel of *the Lord* (*YHWH*).'[33]

On the other hand, there has been a widespread consensus within modern scholarship of a very different kind, though no less generalizing in its construal. This has been that the variations in use of terms for God is indicative of the history of the text: that those passages in Genesis where *'elohim* predominates are part of an Elohist source, distinct from the Yahwist, where *yhwh* predominates. This approach has usually said little about the significance of *'elohim* within the text as it now stands, although, as with the traditional Jewish model, there has often been flexibility of application.

I have discussed this latter position elsewhere (1992: 44–5, 87–9, 176–82), and have argued that although the phenomenon of differing terms for God is indeed indicative of the tradition-history of the text of Genesis, its significance has been regularly misconstrued. The alternation between *'elohim* and *yhwh* is not evidence of different sources with different conceptions of when the divine name *yhwh* was first known, but rather evidence of two conceptual levels within Genesis 12–50. On the one hand, the context is prior to Moses, Sinai, Israel, and a knowledge of God as YHWH, so within its own context the writers naturally refer to God either with the generic *'elohim* or with various titles compounded with *'el*. On the other hand, the patriarchal traditions have been appropriated and retold within a Yahwistic context, where the writers have felt free to use Israel's name for God because of their conviction that it is Israel's God of whom the patriarchal stories tell. The issue at stake in the alternation is the tension between the conviction that Israel's particular knowledge of God as YHWH is a normative understanding of God, and the conviction that Israel's God is the one God with whom those prior to, or outside, Israel relate in some way.

On this basis one might argue that the significance of *'elohim* in Genesis 22 is simply that of the usage of *'elohim* anywhere in Genesis 12–50, part of the logic of the pre-knowledge-of-God-as-YHWH context of the material. Yet the interesting question is why, given that the processes of tradition and redaction have freely introduced the name *yhwh* into the text of Genesis 22, and the story as it stands is the product of extensive moral and theological engagement with the issues it raises, the generic

---

33. Commentary on Genesis 22:12 in *Miqra'ot Gedolot*; cited in Spiegel 1979: 121, 124.

term *'elohim* was retained, when it could easily have been replaced. It seems reasonable that we should find determinate significance for it within the text as it now stands.

Within the story *'elohim* occurs five times (vv. 1, 3, 8, 9, 12), as does *yhwh* (vv. 11, 14 (2×), 15, 16), and all but one of the uses of *'elohim* precede the uses of *yhwh*. The one usage of *'elohim* that occurs after the introduction of *yhwh* is the key concept, 'one who fears God' in verse 12. This is probably best understood by analogy with Job 1:1–2:10. Abraham is presented in the generic category, 'one who fears God', to show that the logic and dynamics of what is portrayed is not peculiar to Yahwism. Divine testing and the need to become a person who 'fears God' is not something restricted to Yahwism, but characterizes God and humanity *qua* God and humanity. However, it is as and when God is known as YHWH that the full significance of divine testing and human fearing becomes apparent. Abraham's initial '*'elohim* will see/provide' (v. 8) becomes the specific '*yhwh* will see/provide' (v. 14a).[34] It is not that there is any doubt in the story that it is YHWH throughout. Rather, the usage of language turns on the subtlety of Israel's conception of the one God, definitively known within Israel as YHWH yet generically known to humanity.

### Abraham's 'fear of God': a preliminary conclusion

What, then, is the content of Abraham's 'fear of God' in Genesis 22:12? Certainly it entails obedience, obedience of the most demanding kind, where God's claim on that which is most precious to Abraham, his son, must be acknowledged. In probing further than this, we saw that construals of 'fear of God' in terms of Otto's *mysterium* or of fear of unpleasant consequences import extraneous concerns which obscure the term's primary connotations. Rather, the term depicts human integrity, an integrity rooted in responsive recognition of God, in which the potential of human life can be realized. Abraham's 'fear of God' is also illuminated by his words that 'God will see/provide' (v. 8), which represent a fundamental trust in God as the context within which adherence to God's will is worked out. Abraham's embodiment of this appropriate human response to God is also enriched in content through its links, tacit within Genesis

34. There is some uncertainty here in terms of the history of the text, in that a Qumran text has the generic *'elohim* in verse 14 (Davila 1991). But while such uncertainty may qualify the emphasis to be laid upon this point, biblical textual criticism needs to take account of reception as well as origin in arguments as to what constitutes a best text.

22 itself but clearer in a canonical context, with God's election of Israel and the covenant at Sinai.

Within a canonical context it is possible to find other important resonances also. One can, for example, see possible links between Genesis 22 and the paradigmatic story of human disobedience to, and alienation from, God in Genesis 2–3 (see Moberly 1988a); Abraham's genuine 'fear of God' provides a definitive alternative to the way of Adam and Eve. It also, as we will see, has important resonances with the portrayal of Jesus in Matthew's Gospel. But first we must turn to the term within the narrative which we have already noted to be explicitly correlated with Abraham's fear, that is God's 'test' (v. 1).

### The meanings of testing

#### (1) Caveat and terminology

Within Genesis 22 God's test of Abraham and Abraham's fear of God are intimately linked, the one being the means to the other. As with 'fear', 'test' is best understood if set within the context of other Old Testament usage. A first step within this is to note the varied Hebrew terminology;[35] after a preliminary caveat.

The caveat is that there is a recurrent tendency among commentators on Genesis 22 to qualify God's test of Abraham with 'only'. Von Rad, for example, says that 'the story concerns a temptation given by God, a demand which God did not intend to take seriously. But for Abraham the command that was directed to him was deadly serious.' And the climax of his exposition is that the story 'has to do with a road out into Godforsakenness, a road on which Abraham does not know that God is only testing him'.[36] Despite von Rad's concern to do justice to both the ignorance of Abraham and the insight which the narrator gives to the reader, the effect of the 'only' together with God 'not intend[ing] to take [the demand] seriously' is a reductive qualification which risks undercutting serious imaginative engagement with the biblical text. For to depict a test as 'only a test' gives priority to a detached perspective (a third-person account) which diminishes the essence of a test to a person being tested (a first-person account) as a *real* test in which the future is unknown and in which there is no reason to suppose that the test will have a benign outcome.

---

35. It is not, of course, that specific terms are the sole guide, for we have already noted the story of Job where no word for test is used, and yet the concept clearly informs the story.
36. 2 1972a: 239, 244. The German is 'nur versucht'.

And to know, with the narrator, that God is testing Abraham is no guarantee that one understands what 'test' means, even if one already knows the outcome. In terms of the narrative, God's own 'now I know' (v. 12) is, as we will see, an idiom which functions to prevent a reductive flattening of what testing means.

There are three primary Hebrew verbs for 'test': *nissah, bahan, tsaraph*. Of these *nissah* is the most important, and is used consistently with God as subject.[37] Several features are apparent. First, the object of testing is consistently Israel, with the exception of Abraham (Gen. 22:1), Levi (Deut. 33:8), the psalmist (Ps. 26:2), and Hezekiah (2 Chron. 32:31). Secondly, the contexts are usually of considerable significance – the climactic moment in Abraham's life (Gen. 22:1); the beginnings of Israel's life as the people of YHWH as soon as they are finally delivered from Egypt (Exod. 15:25; 16:4); the purpose of the giving of the Ten Commandments (Exod. 20:20); the significance of Israel's forty years in the wilderness (Deut. 8:2, 16); the construal of prophecy, attested by signs, which encourages apostasy from YHWH (Deut. 13:4 (ET 3)); the appointment of Levi to the priesthood (Deut. 33:8); the significance of continuing opposition to Israel's possession of the promised land (Jdg. 2:22; 3:1, 4). Only the tests of the psalmist and Hezekiah lack special contextual significance. Thirdly, the purpose of the test is always, at least implicitly (Deut. 33:8–9, Ps. 26:2–3), adherence to YHWH. Fourthly, the choice of language to depict such adherence is particularly characteristic of Deuteronomy.

The verb *bahan* is regularly used of God's engagement with an individual's heart or mind.[38] The verb is used to depict a divine inspection of a person, a kind of quality control process. It is regularly invited in the confidence that the person so tried will be found acceptable to God, with the expected consequence being vindication of that person and the judgment of their enemies. The verb *tsaraph* denotes primarily the process of working with and refining metals,[39] but is regularly used metaphorically either of people,[40] or of God's promise as having stood the test.[41] Although there are differences between the usages of these verbs, there is no absolute difference, for sometimes the verbs are used in close conjunction with each other.[42]

37. Gen. 22:1; Exod. 15:25; 16:4; 20:20; Deut. 8:2, 16; 13:4 (ET 3), 33:8; Jdg. 2:22; 3:1, 4; Ps. 26:2; 2 Chron. 32:31.
38. Jer. 11:20; 21:3; 17:10; 20:12; Ps. 7:10 (ET 9); 11:4–5; 17:3; 26:2; 139:23; 1 Chron. 29:17.
39. Isa. 40:19; Ps. 12:7.    40. Jdg. 7:4; Isa. 1:25; 48:10; Ps. 105:19.
41. Ps. 12:7; 2 Sam. 22:31//Ps. 18:31 (ET 30); Ps. 119:140.
42. Ps. 26:2 (*bahan; nissah, tsaraph*); Ps. 17:3 (*bahan, tsaraph*); Jer. 9:6 (ET 7) (*tsaraph, bahan*).

## (2) The analogy with metalworking

What does testing mean? It will be helpful initially to focus on the analogy with the processing of metals. This is the single most recurrent metaphor, and the one which is most readily comprehensible. It occurs solely within poetic contexts, perhaps because poetry most readily encourages such metaphor through analogy.[43] Typical is Proverbs 17:3: 'The crucible is for silver, and the furnace is for gold, and Y H W H tries (*baḥan*) hearts.'

There are some problems in knowing the precise nature of the metaphor, because of uncertainties about the nature of metalworking within ancient Israel. Many precious metals were imported into Israel, and may have been purified before they arrived, so that the processes familiar within Israel may have been more of the nature of assaying and moulding rather than purifying. Nonetheless, it remains possible that Hebrew writers could presume familiarity with the full range of activities involved in metalworking.

In any case, the analogy is a comprehensive one in which the metaphor readily extends itself. If refining is the basic image, then the sense is that just as metal comes naturally in the form of a mixture of ore and metal, and needs a process of intense heat for the metal in its purity to be extracted and made serviceable, so too do human lives. Human life is, by implication, a mixture of the pure and impure, a mixture of that which can be of service and that which is dross. If moulding is the basic image, then the sense is that metal comes in awkward shapes and sizes, and it is only as it is melted and formed into a particular shape that it becomes useful to anyone. Human life, on this model, can lack form and direction until it is reshaped by God into that which can give true service.

The fire which melts the metal has two primary resonances. First, it is a natural idiom for a costly and demanding process, for metal must be melted by fire from solid into liquid form before it can become hard and firm and take serviceable shape. Secondly, fire is a common symbol of YHWH, supremely at Sinai (Exod. 3:2; 20:18; 24:17; Deut. 4:11, 12, 15; 5:4, 22–6). Although the biblical writers do not themselves explicitly link the metalworker's fire with the fire of God's presence at Sinai, they do understand fire as symbolic of the presence and action of God, and so the linkage with Sinai is a natural imaginative link to make (implicit perhaps in Exodus 20:18–20).

---

**43.** Jer. 6:27–30 (*baḥan*, v. 27, *tsaraph*, v. 29); Zech. 13:7–9 (*tsaraph*, *baḥan*, v. 9); Mal. 3:1–5 (*tsaraph*); Ps. 66:10 (*baḥan*, *tsaraph*); Prov. 17:3 (*baḥan*); Job 23:10 (*baḥan*). Probably also Isaiah 48:10, though the text is not straightforward.

The metalworking analogy represents a demanding vision of humanity and God, both because of its implication of the necessity of transformative growth in human life and because of its implication that God may be especially at work in those situations which are humanly unwelcome and painful. It is also a positive and hopeful vision, because it sees the possibility of human life becoming most truly itself, as is metal that has been refined, moulded, assayed. In all these senses the metaphor has been common within Jewish and Christian writings down the ages.

### (3) The distinctive idiom of *nissah*

We should note, however, that none of the passages which utilize the metalworking analogy use the verb *nissah*. Although it would be easy simply to subsume *nissah* under the metalworking analogy, we must consider whether *nissah* may not have a distinctive and complementary sense of its own. If we prescind from Genesis 22 and Exodus 20:20, the most informative context for *nissah* with God as subject is Deuteronomy 8. This is partly because the term is, as noted, characteristic of Deuteronomy,[44] so Deuteronomy is a good place to go to try to understand it; and partly because the context of Deuteronomy 8 links *nissah* with various other terms which facilitate its interpretation.

Our prime text is Deuteronomy 8:2–3:

> You shall remember the whole journey in which YHWH your God has led you now for forty years in the desert, to humble you, to test [*nissah*] you, to know what was in your heart, whether you would keep his commandment[s] or not. For he humbled you, and he made you hungry, and he gave you to eat manna, which you did not know (nor did your fathers know), to bring you to the knowledge that not by bread alone do people live, but that by everything that comes from the mouth of YHWH do people live.

The context of *nissah* in Deuteronomy 8:2 is a construal of the significance of Israel's forty years in the desert. It is a passage which interprets the forty years positively as serving God's purposes, despite the unanimous pentateuchal tradition that the extended wilderness period was caused by Israel's faithlessness when it had the opportunity to enter the

---

44. A case could be made that all uses of *nissah* with God as subject were written under the influence of Deuteronomy (apart from Ps. 26:2 and 2 Chron. 32:31, the latter of which is a clear reuse of deuteronomic language). In a classic documentary analysis, Genesis 22:1 and Exodus 20:20 were ascribed to E rather than D, but affinities between E and D were regularly noted. The documentary affiliations of Exodus 15:25 and 16:4b were never clear; there was a tendency to ascribe them to E, partly because of Exodus 20:20 and partly because of a general reluctance to find D within the narrative portions assigned to J, E, and P.

promised land.[45] It is a striking example of a characteristic biblical understanding of how God can bring good out of bad.

Within this context there are at least three things associated with *nissah* which draw out its significance.[46] First is that which is otherwise taken for granted but which is stated explicitly in verse 16, 'to do good to you in the end'. The process associated with *nissah* is for Israel's good, to enable them to be the kind of nation that they could not be otherwise.

Secondly, each usage of *nissah* is closely linked with *'annah* (vv. 2b, 16b), traditionally rendered 'to humble'. 'To humble' (*'annah*) means to induce the quality of being 'humble' (*'anaw*), a quality which characterizes Moses himself more than anyone else (Num. 12:3). What this means in Deuteronomy 8 is spelt out in verse 3, a verse which can be read as an exposition of the meaning of the repeated 'he humbled you' with which it begins. What is envisaged is essentially a process of learning a fundamental truth about human life as nourished by obedience to God (v. 3b) through the hardship of hunger and the resolution of that hunger through the provision of something unfamiliar and unprecedented (v. 3a); for the unprecedented nature of manna is expressed by its very name (cf. Exod. 16:15). Human living – the repeated *yihyeh ha'adam*, verse 3b, which notably does not use the particular 'Israel' but the generic 'people/humanity' – is defined in a resolutely non-reductive way ('not by bread alone') in terms of obedient attention to YHWH; a point which is reiterated later in the context of emphasizing that the lesson learned is one which may be unlearned (vv. 11–18, esp. 17–18). The meaning of 'being humbled' is thus the painful learning and appropriating of a particular way of human living in relation to God, as particularly exemplified by Moses. The purpose of YHWH's testing (*nissah*) is to promote such a way of living.

Thirdly, YHWH's testing is 'to know what was in your heart, whether you would keep his commandment[s] or not' (v. 2b). This expression of YHWH's wanting 'to know' (*yada'*) about the obedience of the one he tests (*nissah*) as the explicit purpose of the test is a recurrent idiom,[47] present

---

45. Num. 13–14; Deuteronomy 1:19–46.

46. The continuing exhortation in verse 5 also summarizes YHWH's dealings with Israel in terms of the way a father brings up his child through discipline (*yissar*), that is, an educative process in which moral formation of the personality is primary. The pattern of individual formation is seen as analogous to the pattern of national formation. The LXX rendering of *yissar* by *paideuo* reminds that this pattern of moral character formation was not peculiar to Israel but was also characteristic of ancient Greece in its famed *paideia*, though the content varies between the differing religio-cultural contexts.

47. Exod. 16:4; Deut. 13:4 (ET 3); Jdg. 2:22; 3:4; 2 Chron. 32:31. In Exodus 16:4 and Judges 2:22 *yada'* is not used, but the posing of choice by the interrogative particle *ha* retains the same idiomatic sense.

also at the key moment in Genesis 22:12.[48] It is an idiom that distinguishes *nissah* from *baḥan* and *tsaraph*, and that poses interesting interpretative issues.

### (4) Divine testing 'in order to know'

Traditional Jewish and Christian exegesis found the idiom problematic because it appears to deny divine omniscience. Thus ancient and medieval commentators tended to emphasize that the need to grow in knowledge really characterized the people being tested rather than God. Augustine's brief comment on Genesis 22:12 – 'Now I have caused you to know'[49] – is typical, as is his fuller comment on the related material in Judges 3:4: 'Not so that God, who knows all things, even the future, should know, but so that they themselves should know, and in their own self-knowledge should either boast or be confounded.'[50] Likewise the discussion of Maimonides:

> The sole object of all the trials mentioned in Scripture is to teach man what he ought to do or believe; so that the event which forms the actual trial is not the end desired; it is but an example for our instruction and guidance. Hence the words 'to know (*la-da ῾at*) whether ye love', etc., do not mean that God desires to know whether they loved God; for He already knows it; but *la-da ῾at*, 'to know', has here the same meaning as in the phrase 'to know (*la-da ῾at*) that I am the Lord that sanctifieth you' (Exod. xxxi.13), i.e., that all nations shall know that I am the Lord who sanctifieth you. (1956: 304)

On the basis that 'to know' means 'that all people may know' Maimonides interprets Genesis 22:12 accordingly: 'The angel, therefore, says to him, "For now I know", etc., that is, from this action, for which you deserve to be truly called a God-fearing man, all people shall learn how far we must go in the fear of God' (p. 306).

Modern commentators, by contrast, tend either to ignore the issue or to see it in purely literary terms. Thus Childs (no enemy of a linkage between exegesis and dogmatic theology), in his discussion of Genesis 22, comments:

> There has emerged a consensus on some features of the biblical text. First, there is general agreement that any modern exegesis must take

---

48. A related idiom may be that of 'finding to be faithful' (*matsa᾽ ne᾽eman*) (Neh. 9:7).
49. 'Nunc te feci cognoscere' (*Questions on the Heptateuch: Genesis* §58).
50. *Questions on the Heptateuch: Judges* §17.3. The Latin reads 'non ut sciret Deus omnium cognitor, etiam futurorum, sed ut scirent ipsi, et sua conscientia vel gloriarentur, vel convincerentur'. I have rendered *conscientia* as 'self-knowledge' to preserve the linkage with the two preceding uses of *scio*.

seriously the nature of the narrative and not turn the debate into dogmatic propositions. As even Calvin clearly recognized, such a phrase as 'now I know' which is placed in the mouth of God, is a literary convention and requires no theological discussion of God's omniscience. (1992: 326)

But although it is indeed right that the conventions of narrative must be respected, and the difference from the genre of dogmatic theology be observed, I think it doubtful that the placement on the lips of God of 'now I know' (or, in texts other than Gen. 22, 'in order to know') is a good example of the point. As a literary convention, it is not a mere pleasing and passing turn of phrase, but rather an idiom which raises intriguing questions about the implications of narrative form for the biblical portrayal of God. This is not least because of the rediscovery of the 'omniscient narrator' (see Sternberg 1985), so characteristic of the narratives of Hebrew scripture. If the narrator, unconstrained by the mundane coordinates of space and time, knows the end of the narrative simultaneously with its beginning, would not the deity, whose mind the narrator expresses, know at least as much as the narrator? This is not the place to explore this particular conundrum. My present point is simply that the issue of divine knowledge is far from being an extraneous dogmatic imposition upon the biblical text but rather is itself intrinsic to its narrative idiom and conventions.

The apparent consensus that 'now I know' requires no discussion of God's omniscience is also not entirely borne out by recent literature. James Crenshaw (1984: 2) introduces a discussion of divine testing in the Old Testament:

> The fundamental assumption lying behind divine testing is that God lacks a certain kind of knowledge, that is, precisely how men and women will act in trying circumstances. Of course, such ignorance arises from human freedom, which is itself a gift from the transcendent one. Therefore, the divine act of self-limitation has created the necessity for such testing.

Crenshaw's assertion that the fundamental assumption behind divine testing is God's lack of a certain kind of knowledge is in fact mistaken, for, as we have seen, the notion is entirely lacking, and indeed unnecessary, in passages which use the analogy of metalworking. Rather, the issue of divine knowledge appears only in conjunction with *nissah*, though here it is indeed characteristic. What is interesting, however, is the move that Crenshaw makes. On the one hand, against the tradition represented by Augustine and Maimonides, he wants to take the language implying divine ignorance at face value – God really does not know. On the other hand, the reason for God's not knowing is the genuine human freedom which is itself a gift of God, representing God's own freely chosen self-limitation – so all remains within the purposes of God. Whether or not this is fully satisfactory as an explication of the biblical text, it is an interesting attempt, informed by wider theological debate, to hold together divine sovereignty and human freedom.

In a way not dissimilar to Crenshaw, Walter Brueggemann has an interesting account of the issue in the course of his commentary on Genesis 22:

> Verse 1 sets the test, suggesting God wants to know something . . . It is not a game with God. God genuinely does not know. And that is settled in verse 12, 'Now I know.' There is real development in the plot. The flow of the narrative accomplishes something in the awareness of God. He did not know. Now he knows. The narrative will not be understood if it is taken as a flat event of 'testing'. It can only be understood if it is seen to be a genuine movement in the history between Yahweh and Abraham. The movement is from 'take' (v. 2) to 'you have not withheld' (v. 12), and from 'test' (v. 1) to 'now I know' (v. 12). The move in both forms is accomplished by the affirmation in verse 8, an enigmatic statement of unqualified trust. It is only verse 8 that permits the story to move from its problem to its solution. The verse contains the primary disclosure about God: 'God will provide.' In the same verse, we also have the main disclosure about Abraham: 'he trusts'. (1982: 187)

Like Crenshaw, Brueggemann wants to give full weight to the implicit expression of divine ignorance; unlike Crenshaw, he does not as such appeal to broader theological axioms to resolve the apparent difficulty, and indeed implicitly refuses to see divine ignorance as a difficulty. However, although he remains within the framework of the narrative, he in fact introduces an axiom of a different kind, about the nature of faith: faith is not a 'flat event' but a 'genuine movement' of 'trust' in the history between God and a human being. Appreciation of this wider principle of the dynamics of faith resolves the apparent problem within the text.

The discussions of both Crenshaw and Brueggemann are interesting examples of the way in which contemporary Christian exegetes of the Old Testament interpret the text in terms of wider theological conceptions. However much they distance themselves from the traditional stance of an Augustine, what they do is not to replace a theological axiom by a non-theological axiom, but rather replace one theological axiom by another which they judge more appropriate to the context. This seems to me entirely appropriate. Nonetheless, more can still be said to probe the nature of the subject matter, that is, the significance of language of 'testing' and 'knowing' with regard to God's dealings with humanity.

The interpretation of testing through the analogy of metalworking draws out several aspects of the process: testing is necessary for human beings to become truly themselves, and so is for human good; testing may be a searing and demanding process; testing is the action of God within human life. But the metalworking analogy on its own could imply a primarily passive role for the human within the process. For the analogy says nothing about moral choice and the characteristic biblical understanding that human life and growth is in a significant way constituted by the act of choosing between good and evil. It is this dimension of human choice that is primarily signified by *nissah*, which characteristically, as in Deuteronomy 8:2, poses Israel's response in terms of a fundamental choice – 'testing you to know what was in your heart, whether you would keep his commandment[s], or not'. What marks out Abraham as 'one who fears God' is that he *chose* to obey God. What Deuteronomy holds out as a human possibility, all too often unrealized, is realized in Abraham. Human growth through choosing to obey God is the issue (in this sense the instinct of Augustine and Maimonides that what the biblical text is really about is human learning is surely not unjustified).

But there is one further aspect of testing which is not touched by the metalworking analogy, and that is the nature of God's involvement in the process. That God is involved, and that it is for human good, is clear. But the usage of *nissah* in conjunction with 'know' indicates a further dimension of divine involvement – in essence that the test and its outcome *matters* to God. It is an implication at one with the portrayal of God as one who elects and enters into covenant, in which the relationship thereby constituted is a real relationship which engages God as genuinely as it does Israel. The logic of God's 'need to know' is that of relationship and response.

It may be in some ways a peculiarly modern formulation to suggest that God may be a cold, clinical experimenter or manipulator, 'doing good' at the expense of the suffering of those involved – which would be one possible construal of the imagery of divine testing. In those terms, it would certainly be anachronistic to suggest that the writers of the Hebrew scriptures were aware of such a problem or sought to address it with their consistently anthropomorphic and anthropopathic language about God. Nonetheless, there are at least two recurrent contexts within the Old Testament where the question of God's responsiveness to people is raised.

First, when Old Testament writers express the scepticism of 'unbelievers' about God, it is characteristically in terms of God not making any difference to what happens in the world, so that those people in question may pursue their own purposes with impunity: doubts about God are expressed in terms of their practical consequences in terms of corrupt and oppressive human activity. The paradigm of such denial of God is 'the fool' (*nabal*): 'The fool says in his heart, "There is no God." They are corrupt, they do abominable deeds, there is none that does good' (Ps. 14:1, RSV; cf. Isa. 5:18–19; Zeph. 1:11–12). Questions as to whether human faithfulness and unfaithfulness matter to God are at least at one remove in such a context.

Nonetheless there are contexts in which the question 'Does God *care*?' is explicitly voiced; that is, in passages in which the questioning is the questioning of faith rather than of non-faith, in which the nature of the relationship between people and God is precisely the issue. These are most obviously psalms and prophetic texts of lament/complaint. A good example is the lament of the disheartened Jews in exile in Babylon: 'My way is hidden from YHWH and my longing for justice is disregarded by my God' (Isa. 40:27; cf. 49:14). To be sure, it is likely that the thrust of the exiles' question is 'Why doesn't God *do* something?', for it is in these terms that the prophet responds each time. But it would be anachronistic to distinguish between the nature and action of God in such a way as to separate them. The emotive and relational language ('my God', Isa. 40:27) suggests that the heart of the matter is the relationship between God and Israel, of which God's action on Israel's behalf is an expected outworking.

This context of the dynamics of relationship is one which makes sense of God's need to know. Issues about God within the Old Testament are never posed in separation from the relational dynamic through which Israel knows God. The most explicit raising of the issue of divine omniscience, Psalm 139, raises the issue entirely within the context of the psalmist's relationship with God.[51] It would be a mistake to construe God's 'knowing' in relation to his 'testing' any differently. The concern of the texts is for a deepening of the encounter between God and people. Although the primary emphasis falls upon the appropriate human response, this response is relational at the same time as being moral, and

---

51. The language of the psalmist and God is entirely first and second person – 'I and Thou' – and it eschews the potentially more distanced stance of third person. How many of the conundrums about divine omniscience are created through neglect of the specific form, or 'grammar', of the biblical witness?

this relationship is not conceived as one-sided but rather God is engaged within the encounter in such a way that the outcome is a genuine divine concern. When Abraham is depicted as 'one who fears God', the divine pronouncement 'now I know', rather than 'now people will know', indicates that the deepened relationship is in some way an intrinsic concern of God even as it also constitutes the nature of mature humanity.

### Divine seeing in Genesis 22

### (1) Seeing and providence

A third key motif within Genesis 22 is encapsulated in the verb 'see/provide' (ra'ah). It is this that Abraham affirms God will do, when as yet he does not know how; in response to Isaac's question about a sheep[52] for the sacrifice Abraham says: 'God will see/provide for himself ('elohim yir'eh lo) a sheep for burnt offering, my son' (v. 8). And it is this that becomes a lasting memorial through Abraham naming the place 'YHWH sees/provides' (yhwh yir'eh, v. 14).

The use of ra'ah, the most common Hebrew word for 'see', is initially surprising in this context, for the context seems to require a sense of 'see' other than its usual one.[53] What could 'God will see for himself a sheep for burnt offering, my son' mean for Isaac? The context seems to require that 'see' here has the sense not merely of sight but of sight leading to

---

52. Hebrew seh is a generic term for an animal from a flock (tso'n), of which the ram ('ayil, v. 13) is a specific instance. Traditional commentators, both Jewish and Christian, rendered seh as 'lamb' because of typological associations, not least with the lamb of the tamid (Exod. 29:38ff.) and Jesus as the lamb of God (amnos tou theou, Jn. 1:29); this has continued into some modern translations (RSV, JB, NIV). However, the Hebrew for lamb is kebes, not seh. The typological associations are rich; but the Hebrew text of Genesis 22, where 'ayil not kebes makes specific the sense of seh, gives no warrant for this particular typology; nor does the LXX, which renders seh by the generic probaton.

53. The closest parallel usage of ra'ah elsewhere in the Old Testament is in 1 Samuel 16:1 (other possible parallels are Gen. 41:33; 2 Kgs. 10:3), where YHWH says to Samuel, 'I have seen for myself' (ra'ah le, as in Gen. 22:8) a king among the sons of Jesse. This introduces a story in which one of the central issues is the nature of seeing. Samuel's initial seeing of one of the sons of Jesse is defective, being based on superficial criteria; and this leads to the enunciation of a general principle about the difference between divine and human seeing (1 Sam. 16:6–7). This is then followed by the nice twist that the one who is chosen precisely fits the criteria of appearance by which Samuel made his initial defective judgement (v. 12a); and now YHWH has to tell Samuel that this is the chosen one (v. 12b). Samuel has to learn that if attractive appearance does not determine God's choice, neither does it preclude it. True seeing may need to be carried out precisely in the presence of those features that are most likely to prejudge the seeing.

Although one need not suppose that Genesis 22 is making the same point about seeing that is made in 1 Samuel 16, there is the striking similarity that each time God initially 'sees' something which is not apparent to the human agent, each time the human agent is enabled to see that which God has seen, and each time there is a general principle about divine seeing.

corresponding action – a sense which is certainly in keeping with general Hebrew idiom; for *shama'* regularly means not only to hear but also to act in accordance with what is heard, that is, to obey, and *zakar* regularly means to remember not only as a mental process but as an awareness that initiates action. As Karl Barth comments: 'In this passage "to see" really means "to see about". It is an active and selective predetermining, preparing and procuring of a lamb to be offered instead of Isaac. God "sees to" this burnt offering for Abraham' (1961a: 3). It is customary to render this 'seeing about/seeing to' as 'provide'. The sense of the verb thus determined in verse 8 is then transferred to verse 14, where the place name chosen by Abraham enunciates a theological principle of considerable importance (though only here within the Old Testament is divine provision formulated in an axiomatic way).

Indeed, it becomes a central axiom of Jewish and Christian faith. Barth (1961a: 3, 35) suggests that the concept of divine providence owes to Genesis 22 not only its terminology ('providence' deriving from the Vulgate rendering of v. 8, 'Deus providebit'),[54] but also its substantive sense, in terms of the specific context of the history of salvation giving the necessary content and meaning to the engagement of the Creator with his creation.

In the light of Barth's latter point, it is important not to interpret 'providence' in too abstract a way within this story. For the story makes clear that the divine seeing is marked by the provision of the ram which Abraham sees behind[55] him as soon as the angel has spoken. Abraham's confidence that 'God will provide' is met by his being able to see something that God has provided. The medium of this enablement is Abraham's 'fear of God'. And the divine seeing is memorialized in the name of that specific place.

### (2) Where is 'YHWH sees'?

If the first climax of the story is the divine knowledge of Abraham's fear of God (v. 12), a second climax is Abraham's naming of the place with a name

---

54. It should be noted, however, that the Vulgate uses not *provideo* but *video* in verse 14; that is, the translator reverts to the more common rendering of *ra'ah* by *video* when the context no longer requires an unusual rendering. This suggests that the Vulgate itself does not attribute to *provideo* the significance which it later came to acquire.

55. Hebrew *'ahar* is difficult. *BHS* (ad loc.) prefers a strong MSS tradition which reads *'ehad*, seeing *'ḥr* as a corruption of *'ḥd*, because of the ease of scribal confusion of *resh* and *dalet*. I fail, however, to see the point of *'ayil 'ehad*, for the *'ehad* is redundant if 'a ram' is the sense of the Hebrew. I therefore retain the consonantal text. If *'ḥr* is pointed as in MT then it is an adverb, 'behind' as in Psalm 68:26, which makes good sense. (A possible alternative would be the pointing *'aher*, 'other', with the sense that Isaac is regarded as a sacrificial sheep, and the ram is the alternative, 'another ram'; but this seems to me rather forced.)

that enunciates a general truth about God (v. 14). In fact, two principles are formulated in verse 14: the first, the name Abraham gives to the place (v. 14a), the second, a saying current in the time of the writer (v. 14b). The interpretation of both of these is open to debate, especially the latter where the pointing of the Hebrew text is problematic (see Cooper 1987: 67–73; Moberly 1988b: 307). But their position within the story makes them important. It is clear that the general truth about God is tied to a particular place where that truth is realized. One may therefore reasonably ask, 'Where is this place which is so named by Abraham?'

Perhaps surprisingly, the name which Abraham gives to the place is not used elsewhere in the Old Testament. Can we then know where it is? The problem may be approached through von Rad who, despite his focus on the text in its received form, can find here nothing but a slightly puzzling pun:

> The naming of the place, which Abraham now does, was an important matter for the ancients; for a place where God had appeared in so special a fashion was consecrated for all future generations. Here God will receive the sacrifices and prayers of coming generations, i.e., the place becomes a cultic center. It is strange, to be sure, that the narrator is unable to supply the name of a better-known cultic center. He gives no place name at all, but only a pun which at one time undoubtedly explained a place name. But the name of the place has disappeared from the narrative; only the pun is left . . . What was once the most important point has now become an accessory to the narrative in the form of a pun. Perhaps the ancient name was lost because of the later combination of the narrative with the 'land of Moriah'. (1972a: 242–3)

The pun is not without significance, for by it 'the reader is summoned to give free reign [sic] to his thoughts'; this fits with von Rad's conception of the story as a whole as one which 'is basically open to interpretation and to whatever thoughts the reader is inspired' (pp. 242–3).

Von Rad sees both the importance of Abraham's naming of the place, and the role of wordplay within the text. He sees clues, but cannot piece them together in a coherent pattern. This is a remarkable lapse for so gifted an interpreter, for surely the clues do fit together and the identity of the site within the present text is not in doubt – it is, as Jewish tradition has always recognized, Jerusalem (see Hayward 1981: 132). Von Rad's lapse is, however, in keeping with a mainstream scholarly consensus, which has not identified the site of Genesis 22 with Jerusalem (except as a late gloss, entirely secondary to the meaning of the text otherwise). It is a pleasing irony that a strong consensus of scholars should have attributed to the Elohist,[56] writing in and for the Northern Kingdom, the paradigmatic text in the Old Testament about the propriety of worship in the capital of the Southern Kingdom, in Jerusalem.

What are the clues which identify Jerusalem? First, the saying in verse 14b refers to a/the 'mount of YHWH' (*har yhwh*). The phrase *har yhwh* occurs elsewhere in the Old Testament as a designation for Zion/Jerusalem (Isa. 2:3; Zech. 8:3),[57] though it is also once used for Sinai (Num. 10:33). In itself it would appropriately designate either of these two holy mountains, both of which are central to the Old Testament; but the balance of usage favours Zion. Since the saying in verse 14b presumably refers to the place named by Abraham in verse 14a (for otherwise the reference to this saying in this context would be odd), then Zion (or perhaps Sinai) is indicated as the place named by Abraham.

Secondly, the place to which Abraham goes is only a short journey away, for he sees it 'on the third day' (22:4). 'Three days' is a standard biblical Hebrew idiom for an indefinite short period of time,[58] just as 'forty days' (or 'forty years') is the idiom for an indefinite long period of time. Genesis 22 does not itself specify where Abraham was at the outset, and, in a text such as this, little is to be gained through speculation about possible details of place or time which are passed over in silence. We note, however, that Abraham is located at Beersheba at the end of the previous story (Gen. 21:33) and goes to Beersheba when he returns from the place he has named 'YHWH sees' (22:19). Moreover, the traditions consistently locate Abraham, after his initial presence in Shechem and Bethel,[59] in the southern regions of what became the land of Israel – Mamre, Hebron, Gerar, Beersheba.[60] Both the length of journey and an implicit likely location of Abraham in the Beersheba/Negev region tell against Sinai as the goal of his journey. For the journey to Sinai/Horeb is depicted specifically as a long journey, 'forty days and forty nights', even from Beersheba (1 Kgs. 19:3, 8). Abraham's journey is to somewhere more accessible, more central. Zion fits perfectly.

---

56. 'The attribution of Genesis 22 to E has been a commonplace of source criticism', 'Past critics . . . attribute this tradition to E almost unanimously' (Jenks 1977: 24; Campbell and O'Brien 1993: 170, n. 20).

57. The identity of the *har yhwh* in Isaiah 30:29 must, within the context of the book of Isaiah, be Jerusalem, for the nature and destiny of Jerusalem is a dominant theme in the book as a whole and in its parts (cf. for immediate context 30:19; 31:4–5). The location of the *har yhwh* in Psalm 24:3 is presupposed rather than specified within the psalm, but that this presupposition is Jerusalem is widely accepted.

58. E.g. Josh. 1:11; 2:16, 22; 2 Sam. 20:4; Jon. 1:17; 3:3.    59. Gen. 12:6, 8; 13:3.

60. Gen. 13:18; 18:1; 20:1; 21:22–3, 31–2; 23:1.

Thirdly, the unusual name Moriah[61] occurs in only one other passage in the Old Testament (2 Chron. 3:1), where Mount Moriah is said to be the site of Solomon's temple. To be sure, Genesis 22:2 refers to the land of Moriah rather than Mount Moriah, but this difference is less likely to be significant than the commonality of the name Moriah. The 'land of Moriah' is, as we will see, a symbolic name, comparable to the 'land of Nod' (Gen. 4:16), that is, the land of wandering (*nod*) where Cain will fulfil his destiny of being a wanderer (Gen. 4:12, 14). The mountain of Moriah, where the temple stands, has a symbolic significance comparable to that of other holy mountains in the ancient world – a 'centre of the world' where heaven and earth meet,[62] an 'intersection of the timeless with time'. Since the story of Abraham envisages his going to a specific mountain within the symbolic land of Moriah, and since Abraham names that particular place with (most likely) the same verbal root as that of Moriah, there is little difficulty in seeing Mount Moriah as another name for the same place.

Fourthly, if the name Moriah has a meaning, what is the meaning? This is an ancient crux, the problem being the identity of the verbal root. Since it is common Hebrew practice to form a noun from a verbal root by the addition of a nominal preformative, *mem*, it is likely that this is the case here; though one cannot be sure that the initial *mem* is not integral to the root. The matter may be less intractable, however, if we prescind from questions of etymology in their philological form and focus rather on the associations that the word is likely to have had for the biblical writer within the context of Genesis 22. Here the regular use of *ra'ah* ('see'/'provide') makes it likely that Moriah is to be understood as a noun formed from the verbal root *ra'ah* (and there is a similar linkage in 2 Chron. 3:1, *nir'ah*). This is not beyond question, as the spelling of Moriah in the Hebrew text, *hammoriyyah*, lacks an *'aleph*, the middle radical of *ra'ah*;[63] but it is unlikely that such a spelling problem would matter for such a contextual meaning. If the linkage is not with *ra'ah* then it would be with the other key verb, *yare'* ('fear'; though an *'aleph* would still be missing).[64]

---

61. The presence of the definite article is not incompatible with 'Moriah' as a proper name, for there are other Hebrew names which take a definite article, e.g. Jordan (*hayyarden*), Lebanon (*hallebanon*), Ai (*ha'ay*).    62. See Eliade 1958: ch. 10; Levenson 1985: pt. 2.
63. The *'aleph* is present in some Hebrew MSS (see BHS ad loc.).
64. A traditional Jewish interpretation is to link *Moriah* with the root *yrh*, from which comes *torah*, that is, Moriah means 'place of teaching/guidance' (Hirsch 1959: 368; more recently Janzen 1993: 78). The reason for not making this move is that Genesis 22 does not do so. But in a wider canonical context – initially such biblical texts as Isaiah 2:3//Micah 4:2, and more broadly the contextualization of Hebrew scripture within rabbinic Judaism – such a sense would not be inappropriate.

It may even be, if the meaning is associative rather than philological, that one need not choose between *ra'ah* and *yare'* but can embrace both associations. Thus Moriah, if it is seen as a noun linked with *ra'ah*, would mean 'place of seeing'; and perhaps also, if linked with *yare'*, 'place of fearing'.

If one asks in the light of the rest of the Old Testament where 'the place of seeing' is to be found, the answer is that there are two places where it is said that God is seen, and where, by inference, God may be thought to be present and to see in a particular way. Either of these places might therefore be appropriately named 'YHWH sees'. They are Sinai (Exod. 24:9–11) and Zion (2 Sam. 24:15–17; Isa. 6:1; Ps. 84:6, 9 (ET 5, 8)). If Sinai is too distant, then Moriah is Zion. If one asks in the light of the rest of the Old Testament where the 'place of fearing' is to be found, the answer is initially less obvious. Yet it would presumably be that place where Israel worships YHWH according to the commandments that YHWH has given; which is, as we will see, Jerusalem. Thus, again, Moriah is Zion.

Fifthly, the concerns of Genesis 22 naturally resonate with those associated with the temple in Jerusalem. Abraham is told to go to a place to which God will direct him, there to offer sacrifice, just as Israel is to offer its sacrifices at the place which YHWH chooses for them (Deut. 12:5–6, 13–14). Deuteronomy itself does not specify where this place is, but elsewhere in the Old Testament the one place which is explicitly associated with the language of Deuteronomy 12 is Jerusalem (1 Kgs. 14:21). Abraham offers a ram as a burnt offering (*'olah*), just as Israel offers the *tamid*, the twice daily sacrifice of burnt offering (*'olah*, Exod. 29:38–46). Abraham's sacrifice is the outworking of an obedience to God, just as those who come to sacrifice in the temple at Jerusalem should display obedience to God in their lives (Ps. 15; 24:3–6; Jer. 7:1–15). That is, as we have already noted in the linkage between Genesis 22:1, 12 and Exodus 20:20, Abraham is a type of Israel. His fear of God and sacrifice on Moriah is the pattern for Israel in Jerusalem.

### (3) Jerusalem and tradition history

Why is it that the linkage with Jerusalem has not been seen by so many modern scholars? Or, more precisely, why has it been seen only as a late gloss,[65] arbitrary and irrelevant to the meaning of the story in itself? It is

---

65. It is not clear what constitutes the gloss. The primary candidate is verse 14b, which on any reckoning is a comment that stands outside the story line. It is debated whether the gloss also includes the name 'Moriah', introduced secondarily under the influence of 2 Chronicles 3:1; though Moriah might be original if it is dissociated from the identity given it by the Chronicler. The essence of the argument, as far as I can see, is that whatever identifies Genesis 22 with Jerusalem must be part of the gloss, on the assumption that Jerusalem could not be the story's intended location.

hard to say. But the primary reason is probably a sense that such a patriarchal story, which appears to be ancient, would not have referred to Jerusalem prior to Josiah's reform in the seventh century; most likely, therefore, it once was located elsewhere.

If we explore the possibility that Jerusalem is not original to the story and has displaced some other place, can we locate this other place? Given the attribution of Genesis 22 to the Elohist, one might have supposed that the story would have been ascribed to a major cultic site in the Northern Kingdom. This could be Bethel, which became the primary shrine of the Northern Kingdom, 'the king's sanctuary, a royal shrine' (Am. 7:13), and is associated with Abraham (Gen. 12:8; 13:3–4). Or it could be Shechem, a 'sanctuary of YHWH' (Josh. 24:26), site of the symbolic tree of Moreh (reminiscent of Moriah),[66] and also associated with Abraham (Gen. 12:6–7). Here Mount Gerizim has been identified as the location of the story in Samaritan tradition. Yet remarkably these sites have had few advocates in the twentieth century.[67] This is probably because the most influential guess has been that of Gunkel (1997: 238) who appealed to the wordplays in the text as indicating the otherwise wholly obscure site of Jeruel (cf. 2 Chron. 20:16). The fact that a site which is not otherwise attested as a sanctuary, and is located within the Southern Kingdom, should have been widely accepted as the likely original location of the Elohist's text says more about scholars' respect for Gunkel's ingenuity than it does for the intrinsic likelihood of the hypothesis. Even if Gunkel's hypothesis was accepted, one would still expect scholars to have argued that the original Jeruel was pre-Elohist and that the story was relocated to a shrine in the Northern Kingdom by the Elohist before it was finally transferred to Jerusalem. On many of the common assumptions of tradition-history, this is as likely a tradition-history as one could imagine. Yet it is not in Noth's *History of Pentateuchal Traditions* nor in Kilian's traditio-historical monograph on Genesis 22 (Kilian 1970).

The details of Gunkel's argument, and of alternatives to it, have been well set out in a recent discussion by Jon Levenson (1993a: 114–23). As Levenson succinctly puts it: 'Gunkel and those who follow him err not in drawing our attention to the wordplay on *rā'â* and *yārē'*, but in resorting to the obscure place-name Jeruel to explain it' (p. 117). Levenson

---

66. *Moreh* looks like a *hiphil* participle of *yrh*, usually rendered 'direct', 'teach'. But it might be formed from *ra'ah*. Conversely, Moriah could be argued to be linked with *yrh*, and mean 'place of teaching', as noted above.

67. Otto Procksch's argument for Shechem/Gerizim as the original site, later changed to Jerusalem, is a notable exception (1924: 315–16).

(pp. 119–21) even extends the wordplay by suggesting linkage between *yir'eh* and *yare'* and the first half of the name Jerusalem (*yerusalaim*). Even if, for the sake of argument, one allows that verse 14b and the name Moriah may belong to a late level within the tradition-history of the story, it does not follow that these later additions are not making explicit what is already implicit in the text.

However, the interesting issues at stake in this discussion may be lost if the argument is simply set up in terms of wordplays as clues to an historical conundrum. The tracing of a possible tradition-history underlying the text is a legitimate exercise in historical hypothesis. However, a more fruitful approach may be to consider the language of the text as symbolic language. It is not that Genesis 22 could not refer to somewhere other than Jerusalem; its designations for its location ('land of seeing/fearing', 'YHWH sees', 'Mount of YHWH') are symbolic terms which could refer to any Yahwistic site of significance. It is just that within the Old Testament there are only two places whose significance is developed in such a way as to resonate with the wordplays and assumptions of Genesis 22, and of these Sinai is too distant.

Three further reflections on this issue: first, if Genesis 22 envisages Jerusalem, then this is in the first instance an insight into the nature of the Hebrew scriptures as a canonical collection more than into the origins and development of Israelite religion. That is, the Hebrew scriptures as a canonical collection accord a precedence to Jerusalem and to the perspectives of Deuteronomy such as to form an interpretative context which has classically guided the religious interpretation and appropriation of the material. It does not follow from this that Israelite religion always had this perspective. Indeed, it has been one of the enduring achievements of the last two centuries of historical study to show something of how complex the processes may have been which underlie the present canonical formation. The discovery of these processes for a long time all but eclipsed the significance of the present canonical formation. It is to the credit not least of Brevard Childs that its significance, at least for those Jews and Christians who seek to fashion their lives in continuity with the biblical text, has been restored to the scholarly agenda. The point is that attention to the received canonical form of the Hebrew scriptures does not of itself either preclude or prejudge questions of tradition-history and of the history of Israelite religion.

Secondly, how old can the text be in its present form? In so far as the text resonates with Jerusalem, the *terminus post quem* for this is David's capture of the Jebusite city (2 Sam. 5:6–10; cf. Jdg. 19:10–12) and Solomon's construction of the temple (1 Kgs. 6). If one wished to argue for an origin for the tradition prior to this, there would be two alternatives: either to sever its links with Jerusalem and relate it to another site, for which Shechem would be the most likely candidate in the light of its significance in Deuteronomy and elsewhere in the Old Testament; or to argue for the story in a form other than that in which we now have it, though this form would be entirely hypothetical. Only the former of these alternatives would enable anything worthwhile to be said.

Thirdly, it may be salutary to remember that the story has a continuing tradition-history within Islam: Abraham is the model of a true believer in God, who antedates both Judaism and Christianity, and whose true significance is only revealed through Mohammed. In this context, Ishmael replaces Isaac as the son of destiny, and Abraham and Ishmael together found the most holy site in Islam, the Ka'ba in Mecca. The desire to link ancient holy figures with contemporary holy places is clear. The specific story of Genesis 22 is recounted in rather different form in the Qur'an (37:83–113, esp. 99ff.):

> Then We gave him the good tidings of a prudent boy;
> and when he had reached the age of running with him,
> he said, 'My son, I see in a dream
> that I shall sacrifice thee; consider, what thinkest thou?'
> He said, 'My father, do as thou art
> bidden; thou shalt find me, God willing, one of the steadfast.'
> When they had surrendered, and he flung him upon his brow,
> We called unto him, 'Abraham,
> thou hast confirmed the vision;
> even so We recompense the good-doers.
> This is indeed the manifest trial.'
> And We ransomed him with a mighty sacrifice,
> and left for him among the later folk 'Peace be upon Abraham!'
> Even so We recompense the good-doers;
> he was among Our believing servants.
> Then We gave him the good tidings of
> Isaac, a Prophet, one of the righteous.
> And We blessed him, and Isaac;
> and of their seed some are good-doers,
> and some manifest self-wrongers.[68]

---

68. Translation in Arberry 1980: 153–4.

The basic contours of the biblical story are clearly recognizable in the divine trial of the sacrifice of a loved son, Abraham's full obedience to the will of God, and subsequent divine blessing. For present purposes, it is two silences within the story that are of particular interest. First, the identity of the son is not specified. Although within early Islamic tradition the identity of the son appears to have been a matter of dispute, in due course a consensus emerged that Ishmael, rather than Isaac, is the son in question (Caspi and Cohen 1995: 95ff.). Secondly, no location for the story is given. But eventually Islamic tradition localized it – as Mecca. It is as good an example as one could hope to find of the unfolding logic of the central symbols of a religious tradition which appropriates to itself that which expands and deepens its identity.

One question which therefore arises is whether the development of tradition within the Old Testament is to be envisaged as essentially different from that within Islam. There is, however, little to add to what has already been said. It is possible and not unreasonable to assume that a story which could originally have been located elsewhere has become located in Jerusalem. A Samaritan claim for Gerizim/Shechem can find some warrant within the biblical text (certainly more than Jeruel). But although one can hypothesize various not implausible tradition-histories, we simply do not have the evidence to test conjectures or produce accounts that do more than simply instantiate their working assumptions. The fundamental question is how one understands and evaluates the overarching context of Hebrew religion as depicted within the Old Testament, within which the symbolic meaning of the story of Genesis 22 is now contextualized.

### The significance of Jerusalem as 'YHWH sees'

If Jerusalem is the place where 'YHWH sees', what does this imply for understanding the text (beyond Barth's observation, noted above, about a particular history giving content to the general notion of providence)? Two possibilities may be mentioned.

First, it would imply a striking canonical convergence between traditions of the fear of God and of Jerusalem, a convergence which makes Genesis 22 a kind of hermeneutical key to the Old Testament. On the one hand, 'fear of God/YHWH' is a term that occurs in all the major strands of the Hebrew scriptures as that response to God appropriate both to humanity in general and to Israel in particular. As such it is one of the most obviously unifying concerns in the canonical collection. Certainly, 'fear of God/YHWH' need have no specific linkage with *torah*. Nonetheless, its connection in Genesis 22 with divine testing, and the connections of Genesis 22 with God's giving of the Ten Commandments to Israel and God's testing of Israel, suggest that Abraham's 'fear of God' may in some way represent the tradition of 'Sinai'.[69]

On the other hand, Jerusalem is *the* city of God in Hebrew scripture. Remarkably, it is never mentioned by name in the Pentateuch (a silence for which there are many possible explanatory hypotheses). But it is the place of Israel's worship, as prescribed in Deuteronomy 12 (cf. 1 Kings 14:21), it is celebrated in lyrical terms in the psalms, and its fate becomes a central issue in the prophets and deuteronomistic history. It is for Jerusalem that the psalmist longs in exile (Ps. 137), and Jerusalem's destruction turns joy into anguish and reproach (Ps. 48:3 (ET 2); Lam. 2:15). It is not only the place chosen by God, but its choice is closely associated with God's choice of the house of David as its ruling dynasty (2 Sam. 6–7; Ps. 78:67–72; 132). This whole complex of tradition could be summed up as 'Zion'. And Genesis 22, as the prime story about the divine choice of Jerusalem,[70] and about Jerusalem's significance as the place where 'YHWH sees/provides', could be seen to represent this tradition.

The respective nature of Sinai and Zion, and of the relationship between them, has been a major issue in scholarly study (Levenson 1985: pt. 3), but the possible significance of Genesis 22 has not, I think, been noted. For the purpose of Sinai is fulfilled in Abraham's worship on a mountain which is Zion. That is, whatever the relationship between Sinai and Zion within the development of Israel's religion, within the Hebrew scriptures as a canonical collection we are presented with an intrinsic congruence and coherence between the one and the other. Genesis 22 stands as a foundational account of Israel's life with God, a life centred around worship in the place of divine seeing, which in the Old Testament is Jerusalem.

Secondly, Genesis 22 becomes the primary account within the Old Testament of the meaning of animal sacrifice (as practised in the Jerusalem temple). It has long been a puzzle that the extensive pentateuchal

---

69. One may compare the rabbinic linkage, already noted, between Abraham's love of God and Israel's love of YHWH as prescribed in the Shema.

70. 2 Samuel 24 is another story about the choice of the site of the temple, the link with the temple being made more explicit in the retelling of the story in 1 Chronicles 21, especially 1 Chronicles 22:1. Given the intrinsic importance of the site of the temple, it is not surprising that it should be related to more than one of the key figures in Israel's history.

prescriptions for sacrificial worship say so little about the meaning of what is prescribed. One explanation, at least in terms of the Pentateuch as a canonical collection, is that the meaning of sacrifice has been so clearly depicted in Genesis 22 that further explanation becomes superfluous.

To be sure, Israel offers a range of sacrifices of differing kinds. Nonetheless the primary sacrifice, that which stands at the head of the list both in Leviticus (Lev. 1) and Deuteronomy (Deut. 12:6, 11, 13, 14, 27), is the whole burnt offering ('*olah*); and this is the sacrifice which Abraham makes (Gen. 22:2, 13). Within Genesis 22 Abraham's sacrifice of the ram stands in place of his sacrifice of Isaac. Once Abraham sees the ram, he does not need to be told what to do, but directly grasps its significance and so he sacrifices the ram instead of Isaac. The meaning of this substitution of animal for child is provided by the preceding narrative of God's testing, Abraham's fearing, and God's providing. That is, the whole burnt offering is symbolic of Abraham's self-sacrifice as a person who unreservedly fears God. Sacrifice could, and no doubt did, mean other things within Israelite history (not to mention other contexts). But the canonical and received meaning is that of Genesis 22, where visible religious action and inward spiritual significance are knit together as one.

### YHWH's oath of blessing

#### (1) Role within structure of story

The last major segment of the narrative is the second call of the angel of YHWH from heaven. Hardly surprisingly, it is the most neglected part of the story because of the sense of climax and resolution already by verse 14. Nonetheless, it spells out important implications of Abraham's fear of God and of God's seeing/providing, both within the immediate context and within a wider canonical context. It contains the fourth key word of the story, that is 'bless'.

The fact that the angel speaks words of blessing (22:16–18) means that Abraham's encounter with God ends (in certain significant ways) as it began (12:1–3). The whole story of Abraham's encounter with God is framed by promises of blessing. What does this signify?

In general terms we may note that the underlying logic of what this unit contributes to the story is akin to that expressed in other famous biblical passages. Solomon asked for wisdom, and was given also riches and honour which he had not asked for (1 Kgs. 3). A typical formulation comes on the lips of Jesus: 'Seek first God's kingdom and his righteousness, and all these things [basic human concerns for provision and security] will be added to you' (Matt. 6:33; cf. Lk.12:31). The point is that when a person does the will of God, God provides for their other concerns also. So Abraham lived as one who fears God, even when that imperilled his love for Isaac and the promise of descendants through Isaac. This confirmed his confidence that 'YHWH sees'; and the renewed oath of blessing is an outworking of that divine seeing/providing. This principle of divine blessing is, of course, easily corrupted when it is treated as a goal or an entitlement rather than a gift; and the invincibly suspicious may suppose that this is always the case. But it is the purpose of the portrayal of Abraham in Genesis 22, as it is also (to anticipate our thesis) of Jesus in Matthew's Gospel, to show what seeking God for God's sake might in fact entail. In neither context is the divine blessing bestowed except after searching testing of faithfulness to the will of God. Neither human integrity nor divine gift are trivialized.

In an earlier study (Moberly 1988b), I offered a detailed exegesis and interpretation which focussed on the uniquely emphatic form of this particular blessing and the fact that only here is God's blessing in some way dependent upon Abraham's obedience ('because you have done this thing (v. 16b) . . . because you obeyed my voice (v. 18b)'). Elsewhere, the only specified reason for blessing is YHWH's election of Israel, his commitment to a particular people because of his purpose that they should live out on earth a lifestyle of conformity to the 'way of YHWH' (Gen. 18:19). But the initial giving of the promise (Gen. 12:1–3) precedes Abraham's obedient response, and is not said to be conditional upon such response ('if you are obedient, then I will bless you'), despite the fact that in the Old Testament divine promises regularly are said to be contingent upon appropriate response (most extensively in Deuteronomy 28). How then should the angel of YHWH's words be related to the already-existing promise of blessing?

On the one hand, there is a sense in which the basis for God's blessing has changed. As I put it in my earlier study:

> Abraham by his obedience has not qualified to be the recipient of
> blessing, because the promise of blessing had been given to him
> already. Rather, the existing promise is reaffirmed but its terms of
> reference are altered. A promise which previously was grounded solely
> in the will and purpose of YHWH is transformed so that it is now
> grounded *both* in the will of YHWH *and* in the obedience of Abraham.
> It is not that the divine promise has become contingent upon

Abraham's obedience, but that Abraham's obedience has been incorporated into the divine promise. Henceforth Israel owes its existence not just to YHWH but also to Abraham.

Theologically this constitutes a profound understanding of the value of human obedience – it can be taken up by God and become a motivating factor in his purposes towards humanity. Within the wider context of Hebrew theology I suggest that this is analogous to the assumptions underlying intercessory prayer. Here too faithful human response to God is taken up and incorporated within the purposes and activity of God. (1988b: 321)

Thus the angel's words draw out an implication of the story which is fully consistent with the close interrelationship between divine and human action – God's testing, Abraham's fear of God, God's providing – already noted within verses 1–14.

On the other hand, Abraham has not used God's promise of descendants through Isaac (17:15–19; cf. 18:18) as a reason for not heeding YHWH's voice. He does not say 'I cannot sacrifice my son because he is the destined channel of your promise.' His response shows the logic of trust in its most sharp and paradoxical form. The reaffirmation of the divine blessing is therefore an affirmation of the rightness of Abraham's construal of the promise. Here we should note also that God does not just promise to Abraham but swears an oath to him. David Blumenthal has recently discussed the importance of God's oath to give the land of Israel to the Jewish people within scripture and rabbinic Judaism, and he observes that 'all the references in the Torah to God having sworn to do something for the forefathers go back to one instance', that is, Genesis 22:15–18 (1998: 38–42). Whatever precisely one makes of this, it underlines the foundational nature for Israel's life of Abraham's response to God which takes trust to its extremity.

## (2) The content of YHWH's blessing

The content of the blessing is spelt out in three ways. Abraham's descendants (*zera'*) will become so many that they will not be able to be numbered (v. 17a), will have dominion over their enemies (v. 17b), and will be a widespread expression of blessing (v. 18a). There is a consistent emphasis on Abraham's descendants, as distinct from Abraham himself as in the initial blessing (12:1–3). Or, to be precise, God says 'I will greatly bless you [i.e. Abraham]' and the form that this blessing of Abraham will take is the multiplying and enhancing of his descendants. That which will mean most to Abraham is something directed not to himself personally but to Isaac and Isaac's descendants – that which he was requested to relinquish in his adherence to God's will.

Of particular interest is the third element of the promise, 'and all peoples of the earth shall bless themselves by your descendants'. This promise is a reiteration of the initial promise to Abraham (12:3b), in which context it has received enormous attention, and so will be the focus of our own discussion. There are interesting exegetical and interpretative issues at stake, where semantics and the history of interpretation are so intertwined, that an approach from the historic use of the text is probably most fruitful.

From a Christian perspective, Paul's use of the promise in Galatians 3:8 has been foundational. Here Genesis 12:3 is seen as an anticipation of the gospel, and the Hebrew verb *wenibreku* is rendered, following LXX, with a passive (*eneulogethesontai*): 'All the nations will be blessed in you.' The gospel is mediated through Abraham and through his descendant, Christ. Abraham is not a model of blessing to which others aspire, but a channel of blessing to which others, through faith, attain. Although this interpretation has, unsurprisingly, been criticized frequently on the grounds that the Genesis text does not mean what Paul says it means, it nonetheless retains considerable influence over a Christian imagination (even if the influence is often oblique) when the story of Abraham is read in conjunction with the story of Christ and early Christian mission. For the general tenor of Paul's interpretation has been revived in recent times by Wolff (1966) and von Rad, both of whose comments are so interesting that they merit extensive discussion, though I shall restrict myself to von Rad whose exegesis and hermeneutics are a special concern of this study. Von Rad (1972a: 160–1) says, with reference to Genesis 12:1–3:

> The question has been raised at vv. 2b and 3b whether the meaning is only that Abraham is to become a formula for blessing, that his blessing is to become far and wide proverbial (cf. Gen. 48.20). In favor of this conception . . . one can refer to Zech. 8:13. It is, however, hermeneutically wrong to limit such a programmatic saying, circulating in such exalted style, to only *one* meaning (restrictively). In Isa. 19.24, for example, this conception is no longer applicable. In Gen. 12.1–3 its effect is trivial in God's address which is solemnly augmented – completely so in the final strophe! The accepted interpretation must therefore remain. It is like 'a command to history' . . . Abraham is assigned the role of a mediator of blessing in God's saving plan, for 'all

the families of the earth'. The extent of the promise now becomes equal to that of the unhappy international world . . . an idea that occurs more than once in the Old Testament. Both Isaiah (ch. 2.2–4) and Deutero-Isaiah have prophesied about this universal destiny of Israel. The unusual *nibreku*, to which the Yahwist gives preference against the *hithpael* for this promise, can be translated reflexively ('bless oneself'); but the passive is also possible . . .

This prophecy, which points to a fulfillment lying beyond the old covenant, was especially important to the retrospective glance of the New Testament witnesses. We find it cited in Acts 3.25f.; Rom. 4:13; Gal. 3.8, 16.

The full force of von Rad's comments is best appreciated when they are taken in conjunction with his view of Genesis 12:1–3 as the key to the universal, primeval history of Genesis 1–11:

The story about the Tower of Babel concludes with God's judgment on mankind; there is no word of grace. The whole primeval history, therefore, seems to break off in shrill dissonance, and the question . . . now arises even more urgently: Is God's relationship to the nations now finally broken; is God's gracious forbearance now exhausted; has God rejected the nations in wrath forever? . . .

From the multitude of nations God chooses a man, looses him from tribal ties, and makes him the beginner of a new nation and the recipient of great promises of salvation. What is promised to Abraham reaches far beyond Israel; indeed, it has universal meaning for all generations on earth. Thus that difficult question about God's relationship to the nations is answered, and precisely where one least expects it. At the beginning of the way into an emphatically exclusive covenant-relation there is already a word about the end of this way, namely, an allusion to a final, universal unchaining of the salvation promised to Abraham. (1972a: 153, 154)

Von Rad's interpretation has been influential (often in less nuanced form than he himself expresses it). Childs, for example, utilizes it when he says of God's election of Israel: 'This relationship was toward the purpose of shaping this people into a holy and righteous vehicle by which to reconcile himself to the world (Gen. 12.1ff.)' (1992: 445). It can provide an attractive framework for Christian interpretation of the Old Testament as a whole. As Christopher Wright (1992: 4) puts it:

God called Abram as the starting point of his vast project of redemption for humanity . . . Through that people of Abram God would bring blessing to *all nations* of the earth. So although Abraham (as his name was changed to, in the light of this promise regarding the nations) stands at the head of the particular nation of Israel and their unique history, there is a universal scope and perspective to him and them: one nation for the sake of all nations.

An implicit promise of 'universal meaning for all generations on earth', given to Abraham at the outset, and reaffirmed as the final word of God in Genesis 22:16–18, would indeed make a fine climax for a Christian interpretation of Genesis 22. However, we must linger longer over the question, 'Does the text really mean this?'

The initial problem is the construal of the Hebrew form of *brk*, 'bless'. In Genesis 12:3, as in 18:18 and 28:14, the verb is a *niphal*, *nibreku*. The sense of the *niphal* can be both reflexive (i.e. 'bless themselves') and passive (i.e. 'be blessed') (Kautzsch and Cowley 1910: §51, c–h; Joüon and Muraoka 1991: §51). In Genesis 22:18, as in 26:4, the form is a *hithpael*, *wehithbareku*, the sense of which must be reflexive. On the assumption that no difference in the meaning of the blessing is intended in 22:18 from 12:3 – and the context gives no reason to assume any difference (*contra* Sailhammer 1990: 113–14) – then the ambiguous *niphal* must be resolved by the unambiguous *hithpael*. Such a usage of the *niphal* as reflexive and interchangeable with the *hithpael* is not unique within biblical Hebrew.[71] The sense of all five passages is then in conformity with the Hebrew idiom of the invocation of a specially favoured recipient of divine blessing in the context of a prayer to be like them (Gen. 48:20; Ruth 4:11–12; Ps. 72:17; Zech. 8:13). All this was succinctly expressed by Rashi in his commentary on *wenibreku beka* in Genesis 12:3b:

> There are many Agadoth concerning this but the plain sense of the text is as follows: A man says to his son, 'Mayest thou become as Abraham.' This, too, is the meaning wherever the phrase *wenibreku beka* 'And in thee shall be blessed' occurs in Scripture, and the following example proves this: (Gen. xlviii.20) *beka yebarek* 'By thee shall Israel bless their children saying, "May God make thee as Ephraim and Manasseh."'
> (Rosenbaum and Silberman 1972: 49)

When this idiom is connected with the context of Abraham's story, the purpose of the divine promise is clear: assurance to Abraham.[72] He is a solitary figure, who in response to God is leaving behind the usual

---

71. For a similar interchange between *niphal* and *hithpael* see Genesis 3:8, 10, where the *niphal wa'ehabe'* (v. 10) must have the same reflexive sense ('and I hid myself') as the *hithpael wayithhabe'* (v. 8, 'and he hid himself').

72. This is the clear tenor of the earliest extra-biblical commentary on Genesis, the Book of Jubilees. Jubilees expands God's call of Abraham with the words 'And I will be God to you and your son and your son's son and to all of your seed. Do not fear. Henceforth and for all generations of the earth I am your God' (Jub. 12:24).

securities of territory and family (12:1). As such, he may fear rapid extinction and oblivion. But God will make this solitary figure into a great nation (12:2a), whose name will be so renowned that it will become a well-known pronouncement of blessing (12:2b). God will so commit himself to Abraham that those favourable or hostile towards him will encounter God's favour and hostility accordingly (12:3a). This will be so marked that everyone who hears of how God has blessed Abraham will wish to be similarly blessed themselves, and so will say to each other, 'May God make you like Abraham' (12:3b).[73] Because of God's blessing the solitary and vulnerable Abraham will become a nation to be reckoned with, and the object of extensive respect and prayer for emulation.[74]

The point of the renewed blessing in the context of Genesis 22 is that because Abraham has feared God, that which he has been prepared to relinquish is restored to him definitively. God's blessing of Abraham will take the form of making the number of his descendants far beyond all counting (v. 17a). Their lot will not be that of the downtrodden but, on the contrary, they will have dominion over the cities of their enemies (v. 17b). And nations will so recognize God's blessing of Abraham's descendants that they will say to each other, 'May God make you like Israel' (v. 18a). For Israel, however, the context of the promise within Genesis 22 is an enduring reminder that their existence as a blessed nation, a cynosure among the nations, is poised on the knife edge of unreserved response to God in the mode of Abraham.

If this is an accurate rendering of the Hebrew, von Rad is incorrect to say that a reflexive sense makes the text 'trivial'. The notion that other peoples should recognize God's blessing on Abraham and his descendants, and find it worthy of respect and aspiration, is not trivial for Israel, as a small people seeking to live faithfully to their God in a large and often hostile world. They need the reassurance that this is what God wants of them and that their life with God will in fact be recognized by those who do not share it. To put what I think is the same, or a closely related, point in rabbinic terms, Israel's vocation is to be Israel. God has chosen Israel, and his primary concern is to reassure Israel of that divine purpose. God is

73. Verses 3a and 3b are thus parallel to verses 2a and 2b, each expanding the initial content.

74. The question of how extensive this admiration is depends on how narrow or broad a meaning is given to 'earth' ('erets) in the phrase 'all the families of the earth'. It could envisage solely the clans of Canaan, those nations which are displaced by Israel (cf. Deut. 7:1); or the peoples surrounding Israel; or the whole world as then known (cf. Gen. 10); or the whole world as subsequently known. The implications of 'erets in the divine promise are genuinely open to vary according to the wider context within which it is construed.

not unconcerned for other nations, but Israel will only be significant for other nations in so far as she is truly Israel; that is, taking Genesis 12 and Genesis 22 together, as long as there is obedient response to the call of God, and the fear of God is practised and focussed in worship at Moriah.

Why then does interpretative debate about the scope and purpose of God's blessing continue? Interestingly, it is not the case that a passive rendering, 'will be blessed', together with a perspective of universal concern, is simply a foible of Christian misreading. For three twentieth-century Jewish commentators, Benno Jacob, Umberto Cassuto, and Nahum Sarna, all consciously writing from a Jewish perspective, have adopted some such construal of the text. For example, Sarna, in his recent Jewish Publication Society commentary on Genesis, has in his translation the JPS rendering of *wenibrekhu* as reflexive and appropriately notes its meaning, 'People will take your own good fortune as the desired measure when invoking a blessing on themselves.' However, he goes on to say (1989: 89): 'A more likely translation of the verb is as a passive: "shall be blessed through – because of – you".' God's promises to Abram would then proceed in three stages from the particular to the universal: a blessing on Abram personally, a blessing (or curse) on those with whom he interacts, a blessing on the entire human race.'[75] One crucial factor is the context of God's blessing juxtaposed with the primeval history of the world in Gen. 1–11. The interpretative problem may be seen if we ask, '*For whose benefit* is the promise of blessing made?' Von Rad is clear that the promise is for the benefit of the nations, as, in a different way, is Sarna. Yet in fact, within Genesis, the nations form the backdrop against which the promise is made for the benefit of Abraham and his descendants. In the context of a hostile or indifferent world, that is, despite the nations, Abraham is promised that his walk with God will not lead to oblivion; it will lead to a

---

75. Both Jacob and Cassuto explicitly interpret Genesis 12:3 in the light of Jewish 'universalism' as given expression by the prophets. Jacob understands the verb as reflexive but strongly emphasizes the universal implications of the text: 'Es ist eine zweite Welt, die mit Abraham ins Dasein gerufen wird, die Welt des Segens durch Menschen für Menschen. Es kommt darin der grossartigste religiöse Universalismus zum Ausdruck, den kein Prophet hat übersteigern konnen, und den man (z. B. Holz, Gu.) vergebens zu verkleinern sucht. Am Anfang der Geschichte Israels stehend, ist sich die Tora voll des Letzten bewußt, worauf sie hinausgehen soll' (1934: 339); Cassuto comments on verse 3b: 'According to some commentators the meaning here is that Abram's name will serve as a classic example in formulating benedictions; but this explanation, which is apparently correct for the words *so that you will be a blessing*, in v. 2, does not accord with the phrasing of this verse . . . It appears preferable to take the meaning to be that the father of the Israelite nation will be privileged to become a source of benison to all peoples of the world, and his merit and prayer will protect them before the Heavenly Court of Justice. We have here the first allusion to the concept of universalism inherent in Israel's faith, which would subsequently be developed in the teaching of the prophets' (1964: 315).

people whose walk with God can receive the respect of others and a desire for emulation. The concern is not to 'save' or 'reconcile' other nations. It is to establish Israel in their midst, a people where the reality of God's presence may be acknowledged by others.

This notion that people should bless one another with the name of Abraham or Israel bears striking affinity to Deuteronomy's vision of Israel among the nations (Deut. 4:5–8). It also includes an unblushing assumption that God's blessing includes dominion over neighbours and enemies. This is the meaning of the two pentateuchal stories which explore the implications of God's commitment to Israel as expressed in Genesis 12:3a – wording which reappears at the climactic moment of Isaac's blessing of Jacob (Gen. 27:29) and Balaam's blessing of Israel (Num. 24:9), stories in each of which Israel's dominion is established by God at the expense of Israel's neighbours, Edom and Moab (Gen. 25:23; 27:29a; Num. 24:8, 17–19). In Genesis 22 the promise of nations blessing themselves by Abraham's descendants follows directly after reference to those descendants 'possessing the gate of their enemies'.

The restrictive nature of the promised blessing to Abraham and Israel, and its close linkage with temporal supremacy, are both elements of the text that many Jews and Christians, for different reasons and in different ways, have felt uncomfortable with and so have tended to construe in new ways. Jews no less than Christians have wanted to stress that their faith in God is somehow for the benefit of the world, even though they have not generally construed this in the missionary form that is constitutive of Christian faith. And both Jews and Christians have found much in scripture and their own living through history which indicates that God's blessing and victory over one's enemies may be distinct categories, realized in greater or lesser independence from one another. This means that when the pentateuchal promises are read in a wider context there are important factors to promote various kinds of rereading. To be sure, Israel's call to be Israel in spite of the nations is in no way incompatible with a call to be Israel for the sake of the nations, for both may be true simultaneously. But the two conceptions must still be distinguished. I am in full agreement with von Rad about not restricting an important and resonant text to only one meaning (though the way in which he formulates this principle is open to question). But this should not mean that one fails to acknowledge the reflexive idiom of *wenibreku* and the sense that belongs to the text within its pentateuchal context, or to make clear that the prime reason for reinterpreting the passage is its broader canonical context and its reception within Jewish and Christian faiths.

This raises larger issues about interpretation and reinterpretation when the story of Genesis 22 is preserved as scripture. We have already touched on this issue when discussing the relationship of the story to Jerusalem, and we now need to consider it further in relation to other aspects of the story, as we move on from discussing the four key verbs.

### The problem of child sacrifice

One recurrent issue in modern study of Genesis 22 has been the question of its relation to the practice of child sacrifice in the ancient world. Particularly because of the moral problem this may pose ('How could God want Abraham to take the life of a child?'), a discussion of the issue is a necessary complement to our exegesis. On this whole question the starting-point must now be the fine recent study by Jon Levenson (1993a), *The Death and Resurrection of the Beloved Son*.

Levenson argues that Exodus 22:28b envisages that an Israelite father should sacrifice his first-born son to YHWH, but that as a result of prophetic denunciations against all child sacrifice in the seventh and sixth centuries such sacrifice became problematic within Israel. However, the practice was not so much eliminated as transformed by ritual substitutions: God retains an absolute claim on the life of the first-born, but ritual substitutions make that claim compatible with the continued life of the first-born. Further, this pattern of understanding can be found in many narratives of Genesis, not least Genesis 22. Levenson (1993a: 59) says:

> It is the central thesis of this study that a basic element of the self-understanding of both Jewry and of the Church lies in stories that are the narrative equivalent of these ritual substitutions – narratives, that is, in which the first-born or beloved son undergoes a symbolic death. The symbolic death corresponds to the demand that the *rēšît* ['first fruit'] or the *peṭer reḥem* ['first issue of the womb'] be sacrificed to God. That the death is only symbolic, that the son, mirabile dictu, returns alive, is the narrative equivalent of the ritual substitutions that prevent the gory offering from being made.

Several comments are in order. First, this process of positive transformation – 'one that metamorphosed a barbaric ritual into a sublime paradigm of religious life' (1993a: x) – is something deeply characteristic of scripture and the faiths rooted in it. To the unsympathetic it can look like an ever-shifting refusal to confront something unpalatable, which lacks the courage to abandon error and make a fresh start. Sometimes, indeed, it might be such. Yet it represents a confidence in the intrinsic value of given religious tradition, even when it becomes problematic, as containing within itself the resources to tackle the problem constructively. It is a process of resolving problems and enriching the meaning of the tradition by moving into new forms of metaphorical and symbolic modes of understanding (though it is a complex procedure, dependent on numerous norms of critical discernment).

Secondly, a parallel instance of this process can be seen, I suggest, with respect to the other practice within the Old Testament that most affronts modern sensibilities, that is the practice of *ḥerem* (sometimes unsatisfactorily translated as 'holy war'). Within the Old Testament's major exposition of *ḥerem*, the book of Deuteronomy, *ḥerem* is already becoming a metaphor; not a 'mere' metaphor, but rather a specific form of focussing undivided and uncompromising loyalty to YHWH through rejection of compromise with whomever or whatever may dilute Israel's allegiance to YHWH as spelt out in the Shema (see Moberly 1999).

Thirdly, a metaphorical understanding of these texts is most likely already implicit in their preservation and collation within the Pentateuch and the Hebrew canon. For metaphor is the natural key to their continued use. Why else, one may ask, would texts depicting child sacrifice and *ḥerem* be edited and preserved at key points within the compilation of Israel's scripture, when the 'literal' practices were obsolete, unless the texts were understood as able still to be implemented even if in ways different from those previously envisaged?

### Metaphorical language and the problem of Abraham's immorality

The above reflections lead us directly back to the problem noted at the outset – the difficulty some contemporary interpreters have with Abraham's actions in Genesis 22. Is this not a story which, unless subverted and read 'against the grain', could lead people to believe in a cruel and capricious God and perhaps to suppose that they themselves might be justified in abusing or killing a child? This has been a recurrent issue in modern times. Perhaps the most influential voice in understanding the biblical text thus was that of Kant who, in his argument for the supremacy of the moral law over religion, denounced the misguided and immoral nature of Abraham's actions as portrayed in the story. Kant (1979: 115) says:

> In some cases man can be sure that the voice he hears is *not* God's; for if the voice commands him to do something contrary to the moral law, then no matter how majestic the apparition may be, and no matter

how it may seem to surpass the whole of nature, he must consider it an illusion.

The note is added:

> We can use, as an example, the myth of the sacrifice that Abraham was going to make by butchering and burning his only son at God's command (the poor child, without knowing it, even brought the wood for the fire). Abraham should have replied to this supposedly divine voice: 'That I ought not to kill my good son is quite certain. But that you, this apparition, are God – of that I am not certain, and never can be, not even if this voice rings down to me from (visible) heaven.'

Kant's critique has obvious force, not least because it is a central biblical emphasis that the moral is a fundamental element in evaluating the religious. More recently, in a context where child abuse is a burning issue, Terence Fretheim (1994: 494–501; 1995) has used as a springboard for interpreting Genesis 22 the claim by psychoanalyst Alice Miller (1990) that Genesis 22 may have contributed to an atmosphere that makes it possible to justify the abuse of children. These are grave charges. How valid are they?

The history of interpretation of Genesis 22 is well documented, as in D. Lerch, *Isaaks Opferung*, and S. Spiegel, *The Last Trial*. Despite the enormous interpretation and use of Genesis 22 there is no evidence that the above fears were realized. There is *no* recorded example of Jews or Christians using the text to justify their own abusing or killing of a child. Although the implications of the story were endlessly discussed, commendations of immorality or murder were not drawn from it. Interpreters from Kant to Miller have wanted to find a significance within the story which neither Jews nor Christians have ever in fact (until perhaps very recently) found in it. What this means is that within Jewish and Christian contexts, where until recent times the understanding of Genesis 22 was consistently positive, the metaphorical significance of the text was taken for granted, because it was always read within a wider scriptural and communal context which provided guidelines and constraints for understanding and appropriating the story. To disregard the context which enabled the meaningful preservation of a story about child sacrifice, and then proclaim the story a problem for contemporary readers, is to create a more or less artificial problem. It exemplifies the truism that context is crucial for meaning. It is unsurprising that if you transfer a story from its own context within the scriptural canon and within Jewish and Christian (and Muslim) faiths to an entirely different context in which the story is read solely in terms of the concepts and concerns of the modern world in

relation to a putative 'original meaning', then its meaning and significance changes drastically; the dialectical tension between the differing
horizons of past and present is prematurely, and unfruitfully, dissolved.

To say this does not, of course, solve all problems. Possible misunderstanding and misuse of the Bible is an inevitable danger in every age; and
in a contemporary context, where the relationships between tradition
and modernity are complex, and where the understanding and appropriation of any great text of the past (not just the Bible) seems increasingly
problematic, difficulties are hardly going to decrease. Moreover, old reso-
lutions of problems may be judged unsatisfactory (though this can hardly
be done before they have been thoroughly engaged with) and new, unanticipated problems may arise. We will therefore return to some of the difficulties posed by Genesis 22 in chapter 5. Nonetheless, unless the
metaphorical significance of child sacrifice, together with the potential of
the metaphor for creative developments, is taken seriously, there is little
prospect of making headway with the deep disagreements which characterize contemporary evaluations of Genesis 22. It may indeed be the case
that the metaphor is a 'dangerous' one, open to abuse on the part of the
misguided or the unscrupulous. But not only do we need to attend to how
the metaphor is meant to be understood within its own context of preservation and use. We need also to ask whether any metaphor will sufficiently capture the dynamics of true response to God without being in
some way 'dangerous'.

### Isaac as beloved son and bearer of God's promise

Even if the proposed sacrifice of Isaac is to be understood metaphorically,
it remains important to determine the significance of Isaac within the
story, so that the metaphor may be accurately understood.

The significance of Isaac is conveyed in two ways. First, he is depicted
in verse 2 as 'your son, your only one, whom you love, Isaac'. This fourfold
depiction, where the specific name 'Isaac' comes last in climactic position
has regularly engaged the imagination of commentators, especially in
Jewish tradition (Levenson 1993a: 127–9). Whatever precise significance is
attributed to the fourfold depiction, its meaning is clear – that Isaac is
supremely valued by Abraham. It is the one he loves dearly (implicitly,
more than any other) who is to be offered in sacrifice.[76]

---

76. Something of the meaning of the loss of Isaac as the 'only' (*yaḥid*) son can be learnt from
the depiction elsewhere in the Old Testament of 'mourning for an only son' (*'ebel yaḥid*) as
the most bitter and terrible of all mourning (Jer. 6:26; Am. 8:10; cf. Zech. 12:10).

Secondly, the wider context of the Abraham narrative makes Isaac the heir of Abraham and bearer of God's promise of blessing in the form of descendants beyond count who would be invoked as a blessing by others (Gen. 12:1–3; 15:1–6; 17:15–19), a promise renewed at the end of the story (22:15–18). Although the earlier parts of Abraham's story may raise the possibility of others, such as Lot or Ishmael, being the heirs of Abraham and bearer of the promise (see Steinberg 1993: ch. 2), it becomes unmistakably clear in chapters 17–21 that it is Isaac, and no one else, who is to be this. He who is only born after years of waiting and after the specific action of God when Sarah is too old to bear a child, who becomes the son of Abraham through whom God's promises to Abraham will be fulfilled – he is the one to be reduced to ashes and smoke through an act of sacrifice.

These two facets of Isaac's significance to Abraham give him a metaphorical meaning that is limitless. For Abraham is required to sacrifice to God not only the centre of his affections but that which he has lived for and is the content of his hope and his trust in God. It is not the situation of David who chose not to offer in sacrifice, in the place where the temple was to be built, that which had cost him nothing (2 Sam. 24:24). Abraham is required to offer in sacrifice, in the place where the temple was to be built, that which would cost him everything.

What this might mean in contexts other than that of Genesis 22 cannot be prescribed in advance. Suffice it to say that for those for whom the story functions as scripture, for whom the metaphor is a paradigm of life with God, the issues it raises, if it comes alive, will touch the very depths of their being.

**4**

---

# Ancient and modern interpretations of Genesis 22

Thus far we have offered an exegesis and interpretation of Genesis 22 as a first step in working out a specific example of the kind of biblical interpretation which might exemplify the more general hermeneutical stance for which we are arguing. The next step will be to consider some of the significant work already existing in this area, so that the articulation of our own thesis may be properly contextualized as a contribution to an ancient and continuing debate. The prime focus will be Christian approaches to Genesis 22, though the chaper will conclude with some brief comments on Jewish approaches.

Because the discussion of Christian approaches to Genesis 22 could itself easily take up a whole book, we will set (convenient though slightly arbitrary) limits by confining discussion (more or less) to the New Testament and two well-known twentieth-century Protestant interpreters, Wilhelm Vischer and Gerhard von Rad. Such a bypassing of centuries of intervening interpretation, much of it of great interest and profundity, is not intended to derogate from the continuing hermeneutic potential of such material. It is primarily because I wish to keep a focus on the developments of recent debate as the prime context for my own exposition. In particular, the widely acknowledged stature of von Rad makes his work an obvious marker in relation to which other contributors need to situate themselves at the outset of the twenty-first century.

## Genesis 22 in the New Testament and in the Fathers

The New Testament explicitly engages with the story of Genesis 22 in two passages, Hebrews 11:17–19 and James 2:18–24. Each writer uses the story as a paradigm of their understanding of the key Christian term for appropriate human responsiveness to God, namely 'faith' (the NT equivalent to OT 'fear of God'). Abraham's faith in God's power to resolve in the future that which seemed impossible in the present, illustrates the nature of faith as an active engagement with that which is future and unseen (Heb. 11:1) – Jesus being the supreme example of such a confident looking forward (Heb. 12:2). Abraham's willingness to act in obedience to God provides the critical test whereby the reality of a confession of faith, which might just be words impossible to substantiate or unrelated to the way one lives, is shown to have genuine substance (Jas. 2:18–20). Both of these are powerful construals of Genesis 22 which relate Abraham's responsiveness to God with that expected of the Christian. It is not that they suppose that Abraham was a Christian; rather they see that which characterizes Abraham as that which must also characterize the Christian, and which is best understood by Christians in the context of their own primary vocabulary of responsiveness to God, namely faith. The hermeneutic of these New Testament writers, which assumes a subtle dialectic of both continuity and difference in divine revelation and human response, is characteristic of Christian faith generally.

It may be, however, that it was Paul's possible allusion in Romans 8:32, 'He who did not spare his own son but gave him up for us all . . .', that was historically most influential. Whether or not Paul intended an allusion to Genesis 22 is unclear,[1] but Paul's language naturally lends itself to a typological parallel between Abraham and Isaac and God the Father and God the Son. The theme of a father giving up a son to sacrificial death, with consequent blessing for all the nations of the earth, readily resonates with the Christian story of God the Father giving his Son to die with a consequent Christian mission to proclaim salvation to the whole world. This means that, in the light of the gospel portrayal of the Son who is obedient even to death, imaginative attention is given to Isaac as well as to Abraham, as the beloved son who willingly offers himself up to death (which is a perfectly natural, though not the only, reading of Isaac's role). This typological parallel can be augmented by two imaginatively suggestive points of detail. On the one hand Isaac bears the wood for the sacrifice (Gen. 22:6) just as Christ carries his cross (Jn 19:17). On the other hand, both stories climax in Jerusalem, the holy city, the city of destiny (although this is only

---

1. The issue is uncertain primarily because there are not the precise verbal links that one might have expected. The Hebrew adjective qualifying 'son' in Genesis 22: 2, 12, 16, *yaḥid*, is appropriately rendered by Paul's *idios*, but the LXX, which might be expected to have influenced Paul had he had Genesis 22 in mind, uses *agapetos*.

implicit in the symbolic language of Genesis 22). It is not difficult, therefore, to see why Genesis 22 came to be considered by Christians as one of the clearest anticipations of the Christian story of salvation in the whole Old Testament.

There is of course the important difference that Isaac was never in fact put to death as Christ was. But the fact that a ram was sacrificed, and that the ram could also be seen as a type of Christ, meant that despite a certain looseness the imaginative parallel with the death of Christ could be maintained.

Christian usage of Genesis 22 thus established a possible double typology, with Abraham as a type of the Christian and Isaac as a type of Christ. Although both led to many interesting interpretations, one problem inherent in the second typology is that it could be relatively superficial in the extent of its engagement with the issues that the Old Testament text poses. Although, for example, the parallel carrying of the wood of sacrifice and of the cross is imaginatively suggestive, it has no bearing on the issues of moral or theological importance in the text. Likewise, discussions about the ways in which both Isaac and the ram could represent Christ certainly have a logic of their own, but it is a logic which may too easily distract from more important concerns. To be sure, Isaac's willing self-offering is a substantive issue; but because the Genesis text focusses self-offering on Abraham more than on Isaac, a focus on Isaac will tend to draw its strength from elsewhere than the Genesis text.

In any case, for detailed analysis I do not wish at present to engage with classic Christian interpretations of Genesis 22 but rather to pass directly to twentieth-century interpretations, where, as will be seen, some of the classic issues, *mutatis mutandis*, reappear.

### Genesis 22 in the work of Vischer

#### (1) Hermeneutical presuppositions
Among modern scholarly examples of Christian approaches to the Old Testament, one of the most consistently Christ-centred is that of Wilhelm Vischer, especially in his *The Witness of the Old Testament to Christ* (1949). Vischer drank deeply from major Protestant theologians. His understanding of scripture shows evident indebtedness to Karl Barth, and the interpreters he most frequently cites are, first and foremost, Luther, and then Calvin.[2]

2. 'Above all, to keep on the highroad of exposition, we shall follow the footprints of Luther and Calvin' (1949: 32).

When the book first appeared, within the context of Germany in 1934, it was a bold and timely attempt to reaffirm the importance of Jewish scripture.[3]

Vischer sets out his hermeneutical principles in a twenty-eight-page introduction; an account which, in Rendtorff's judgment, is 'one of the first detailed, modern theological reflections about the relationship between the Old and New Testaments'.[4] The essence of Vischer's approach is contained in the opening words:

> The Bible testifies beyond doubt, with the attestation of the Holy Spirit, that Jesus of Nazareth is the Christ. This is what makes it the Holy Scripture of the Christian Church. For the Christian Church is the company of all those who, on the basis of the biblical testimony, recognize and believe that Jesus is the Christ, i.e. the Messiah of Israel, the Son of the living God, the Saviour of the world.
>
> The two main words of the Christian confession 'Jesus is the Christ' – the personal name 'Jesus' and the vocational name 'Christ' – correspond to the two parts of the Holy Scriptures: the New and the Old Testament. The Old Testament tells us *what* the Christ is; the New, *who* He is – and indeed in such a manner as to make it clear that he alone knows Jesus who recognizes Him as the Christ, and he alone knows what the Christ is who knows that He is Jesus. (1949: 7)

Vischer does not deny the then consensus view about the dating and authorship of the Old Testament, for he sets out a succinct account of J, E, D, and P in a preface ('more than a thousand years have yielded the content of the Torah'; p. 35). But he sees this as insignificant in relation to the theological claim of the Bible as a whole and the implications of a confession of faith. The 'historical-human aspect of scripture', as expounded by modern investigations, is essentially analogous to the Incarnation: 'The *scandalon* of the human contingency of the Bible, which historical and literary criticism has brought to our attention, corresponds precisely to the *scandalon* of the incarnation of the eternal Word in the historical appearance of Jesus of Nazareth at a certain point of time' (p. 15). Vischer sees the death and resurrection of Jesus, the giving of the Holy Spirit, and the continuing life of the one (holy, catholic, and apostolic) Church as the decisive factors which enable Christian interpretation of the Bible. He is thus clear that questions of original historical context, sequence, and development

---

3. Rendtorff 1993 illuminatingly places Vischer in his historical context, and also sets out von Rad's critique of Vischer. Childs 1994 discusses the ecclesial and theological context of Vischer. Baker 1991: 94–104 offers a general account of Vischer's work.
4. 1993: 79. Such a tribute should not, of course, obscure Vischer's indebtedness to the truly ground-breaking work of Barth.

may be relativized and transformed by the impact of Christ. Christian interpretation of the Old Testament is a rereading of Jewish scripture in the light of Christ. Vischer sees in the statement in Ephesians 2:14 about the unifying of Jew and Gentile in Christ a ground for the affirmation that, 'Through His death Christ has transformed the two [Testaments] into one' (pp. 19–20). And he sees the diversity-in-unity depicted in Ephesians 4:4–6 and 1 Corinthians 12 as the pattern of diversity-in-unity for the people of God in both Old and New Testaments, of such a kind that familiar problems of cultural difference and distance are at least partially overcome (and modern assumptions of superiority are rebutted):

> It has not been proved that differences in religious discernment and experience are greater among Christians living at various times than among those living at the same time. Who has not at some time found it grievously hard to be one in spirit with contemporary Christians? And who on the contrary has not found comfort in the fellowship of Christians of past centuries? Is Abraham, the 'Father of faith' really more remote from me than the Christians of today? It is remarkable how many Christians and free religious spirits of our day regard it as self-evident that they know more about God than Abraham, 'the friend of God', simply because they live a few thousand years later. Have they perhaps never reflected that, however creative they may be in such matters, what they say and write concerning God can be at best but a few drops by the side of the living spring which flows joyously through the chapters about Abraham in Genesis, from which through the ages men have allayed the thirst of their hearts? Was not more insight displayed by that extraordinary man [sc. Kierkegaard, in *Fear and Trembling*] who, whenever he accompanied Abraham in thought to Mount Moriah, sank down exhausted, and with hands clasped exclaimed, 'None was so great as Abraham. Who can understand him?' (p. 20)

Vischer is aware of the obvious objection that Christian interpretation distorts the Old Testament ('Does it not "perpetrate upon the Old Testament an unbelievable philological farce" (Nietzsche)?'), and sees that the key question is 'whether it is true; whether the New Testament is the genuine interpretation of the Old' (p. 27). But although he affirms the necessity of faith in answering such questions, he resists any appeal to faith that would evade or negate intellectual credibility:

> If Jesus is really the hidden meaning of Old Testament scripture an honest philological exegesis cannot fail to stumble across this truth; not in the sense that it directly finds Jesus there, but in the sense that it

would be led to affirm that the thoughts expressed and the stories narrated in the Old Testament, as they are transmitted in the Bible, point towards the crucifixion of Jesus; that the Christ Jesus of the New Testament stands precisely at the vanishing point of Old Testament perspective.[5]

And Vischer is aware of the dangers of reading one's own ideas into the text and of the need to 'be instructed by anyone who reads more correctly' (p. 32).

Finally, Vischer addresses the question of a Jewish reading of these same scriptures. He does this through an appeal to Martin Buber's biblical interpretation, in that an 'unpremeditated coincidence at many points' between Vischer's work and that of Buber shows that Vischer's interpretation 'is not so perverse as certain modern experts imagine'. Yet despite the 'considerable concord' between Vischer and Buber, Buber 'remains a convinced Jew', which means that he 'reject[s] Jesus' messianic claims'. But what this shows is essentially the point that Vischer (p. 33) has already made about the interdependence of scriptural interpretation and Christian faith:

> The most cogent proof from scripture cannot constrain him [sc. a Jew] to this [sc. to accept the messianic claims of Jesus and become a confessing Christian]. This confession requires, for Jew and Gentile alike *metanoia*, change of heart, faith.
>
> Is it then impossible to prove from scripture that Jesus is the Christ? Yes; for this proof is given only by the Holy Spirit. The question of the truth of Christianity can be decided only by faith and the election of grace. It is, however, to this decision that the proof from scripture leads.

In general, Vischer clearly states a classic Christian stance. There are, to be sure, problems. Vischer's robust statement tends to become overstatement because of a lack of nuance in relation to obvious difficulties raised by his account. For example, Vischer ignores the issue of how the 'what' of the Messiah is radically transformed within the gospels. He does not address how a Christian interpretation might relate to the meaning of the Hebrew text in its initial pre-Christian contexts. Despite the reference to Buber, Vischer does not reflect at all about the possible meaning and significance of Hebrew scripture within a continuing Jewish context. There is only limited penetration of the meaning of a confession of Jesus

---

5. 1949: 28. The 'cannot fail' is, in my judgment, a clear overstatement, which would be better expressed as 'need not fail'.

as Messiah. And there is only a minimal account of how the faith of which Vischer speaks might relate to contemporary living, and of the hermeneutical interplay between faith and life. Nonetheless, despite all these areas which need elaboration and qualification, Vischer's summary account of Christian biblical hermeneutics is still noteworthy.

Rather than pursuing the hermeneutical issues as such, it would be more fruitful to focus on how the hermeneutics work in practice, not least because it is in the practice that one can see whether Vischer operates with a greater refinement than he spells out in his programmatic statement.

### (2) Exposition

Vischer begins his exposition of Genesis 22 by setting Abraham within the wider Genesis story as interpreted by Paul in Romans 4: 'Abraham's heir, the son of faith, lives only by a miracle of grace. The word of promise called him out of nothing into life, and only the word which raises the dead sustains his life. The patriarch, as the story relates, still possesses his son only in faith' (p. 141). He also notes, albeit briefly, the significance of the literary form of the text: '"The marvellous simplicity of this narrative possesses greater power than the most detailed and elaborate tragedy", remarks Calvin. The manner of the story matches perfectly the matter: it is indeed no tragedy, but a story of the obedience of faith to the uttermost and of the confidence of faith to the end' (p. 141).

In the smooth linking of obedience and confidence Vischer deftly highlights the central concerns within the story of Abraham's fear of God and his affirmation of God's seeing/provision. But he directly (pp. 141–2) moves on to the big issue which the story poses:

> The tamarisk is planted;[6] Abraham has the promised son in whom he has a visible, tangible support to which he may secure the wide net of the promises. Suddenly, by a single word, God robs him of everything: 'Sacrifice him!' By this word God does more than assail Abraham's human paternal love. He lays an axe at the root of the patriarch's faith in God. 'He tempts him.' What does that mean? Chrysostom expounds it thus: 'God contradicts himself, faith contradicts faith, the command contradicts the promise.' And Luther agrees with him: 'God evidently contradicts Himself. For how can the two sayings be reconciled; "In Isaac shall thy seed be called" and "Take thy son and sacrifice him"? . . .

6. This alludes to his imaginative reading of the end of the previous chapter, Genesis 21: 33–4: 'The man who plants a tree intends to remain. So the tamarisk on the southern border of Palestine proclaims Abraham's hope that he will abide for ever in the Holy Land. He plants it in faith' (1949: 141).

'Human reason would infer either that the promise is deceptive or
that this cannot be God's command, but the instigation of the devil.
For if Isaac is slain the promise is null and void; and if the promise
stands firm this cannot be the command of God. Human reason, I say,
cannot conclude otherwise.

'All the more gloriously does Abraham's faith shine forth when he
obeys God with a willing heart . . .' [Vischer extends for another 20
lines this long quotation from Luther, which goes on to relate
Abraham's faith to faith in the resurrection, as in Hebrews 11:19].

But having established the paradigmatic nature of Abraham's faith, Vischer (p. 142) introduces a significant caveat:

> The temptation of Abraham is written for our comfort and
> admonition, yet it would be a mistake to link it too closely with the
> problems of our life of faith. We need to remember, as Luther says, that
> here we have a truly patriarchal temptation which could be withstood
> only by the father of the faithful. More is here at stake than personal
> matters, even the noblest and dearest. What is really at stake is the
> whole divine promise, the whole expectation, the complete salvation
> of the world that was promised Abraham in Isaac.

Having thus far stayed within the logic of the story within its own Genesis
context (however much this is construed through Paul and subsequent
Christian interpreters), Vischer now makes a different interpretative
move, offering an explicit imaginative comparison between Genesis 22
and Jesus:

> Can we not see how this path of sacrifice is overhung with the darkness
> of Good Friday, and how this dark cloud itself is tinged with the
> radiance of the Easter sun? As the stories of the anticipation and birth
> of Isaac become transparent pictures of Christmas when the light of
> the gospel is placed behind them, in similar manner the words of this
> chapter become transparent: . . . [Vischer cites parts of vv. 2, 4, 5, 6, 7]
> . . . Can we read that, and especially the ambiguous 'God will provide
> himself a lamb for a burnt offering', so reminiscent of Johannine
> speech . . . without as it were looking through a window into the far
> distance to see the only begotten Son whom the Father loved following
> the path of the passion from the Mount of Olives through Gethsemane
> as the Lamb who bears the sin of the world?
>
> *And he took the ram, and offered him up for a burnt offering.*
>
> The sacrifice which God spared his 'friend' (James 2:23), the
> patriarch of the people of faith, He made Himself; the eternal Father
> did not spare His own son, but delivered Him up for us all (Rom. 8:32).
> (pp. 142–3)

Finally, Vischer expounds the blessing in the second call of the angel as 'concerned not with religious speculations but with the occupation of a kingdom upon earth', where the concern, not only for Abraham but for all who follow him, is 'the absolute supremacy of God's government over men – "Thy Kingdom come. Thy will be done on earth as it is done in heaven."' And he (p. 144) ties this in to the central paradox of the story:

> Like Abraham, in blind obedience (verse 18), they [sc. 'all who are born of the Word'] follow the voice of their Lord, and serve the politics of the Kingdom of God, which stands in contrast to the politics of the kingdoms of this world and the 'art of the possible', as the art of the impossible.

### (3) Analysis

Vischer's reading is in many ways a *tour de force*, which well exemplifies his hermeneutical principles. It is full of the kinds of resonances which are only possible when Genesis 22 is read within the context of Christian faith. He not only utilizes the explicit (Hebrews 11; James 2) and implicit (Romans 8:32) New Testament renderings of the story, but also draws on two of the most famous Christian preachers, known for their sustained engagement with the biblical text, the Father Chrysostom as well as the Reformer Luther. He takes seriously the Genesis context as well as the imaginative linkage with the Passion of Jesus.

Yet obvious questions need to be asked. What does the Hebrew mean in a Hebrew context, before it is taken into a Christian context? And cannot, and should not, a Christian interpretation learn from and build on the Hebrew meaning? Hebrew wording and its Old Testament usage is not even remotely alluded to or used. When the specific question as to the meaning of God's 'testing/tempting' is raised, the possible meanings and resonances of Hebrew *nissah* (or Greek *peirazo*) are bypassed in direct appeal to Chrysostom. Abraham's fear of God is nowhere mentioned, except in the general category of 'obedience of faith', so the prime Old Testament understanding of appropriate human response to God is ignored. So too with the meaning of divine 'seeing/providing' and divine blessing.

A natural corollary of this disregard for the text as a Hebrew story is that the primary focus of the story changes in Vischer's reading (which stands in a long line of other Christian readings which make the same move). The prime dramatic climax of the story ceases to be God's knowledge of Abraham's fear of God (v. 12) and becomes instead the offering of

the ram in sacrifice, a type of Christ (v. 13). The sacrifice is of course significant within the Hebrew context of the story, where it is integral to the
typology of Abraham's paradigmatic worship which interprets Israel's
worship in the Jerusalem temple; but it is consequent upon Abraham's
fear of God.

In a different way there are difficulties with Vischer's appeal to Luther's
notion of a 'patriarchal temptation'. The point appears to be that the particular position of Abraham within the history of salvation, in which the
whole future of God's purposes is in the balance, cannot be replicated in
the life of any Christian, whose faithfulness will never have such significance attached to it. Therefore the testing/tempting of any Christian will
somehow not be as weighty as it was for Abraham. This seems to stand in
continuity with Luther's own exposition of the text:

> But because Abraham is the foremost and greatest among the holy
> patriarchs, he endures truly patriarchal trials which his descendants
> would not have been able to bear. . . .
>
> I could not have been an onlooker, much less the performer and
> slayer. It is an astounding situation that the dearly beloved father
> moves his knife close to the throat of the dearly beloved son, and I
> surely admit that I cannot attain to these thoughts and sentiments
> either by means of words or by reflecting on them. . . . With the
> exception of Christ we have no similar example of obedience. (Pelikan
> and Hansen 1964: 114)

The point of christological typology, in both Luther and Vischer, appears
to be that just as Jesus achieved something unique and unrepeatable, so
too did Abraham in his willingness to sacrifice Isaac.[7] From a Christian
perspective, the uniqueness and finality of Jesus is indeed basic. Nonetheless, Vischer utilizes this too simply. For, on the one hand, the question of
precisely where and how to draw the line between Jesus and Christian
believers is a difficult one. As we will see in chapter 6, Matthew's Gospel
clearly presupposes and portrays the uniqueness of Christ, yet draws no
clear line, and both explicitly and implicitly prescribes (non-identical)
imitation on the part of disciples. A too easy and clearcut distinction
between the testing of Jesus and that of the Christian risks undercutting
the imaginative seriousness with which Christians construe their lives in
the light of Christ and the fact that we never know the full significance of
our actions. On the other hand, to make Abraham's testing/temptation

---

7. This same notion of a 'patriarchal temptation' is also appealed to as a significant factor
by Childs, but is utilized differently (1992: 327, 334).

peculiar to him cuts against the likely significance of the parallel usage of 'test' and 'fear' in Exodus 20:20, which makes Abraham in some way a type of Israel's response to *torah*. The fact that Abraham's responsiveness takes a form that the wider Old Testament prohibits as a specific practice should move the interpreter to consider the metaphorical dimensions of the material in which the relationship between non-repeatable and repeatable becomes both subtle and demanding.

In sum, there is an immediate force and power in Vischer's exposition because of its strong Christian resonances. As such, this may have well served the needs of German Christians in the 1930s (cf. Rendtorff 1993: 86–7). But the lack of engagement with the Hebrew world of the text brings with it a strong danger of ultimate superficiality. If the Old Testament no longer says something to the Christian in its own right, to which the Christian still needs to attend and on which Christian faith necessarily builds, its actual role within Christian faith will tend to become marginal and optional, no matter what rhetoric is used to urge its importance.  My proposal is not to abandon the principle or practice of a Christian contextual reading such as Vischer proposes, but rather to give it an appropriate foundation in the disciplines of exegesis, and thereby re-establish the dialectic between scriptural text and theological hermeneutic.

### Genesis 22 in the work of von Rad

#### (1) Hermeneutical presuppositions and exposition

We turn now to the work of the scholar who is widely recognized to be the outstanding Christian theological interpreter of the Old Testament in the twentieth century, Gerhard von Rad. As already noted, von Rad had a particular interest in Genesis 22 and wrote a small popular book on it,[8] which makes the interpretation of Genesis 22 an appropriate case study for von Rad's exegesis and hermeneutics. I shall concentrate on the interpretation as set out in von Rad's Genesis commentary (which does not differ from that in the small book),[9] which itself was aimed to appeal to an audience beyond that of the academic specialist.[10]

The key to understanding von Rad's Genesis commentary is given in the introduction, which sums up much that he sets out in other essays, and which he concludes as follows:

8. Von Rad 1971. A useful study of this is Hopkins 1980.
9. 1971: 31–4 gives an account of divine hiddenness and Abraham's Godforsakenness along exactly the same lines as the Genesis commentary. Despite the many editions of the commentary, since its first appearance in 1952, the discussion of Genesis 22 which we will consider remained unchanged.     10. For von Rad's intended readership, see 1972a: 11.

Franz Rosenzweig once remarked wittily that the sign 'R' (for the redactor of the Hexateuch documents, so lowly esteemed in Protestant research) should be interpreted as Rabbenu, 'our master', because basically we are dependent only on him, on his great work of compilation and his theology, and we receive the Hexateuch at all only from his hands. From the standpoint of Judaism, that is consistent. But for us [i.e. Christians], in respect to hermeneutics, even the redactor is not 'our master'. *We receive the Old Testament from the hands of Jesus Christ, and therefore all exegesis of the Old Testament depends on whom one thinks Jesus Christ to be . . .*

In all the variety of the story, can we perhaps recognize some things that are typical of the action of God towards men? Then we must go on to raise the chief question: can we not recognize a common link even between the revelation of God in the old covenant and that in the new, a 'type'? The patriarchal narratives include experiences which Israel had of a God who revealed himself and at the same time on occasions hid himself more deeply. In this very respect we can see a continuity between the Old Testament and the New. In the patriarchal narratives, which know so well how God can conceal himself, we see a revelation of God which precedes his manifestation in Jesus Christ. What we are told here of the trials of a God who hides himself and whose promise is delayed, and yet of his comfort and support, can readily be read into God's revelation of himself in Jesus Christ.[11]

Among the many features of interest here, the key fact for present purposes is that von Rad is explicitly identifying his work of commentary with the classic Christian stance of reading the Old Testament in christological and typological terms. On the one hand, von Rad is in full agreement with Vischer that understanding of the Old Testament in important ways follows, rather than solely precedes, an understanding of Jesus Christ;[12] the historical sequence from Israel to Christ may be reversed hermeneutically when it comes to reading Israel's scripture as Christian scripture (as is classically set out in the Emmaus story). On the other hand, the interpretative exercise relates not to secondary issues but to the most fundamental issue of all, that of the nature of God and of his self-revelation as perceived by humans.

How then does this work in practice? Although the christological

---

11. 1972a: 42–3 (my italics). The comment of Rosenzweig to which von Rad refers is found in a letter on the unity of the Bible, published in 1936 in *Die Schrift und ihre Verdeutschung*, now available in Buber and Rosenzweig 1994: 22–5.

12. Von Rad's substantial differences from Vischer, his strong criticisms of Vischer, and his engagement in the exegetical work of mainstream Old Testament scholarship, should not obscure the fact that in terms of basic hermeneutical stance von Rad stands squarely alongside Vischer.

perspective is not always readily apparent in von Rad's work, it comes strongly to the fore in the interpretation of Genesis 22. First, we may note von Rad's methodological comments in the epilogue to the interpretation:

> In the case of a narrative like this one, which obviously went through many stages of internal revision, whose material was, so to speak, in motion up to the end, one must from the first renounce any attempt to discover one basic idea as *the* meaning of the whole ... Such a mature narrator as this one has no intention of paraphrasing exactly the meaning of such an event and stating it for the reader. On the contrary, a story like this is basically open to interpretation and to whatever thoughts the reader is inspired. The narrator does not intend to hinder him; he is reporting an event, not giving doctrine. (1972a: 243)

Thus von Rad emphasizes that the nature of the material is intrinsically such that it is open to reflection from a christological perspective; though he expresses the matter so loosely, indeed carelessly ('whatever thoughts') that one may wonder what, if any, are the critical norms within the enterprise (a matter to which we will return).

With regard to the central concerns of the story von Rad writes:

> It is decisive for a proper understanding of what follows that one leave to the statement in v. 1 its entire weight (the word 'God' is particularly emphasized in the syntax), and that one does not try to resolve it by a psychologizing explanation ... One must indeed speak of a temptation [*Anfechtung*] which came upon Abraham but only in the definite sense that it came from God only, the God of Israel ... The narrator has not caused his reader any premature excitement regarding a horrible experience. The subject that now engages excited interest is rather Abraham's (and Isaac's) demeanour. For Abraham, God's command is completely incomprehensible: the child, given by God after long delay, the only link that can lead to the promised greatness of Abraham's seed (ch. 15.4f.) is to be given back to God in sacrifice ... One must be careful not to interpret the story in a general sense as a question about Abraham's willingness to obey and accordingly to direct all interest to Abraham's trial ... Above all, one must consider Isaac, who is much more than simply a 'foil' for Abraham, i.e. a more or less accidental object on which his obedience is to be proved. Isaac is the child of promise. In him every saving thing that God has promised to do is invested and guaranteed. The point here is not a natural gift, not even the highest, but rather the disappearance from Abraham's life of the whole promise. Therefore, unfortunately, one can only answer all plaintive scruples about this narrative by saying that it concerns something much more frightful than child sacrifice. It has to do with a

road out into Godforsakenness [*Gottverlassenheit*], a road on which Abraham does not know that God is only testing him. There is thus considerable religious experience behind these nineteen verses: that Yahweh often seems to contradict himself, that he appears to want to remove the salvation begun by himself from history. But in this way Yahweh tests faith and obedience! One further thing may be mentioned: in this test God confronts Abraham with the question whether he could give up God's gift of promise. He had to be able (and he was able), for it is not a good that may be retained by virtue of any legal title or with the help of a human demand. God therefore poses before Abraham the question whether he really understands the gift of promise as a pure gift. (1972a: 238, 239, 244)

### (2) Analysis and evaluation

This interpretation of Genesis 22, especially its key sentence about Abraham being on a road out into Godforsakenness, has been much appreciated by Old Testament scholars. For example, John Scullion, the translator of Westermann's great Genesis commentary, in his own recent Genesis commentary cites von Rad as the climax of his own interpretation;[13] though remarkably he leaves von Rad's 'moving reflection' entirely without comment, either because he considered its significance self-evident or because he failed to recognize what its significance is. James Crenshaw (1978: 120) is more to the point when he says, 'Von Rad writes that God led Abraham to Golgotha!' (though he himself has 'grave doubts about the legitimacy of such a procedure', that is, seeing Christian significance for Old Testament texts; p. 184, n. 11). Since the significance of von Rad's interpretation is not instantly self-evident, it is worth spelling it out and then reflecting on it a little.

First, von Rad was a Lutheran, and at the heart of Lutheran theology stands a theology of the cross which centres upon the cry of dereliction upon the lips of Jesus in Matthew 27:46; Mark 15:34: 'My God, my God, why have you forsaken me?' (rendered in German by Luther as '*Mein Gott, mein Gott, warum hast du mich verlassen?*'). So if Abraham is on a road into Godforsakenness (*Gottverlassenheit*), the primary intended resonance is with the crucifixion of Christ. In the light of what von Rad says in his introduction about types, it seems clear that Abraham is being understood as a type of Christ.

Secondly, the significance of Luther's theology of the cross is that it conveys a particular understanding both of the way in which God reveals

---

13. Scullion 1992: 174. Other examples of appreciative use are Davidson 1983: 52–3 and Sheriffs 1996: 50, 53.

himself and of the way in which God works in human lives. On the one hand, there is the notion of the hidden and paradoxical way in which God works – the test of Abraham comes 'from God only' and is 'completely incomprehensible'; on the other hand, the process of God's working within people is depicted by the complex and elusive term *Anfechtung* – which is the term von Rad uses to depict God's test of Abraham in verse 1. These interrelated concepts of the hiddenness of God and of *Anfechtung* are well described by Alister McGrath:

> For Luther, the sole authentic *locus* of man's knowledge of God is the cross of Christ, in which God is to be found revealed, and yet paradoxically hidden in that revelation . . . In that it is God who is made known in the passion and cross of Christ, it is *revelation*; in that this revelation can only be discerned by the eye of faith, it is *concealed* . . . The concept of a hidden God (*absconditus Deus*) lies at the centre of the theology of the cross . . .
>
> God is particularly known through suffering . . . Luther regards God himself as the source of *Anfechtung*: God assaults man in order to break him down and thus to justify him . . . The 'theologian of the cross' regards such suffering as his most precious treasure, for revealed and yet hidden in precisely such sufferings is none other than the living God, working out the salvation of those whom he loves . . . As Luther remarks, *Anfechtung*, 'in so far as it takes everything away from us, leaves us nothing but God: it cannot take God away from us, and actually brings him closer to us'. It is through undergoing the torment of the cross, death and hell that true theology and the knowledge of God come about. (1985: 149, 150, 151, 152)

Thus the process of testing which Abraham undergoes is interpreted by the dynamics revealed at Calvary and recapitulated in the lives of Christians.

Thirdly, when von Rad speaks of Abraham having to understand the gift of promise as a 'pure gift' which cannot be held onto 'by virtue of any legal title or with the help of a human demand', the language resonates with the Lutheran interpretation of Paul's concept of faith and works; humanity should not make, and cannot have, a claim on God, but rather must receive from God that which can only be received as a gift of grace. Thus Abraham displays the kind of response to God that should characterize the Christian.

This interpretation by von Rad is imaginatively powerful and theologically profound. How might one evaluate it? In the first place, we should appreciate that in essence von Rad is not doing with the story of Abraham anything different from what the Genesis writer has done. That is, just as the Genesis writer has taken the story of Abraham and interpreted it from the perspective of Israel's relationship with God centred on *torah* obedience and worship in Jerusalem, so von Rad has interpreted it from the perspective of the Christian understanding of God centred on Christ crucified. In each case a theological perspective from a context other than that of the story in itself has been used to bring out its meaning. And these theological perspectives are not arbitrary, but rather are those which historic communities of faith, both Jewish and Lutheran Christian, have recognized as central to their existence. One difference, of course, is that Israel's interpretation has become embodied in the text and has become integral to its canonical form, while von Rad's depends on the resonances of the text when read in a wider New Testament and Lutheran context. One is biblical text while the other is theological commentary, and so the one has a status which the other lacks. Yet in both one can recognize different phases of a continuing quest to relate the paradigmatic stories of Abraham to the ongoing life of faith of the various descendants of Abraham.

Secondly, von Rad has creatively reused the traditional typology of Abraham as a type of the Christian by giving this a more explicitly christological focus – it is because Abraham is a type of Christ that he is also a type of the Christian. This means that the relationship is between those two figures on whom the Genesis and New Testament texts most concentrate and whose dynamics are intrinsically open to be linked to each other. This is akin to the argument of the present study (which is in many ways indebted to von Rad).

Thirdly, despite, or perhaps because of, the Lutheran character of von Rad's interpretation, it is the kind of interpretation which could contribute to theological work in the aftermath of the Holocaust. The notion of a divine test focussed in 'a road out into Godforsakenness' could well have deep resonances for many Jews (though of course it would be for them to decide). And the fact that it is articulated by an heir of that theological tradition, which in certain ways helped create the context for the Holocaust in the first place,[14] could help towards that *rapprochement* between

---

14. It is impossible to measure the malign influence of Luther's intemperate polemic against all his rivals, which became worse in his declining years (when he was racked by illnesses which would not have contributed towards equanimity). But Luther's 1543 pamphlet *Of the Jews and Their Lies*, contains material which, in the light of the twentieth-century fate of Jews in Germany, makes the blood run cold (however much other factors also contributed to Nazi anti-Semitism): 'First, their synagogues or churches should be set on fire, and whatever does not burn up should be covered or spread over with dirt so that no one may ever be able to see a cinder or stone of it. And this ought to be done for the honour of God and of Christianity . . . Secondly, their homes should likewise be broken down and destroyed. For they perpetrate the same things there that they do in their synagogues. For this reason they ought to be put under one roof or in a stable, like gypsies . . .' (cited in Gilbert 1978: 20).

Christian and Jew which is a significant element in contemporary theology, not least in the work of von Rad's erstwhile pupil Rolf Rendtorff (1992: chs. 1 and 4). In making this suggestion I am not proposing that von Rad himself had such an intention, as his date of publication (1952), prior to the development of extended theological reflection on the Holocaust, would make such intention unlikely. It is simply that his writing, like the biblical text, may appropriately lend itself to concerns not envisaged by the writer.

Negatively, however, it must be noted that von Rad's interpretation is not as deeply rooted as it might be in an exegesis of the biblical text. It is interesting to consider his treatment of the four key verbs – test, fear, see, bless. On the first two verbs he does indeed offer special excursuses. Yet these are disappointing. With regard to testing, von Rad misses the crucial linkage with Exodus 20:20. Even when he notes the concept of testing as applied to all Israel (Deut. 13:3; Jdg. 2:22), he only uses this to make an historical observation about the notion of the testing of all Israel being older than that of the testing of an individual, an observation which is left hermeneutically mute.[15] Thus the linkage with *torah*, and Abraham as a type of Israel, is missed. Nor is it at all clear how his use of the Lutheran concept of *Anfechtung* relates to such usage of *nissah* as he does note. His main point in this excursus is one drawn from his wider religio-historical supposition of a 'Solomonic enlightenment' to the effect that 'the application of the idea of temptation or testing to the paradoxes of God's historical leading is to be understood as a suppression of the ritual and an exit from the cultic realm, that is, with respect to the history of faith, as a sign of positive maturity' (1972a: 239–40). But how this relates to *Anfechtung*, and vice versa, is simply not addressed. At the crucial moment there is a jump for which no warrant is offered.

The excursus on the 'fear of God' is much more penetrating than that on 'test', though to construe 'fear of God' as 'simply a term for obedience' is a diminished account of its dynamics (1972a: 242). Yet the chief problem again is how von Rad moves from this 'fear of God', which he rightly sees to be central to Genesis 22, to his own central interpretative insight of Abraham as on 'a road out into Godforsakenness'. To be sure, it would not be too difficult to construct a hermeneutical bridge in terms of the potential costliness of obedience, and the need to adhere to God even in those times when God most seems absent; the combination of Job 1:1–2:10 with

15. Similarly Westermann 1986: 362.

Genesis 22 could prepare a path to the Gospel portrayal of Jesus. But von Rad does not make these moves, with the result that his contention that 'a story like this is basically open to interpretation and to whatever thoughts the reader is inspired' may appear to serve as an excuse at the critical moment to leave exegesis behind and to introduce an imaginatively powerful, but in principle unrelated, theological construct.

With regard to 'see' we have already noted how, ironically, von Rad misses the extensive resonances with Jerusalem despite his insistence, *contra* Gunkel, on working with the text in its canonical form. Yet his typology of 'Abraham at Golgotha' would, of course, be greatly strengthened by recognition of Abraham's implicit location at Jerusalem. This means also that possible socio-religious implications of the text, as discussed below in chapter 5, are nowhere in view.

With regard to 'bless' von Rad has nothing to say in the context of Genesis 22, and his discussion of Genesis 12:3 we have already cited and criticized.

### Von Rad and the relationship between Old and New Testaments

In the light of the above we can now relate von Rad's interpretation of Genesis 22 to aspects of the continuing wider debate about the strengths and weaknesses of von Rad's theological interpretation of the Old Testament, especially the question of the relationship between Old and New Testaments. Here von Rad is one of the few Old Testament theologians of distinction within the twentieth century not only to have seen the importance of the question and addressed it in a substantial way, but also to have offered positive proposals in both theory and practice as to how Old and New should be interpreted together, not being content with the easier task of pointing to the flaws in other people's proposals. Von Rad discussed the relationship between Old and New Testaments in a number of important essays,[16] of which perhaps the best known and most accessible are the essays which conclude the second volume of his *Old Testament Theology* (the remarks in the preface to which are also noteworthy; 1965: vii–viii and pt. 3).

One way of approaching von Rad's contribution to understanding the relationship between Old and New Testaments is through responses to it.

---

**16.** Von Rad 1943; 1952. For a recent exposition and analysis, see Watson 1997: 197ff.

Thus we may start with Brevard Childs' recent expression of anxiety about prevalent ways of relating Old and New Testaments, an expression made in the context of Genesis 22 as a case study for Biblical Theology and formulated with specific reference to von Rad:

> There is a widespread appeal in von Rad's insistence that interpretation deal with the text's ability to generate continually a great variety of very different renderings. How one achieves this goal, however, is not altogether clear especially if one does not follow von Rad's *heilsgeschichtliche* scheme for relating the two testaments.
>
> At this point my own criticism of the Old Testament discipline can be voiced. Within the modern debate there seems to be little direction or even concern on how one moves exegetically to include the whole Christian Bible. Often the interpreter feels constrained to move into existential categories, citing from Kierkegaard or recalling a verse from Paul, before then suggesting some loose connection with the New Testament. The implication underlying the uncertainty is that at best the New Testament is linked charismatically with the Old. However, unless more exegetical and theological precision can be brought to bear precisely at this juncture, it is difficult to see how one can proceed in developing Biblical Theology into an actual discipline.
>
> (1992: 326)

Childs' depiction of von Rad's conjoining of Old and New as 'loose' and 'charismatic' and in need of 'more precision' suggests a considerable unease with his approach.[17] Childs (1992: 326–8, 335) goes on to discuss 'canonical guidelines for interpretation which have been structured into the biblical text', but unfortunately does not himself develop them beyond the barest of outlines.

Childs' critique here is reminiscent of an earlier critique by another of the twentieth century's most distinguished theological interpreters of the Old Testament, Walther Eichrodt. When publication of von Rad's *Old Testament Theology* was complete in 1960, Eichrodt added an excursus to his own *Theology of the Old Testament*, in which he offered a preliminary response to von Rad's differing conception of the theological task. Eichrodt discusses various issues on which he is unhappy with von Rad's

---

17. Childs repeats this critique in other contexts. For example, in discussing a growing consensus about figurative understandings of the Old Testament among pre-war German theologians, he comments: 'However, especially with von Rad, his form of typology remained exceedingly nebulous and bordered on a loose appeal to charisma. Consequently few of his many students in the next generation took up his suggestions regarding typology' (Childs 1994: 242). Childs' observation about the lack of scholars following von Rad's lead gives content to a rather impressionistic critique.

approach. It is specifically in relation to the interrelation between the two Testaments, and von Rad's proposal for a revived typology, that Eichrodt raises the question of criteria for such interpretation. With regard to the relationship between Old and New, instead of the understanding (clearly Eichrodt's own) that 'the religious utterances of the OT find in the NT and its Christ a corroboration and development of a factual kind', we find (as Eichrodt construes von Rad) 'discontinuous', 'historically isolated', and 'un-cohesive' prefigurations which 'lean' towards fulfilment in Christ. This makes acute the question of criteria for interpretation. Eichrodt (1967: 515) depicts von Rad thus:

> Not that there is any method of confirming or establishing this interpretation (II, p. 387).[18] Just as in the OT itself there is already a free, charismatic character about the way in which the typological significance of a particular event of weal or woe is understood (pp. 334ff.), so in the NT there is no absolute norm for the Christian understanding of the OT; and this would seem to be confirmed by the differing methods of interpretation used by the NT writers. We must therefore give up all idea of a normative interpretation of the OT, and leave everything to the eclectic charismatic freedom of the expositor, who will constantly be establishing new typological connections between the Testaments in a great variety of ways.

When Eichrodt speaks of leaving things to 'eclectic charismatic freedom' he is clearly depicting something of which he disapproves. The issues at stake here are, of course, manifold and complex. On the one hand, Eichrodt's setting of his own 'factual' approach against von Rad's 'charismatic' approach seriously obscures the genuine intrinsic difficulties over what it means truly to speak of and to perceive God, and the differences between Jews and Christians about such speech and perception in relation to the Hebrew scriptures and the person of Jesus.[19] On the other hand, Eichrodt's pejorative use of 'charismatic', like Childs', bears the weight of long histories of theological controversy in such a way that it becomes well nigh impossible to discuss the appropriateness of such a term without simultaneously tapping into much larger agendas with a high potential for colouring the specific discussion in ways that are at least as likely to be unhelpful as helpful. If the frame of reference within which the criticisms of von Rad are formulated is itself questionable,

---

18. The reference is to vol. II of von Rad's *Theology* whose continuing exposition is interwoven with Eichrodt's critique.
19. The problems raised by Eichrodt's approach are thus characteristic of the kind of approach sketched out with relation to Barr and Barrett in chapter 1.

then no real progress can be made without reconceiving the debate as a whole.

Nonetheless, even if the criticism of von Rad's interpretation as 'charismatic' is itself problematic, may there yet be some fairly obvious sense in which the thrust of the criticism is justified? It seems to me inescapable that this is indeed the case.

If we return to von Rad's own epilogue to his interpretation of Genesis 22, he himself raises the question of criteria for interpretation as soon as he has expressed his point about the story being 'open to interpretation and to whatever thoughts the reader is inspired'. He continues:

> Thus there is only one limitation for the expositor, but it is absolutely valid: the narrative must not be interpreted as the representation of a general unhistorical religious truth. It has been considered the protest of an awakening humanitarianism against child sacrifice; it has even been designated as a monument in human history of religion ... But just as it is difficult to impute to a narrative like this any prejudice or polemic, so it is impossible to suspect it of so theoretical an occupation with the phenomenon of child sacrifice as such or to imagine it capable of such a religious programmatic character. For it describes an event that took place in the sacred history which began with Abraham's call and whose enigmatic character is qualified only by this realm.
>
> The exposition is much more accurate when it discovers in the narrative above all the idea of a radical test of obedience. That God, who has revealed himself to Israel, is completely free to give and to take, and that no one may ask, 'What doest thou?' (Job 9.12; Dan. 4.32), is without doubt basic to our narrative. But one must be careful not to interpret the story in a general sense as a question about Abraham's willingness to obey and accordingly to direct all interest to Abraham's trial ... Above all, one must consider Isaac, who is much more than simply a 'foil' for Abraham, i.e. a more or less accidental object on which his obedience is to be proved. Isaac is the child of promise ... [and the exposition continues with the 'road out into Godforsakenness', already cited]. (1972a: 243–4)

Interestingly, von Rad's concern is not at all the relationship between the Testaments. Rather, he sees the only threat to interpretation as coming from an entirely different direction – the 'unhistorical religious truth', that which is 'theoretical' and 'programmatic'. Here one may recognize von Rad's own charged terminology of critique, a critique aimed fairly clearly at certain kinds of post-Enlightenment sensibility, in which deracinated universalizing tendencies of an abstract kind replace the particularity of engagement with the specific call of God to Abraham and God's promises centred on Isaac. As such it is a powerful critique, one which has learnt constructively from Kierkegaard and has reformulated the issues in a fresh way.

But when von Rad's interpretative reflections are related to the question of the relationship between the Testaments (a procedure to which, given his stated concerns elsewhere, he would not object), and the charge of an unduly subjective ('charismatic') style of interpretation is raised, how does he fare? In some ways, as noted above, very well; on any reckoning his is a moving and profound theological interpretation. The fact that significant and worthwhile interpretations of the biblical text cannot be predicted or anticipated is no argument against their validity; rather, the logic of the Emmaus story suggests that a certain unpredictability and surprise ought to be the case, as the biblical text is ever anew applied to contemporary life and thought in the light of Christ.

Yet it also may be the case that there is something unduly arbitrary in von Rad's approach and that he may even have to some extent replaced one kind of 'unhistorical religious truth' with another. Von Rad's grasp on the pivotal role of God's promise embodied in Isaac, so clear in the Genesis context of the story, is firm. And his sense of the significance of 'one who fears God' is also clear, even if slightly lacking in nuance. But where are all the other concerns of the text, which set it so firmly in its ancient Israelite/Judahite context, and which provide the necessary groundplan for interpretative constructions? Apart from the location of the story in 'the land of seeing', the symbolic context implying Jerusalem, which von Rad sees yet fails to see, what of the significance of divine testing, with its strong resonances of God's action towards Israel, focussed in *torah*, and its purpose of strengthening human life through a demanding deepening of the encounter with God, with the consequent definitive realization of Abraham as 'one who fears God'? How do *Anfechtung* and *Gottverlassenheit* relate to these? It is not that one could not perhaps produce an account of how the Hebrew theology and the Lutheran theology may mutually illuminate each other. It is rather that, at the crucial moments, von Rad allows his Lutheran insights to overwhelm and, in effect, devalue his Hebrew exegesis in the way that often makes those trained in language and exegesis doubtful about the role of theological hermeneutics. Such doubt sometimes may be little more than the mark of an unimaginative pedant, the kind of person who can only ever see the trees and not the wood. But it may be the mark of a genuine and justified dismay about the ease with which the concrete particularity of language and life can be swept away by a grand pattern of things.

Another way of posing the issue (if one may indulge in a convenient simplification) is to say that what is at stake is the age-old problem of what Jews traditionally call *peshat* and *derash*, and what Christians traditionally call 'letter' and 'spirit'. That a close reading of the biblical text should engage with a conceptual framework from beyond the text is not in itself a problem, especially if the text is to have enduring significance and function as scripture. But if we are to have learned from the insights of critical historical awareness and not to retreat from them, a good interpretation must be able to withstand the argued criticism that the text as ancient text does not, indeed could not, mean what that interpretation proposes. In traditional technical terms, *peshat* and *derash*, the 'literal' and the 'spiritual', must not be allowed to come apart from each other: the minutiae of exegesis ('letter', *peshat*) and the wide sweep of theological presuppositions, insights, and goals ('spirit', *derash*) must remain in genuine mutual interaction without either coming into conflict or drifting apart at crucial moments. So demanding is this requirement for Christians, whose understanding of Israel's scriptures is reconfigured through Jesus Christ, that it is not surprising if many renounce the task as hopeless or impossible. Yet it may be that Christian scholars have too often neglected those disciplines which can transform the seemingly impossible into the possible, and so they may not sufficiently grasp the full contours of the interpretative task.

To sum up, von Rad's interpretation of Genesis 22 has genuine strengths as 'spiritual' interpretation, which can be appreciated and appropriated by many.[20] But in so far as, at crucial moments, what von Rad says fails as 'literal' interpretation, it falls short of that goal whose importance von Rad himself so clearly recognized. The challenge not only to follow von Rad, but also to try to do better, remains.

### Abraham in Genesis 18 and 22

#### (1) Two Jewish interpretations

Lest a focus upon Christian interpretations of Genesis 22 be taken to imply unconcern for Jewish interpretations – which would be odd at any time, given the nature of the text, but particularly at the present time when for many reasons there is renewed dialogue and rediscovery of

---

20. These are not solely Lutherans, as the use of von Rad's 'road into Godforsakenness' by the Jesuit Scullion reminds us; quite apart from my own suggestions about its possible significance for post-Holocaust theology.

common ground between Christians and Jews – it will be appropriate to conclude this chapter with some discussion of two recent Jewish approaches to the text (from among the vast number which might be chosen).[21] This will not, however, be directly comparable to the expositions and analyses of Vischer and von Rad, for I wish to use the discussion to reflect on an ancient interpretative challenge within the text of the Abraham narrative, which thus far has been passed over. This is the nature of the relationship between Genesis 18:16–33, where Abraham boldly expostulates with God over justice and keeps coming back to him on the subject, and Genesis 22, where Abraham submits in unquestioning silence to God's astonishing request. The marked difference between these two stances has regularly been observed by commentators down the ages, and has generated renewed interest among recent commentators. Although it is not possible here to provide any serious exegesis of Genesis 18, the uses made of the text may yet be readily comprehended.

One particular way of posing the question, which has attracted some modern interpreters, is to see the two stances of Abraham as two basic types of human stance towards God, one questioning and ethically engaged, and the other submissive and preferring devotion to ethics. Those who pose the question this way usually tend to think that ethical questioning is the truer and more valid stance in relation to God and faith, while submissive devotion may be intrinsically suspect as an invitation to oppression or as too far removed from contemporary sensibilities (in a way analogous to a certain contemporary preference, noted above, for the portrayal of Jesus' crucifixion in Matthew and Mark, with its anguished question in the cry of dereliction, rather than in Luke and John, where Jesus prays and affirms but does not display anguish and does not question). At any rate, some such general context of thought seems to emerge in the writing of Mordecai Roshwald (1991: esp. 396ff.).

Roshwald discusses 'the meaning of faith', in the course of which he sees the Abraham of Genesis 22 as embodying a religion centred on 'faith' while Genesis 18 centres on 'righteousness'. Roshwald (p. 399) robustly promotes Genesis 18 over Genesis 22:

> In the last resort, there can be no compromise between the two stands, so well exemplified in the two stories of Abraham. Abraham of the *akedah* stands for the believer who abdicates his own reason and moral

---

21. Wiesel 1976: 69–97 is a particularly striking reading of Genesis 22 in dialogue with historic Jewish readings, in illustration of Wiesel's thesis that 'here is a story that contains Jewish destiny in its totality' (p. 69).

judgment in the act of faith. Abraham arguing with the Lord about the iniquity of destroying the just with the wicked stands for the human being who shares with God the capacity to think and to judge. His belief is open-eyed, he is personally involved in the ways of God, even if this means questioning Him.

It is this kind of Abraham who represents the noblest in Judaism and in the ethical evolution of man. He is the prototype of the reflective, committed and morally responsible individual. He leaves the Abraham of the *akedah* far behind, at a primitive stage of religious development, where blind trust could lead men to commit senseless atrocities.

A different, and more interestingly nuanced, account of the same issue is offered by Jon Levenson, who compares Abraham in Genesis 18 and in Genesis 22 as follows:

> If Genesis 18 represents the (qualified) autonomy of humanity over against divine decrees, we may take Genesis 22, the binding of Isaac, as the parade example of human heteronomy before the inscrutable will of God . . .
>
> Those two chapters of Genesis, with their contrasting perspectives on Abraham, present us as well with contrasting theologies of the divine–human relationship. In chapter 18 Abraham doubts, questions, argues, and even convinces God to back down from an extreme position. In chapter 22 Abraham demonstrates an absolute and unconditional obedience and as a result wins the reprieve for which he dared not plead. There is a telling analogy between these two chapters and the dimensions of covenant that I have been calling autonomy and heteronomy. Like the autonomous dimension, the theology of Genesis 18 assumes a large measure of validity in human judgment over against the will of God. Divine speech is, or at least can be, in the nature of a proposal that awaits human ratification. It does not demand immediate and categorical submission. Like the heteronomous dimension of covenant, Genesis 22 assumes a theology in which there is no defensible alternative to acceptance of God's will, and human dignity is a function of the completeness of conformity to the divine command. There are, of course, contextual differences between these two chapters, chief among them that in chapter 18 Abraham pleads on behalf of others, whereas in chapter 22 the sacrifice is to be his own: the reprieve he asks for is to be for others, *not* for himself. This granted, it is still the case that the two passages vary tellingly in their view of right and capacity of human beings to understand and second-guess God.
>
> As was the case with the dialectic of covenantal service, so here the

inclusion of the two perspectives in the same Bible, indeed in the same patriarch, yields a subtle and nuanced theology, one that cannot be reduced to either component. By itself the theology of Genesis 18 would soon lead to a religion in which God's will had ceased to be a reality: the human conscience, having filtered out all divine directives that offended it, would produce a God that was only itself writ large, commendable human values practiced because they were right, not because God commanded them. In this highly autonomous theology, no room would be left for obedience, and the personal faithfulness to the suzerain which is the essence of covenant would play no role in the moral life. Left to its own, Genesis 22, on the other hand, would lead to a religion of fanaticism, in which God would be so incomprehensible that even the praise of him as wise or just would be meaningless: no act, no matter how silly or unfair, could be ruled out as the will of God, and faithfulness to him would be indistinguishable from mindless, slavish obedience.

Together, however, the two perspectives delimit a theology in which human judgment neither replaces the inscrutable God who commands nor becomes superfluous within the life lived in faithfulness to him. In this larger, dialectical theology, both arguing with God and obeying him can be central spiritual acts, although when to do which remains necessarily unclear. (1994: 151, 152, 153)

More recently, Levenson has returned to the issue, in the context of discussing the tendency of modern interpreters to impose inappropriate categories of interpretation upon the portrayal of Abraham in Genesis 22. He corrects and elaborates his earlier reference to 'contextual differences' between Genesis 18 and 22 as follows:

The difference is one of context: the context of Sodom and Gomorrah is *forensic*, whereas that of the aqedah is *sacrificial*. In a forensic context, the death of an innocent person is an outrage; in a sacrifical context, since the offering is expected to be blemishless, the innocence of the human victim is no grounds for protest. Abraham raises his voice against God himself at the thought of an unjust *execution*. He is prepared to offer even his beloved son himself to the same God as a *sacrifice*. There is no contradiction in the text. (1998: 272)

### (2) Reflections on Roshwald and Levenson

These two interesting expositions raise many issues, on which I offer some brief reflections which also touch on wider issues of Jewish–Christian dialogue. First, in so far as Roshwald and Levenson are debating the nature of Jewish faith, through setting the biblical text within a wider context of Jewish thought and practice which allows its enduring significance to be fruitfully discussed, they are doing the kind of thing which this book advocates (though as Jews rather than as Christians). Continuing questions about the relative weighting of distinctive elements within the tradition is not something to be regretted, but is a sign of the healthy flourishing of that tradition. Moreover, like many debates within Jewish faith, there are clear analogues with debates in Christian faith, and contributions directed to one context may be significant within another.

Secondly, Roshwald's account seems problematic. His rather easy polarization of 'blind trust' against 'open-eyed personal involve[ment] in the ways of God' problematically divorces ethical reason from religious obedience, in a way that I suspect skews classic Jewish understandings of relationship with God. Roshwald also depends upon an exegetically superficial and somewhat decontextualized reading of the Genesis text and so tends to misconstrue the undoubted importance of engaged questioning of God as an expression of faith.

Thirdly, while I do not wish to lose Levenson's balance between the two stances, I would nonetheless redistribute the balance slightly (though 'balance' may not be the best image for interrelated facets of a single reality). That is, the shape of the canonical portrayal makes Genesis 22 the high point of Abraham's life with God (after which there is no further discourse between God and Abraham). The shape of the story implies that the engagement with God of Genesis 22 is yet more searching than that of Genesis 18.[22]

It is difficult to articulate the nuance accurately here without appearing to downgrade or marginalize that which is represented by Abraham in Genesis 18. The underlying issue is, I think, to do with death, the one absolute certainty confronting human life. There are many and rich things that can be done with life, which in the contexts of scripture and the faiths rooted in it include an engagement with God which makes a real difference to the possibilities and potential of life. Yet a supreme and constantly underlying challenge is to accept, and indeed embrace, death and the many symbolic anticipations of death in the form of obstacles, hardships, and sufferings which cannot be circumvented; and to discover the life-giving reality of God in and through such embrace (a reality definitively disclosed for the Christian in the death and resurrection of Jesus).

22. To anticipate chapter 6, the potential significance of the Genesis shaping of the traditions is underlined for the Christian by the shape of Matthew's Gospel, where a basic issue is Jesus' obedience up to and including death.

It is, I believe, an historic recognition by Christians (a recognition perhaps to some extent shared but understood differently by Jews), that much of the heart of biblical faith lies here. But the faithful articulation of its dynamics is always a challenge. For the balance between a life-enhancing embrace of creatureliness and death and a passionate moral engagement that challenges evil is ever shifting. There are recurrent, and all too often justified, suspicions that embrace of death and its equivalents can be used to undercut and evade, instead of undergird and enable, positive embrace of life and willingness to seek its transformation. Herein lies the enduring task of the ancient and contemporary discipline of moral and spiritual discernment.

Finally, as a kind of thought experiment, I would like to suggest a redescription of the relationship between Genesis 18 and Genesis 22 in categories other than Levenson's categories of autonomy and heteronomy, categories not far removed from Roshwald's reworking of a classic Enlightenment opposition between ethical reason and faith.[23] Thus, I suggest that Abraham in Genesis 18 be viewed as an exemplar of the person who in some way makes a difference to God in God's relationship with his world.[24] Such a person in some way has 'power' with God which is exercised for the benefit of others; in this capacity Abraham engages God for the benefit of Sodom and Gomorrah where Lot is situated. Abraham in Genesis 22 is no less 'powerful' in his engagement with God, which indeed leads to an enduring remembering of God's provision in his chosen place and an invocation of blessing among the nations. But the issue in Genesis 22 is what such 'power' means for himself, and the fact that it can be definitively realized only in the relinquishment of Isaac (with all that Isaac symbolizes).

My purpose in thus redescribing the difference between the narratives is twofold. First, the account just offered may perhaps capture some easily passed over elements of the kind of significance which is likely to have been attached to the story in its composition and reception within

---

23. This is not to deny the potential fruitfulness of reconsidering this major ancient and modern debate through these paradigmatic narratives, but simply to suggest that the issues of God and justice raised by verse 25, 'Shall not the Judge (*shophet*) of all the earth do justice (*mishpat*)?' may fruitfully be considered in more than one context.

24. The primary Hebrew term for such a person is 'prophet' (*nabi'*, Gk. *prophetes*), as in the Emmaus disciples' depiction of Jesus (Lk. 24:19). One prime responsibility of the prophet was to pray for others, as is almost definitionally spelt out in 1 Samuel 12: 19, 23; Jeremiah 27:18. It is in this sense that the term is applied to Abraham (Gen. 20:7). This biblical role is realized, *mutatis mutandis*, in Jewish tradition in the *tsaddiq* or *ḥasid*, and in Christian tradition in the saint.

Genesis (though this is obviously a moot point, which cannot be justified here). Secondly, to anticipate the argument of chapters 6 and 7, I wish to link the two Abraham narratives with the narrative construal of Jesus as Son of God in Matthew's Gospel, as an instance of the way in which Jesus continues and deepens the kind of engagement with God which characterizes Abraham. In Matthew's Gospel a major issue at stake in Jesus' sonship is precisely the appropriate use of the 'power' which it entails. Although Jesus freely uses his messianic power for the benefit of others, he will not, despite the repeated urgings of the satan, use it to benefit himself. Thus the mocking 'others he saved, himself he cannot save' (Matt. 27:42) in deep irony depicts the moment of recognition as the moment of misunderstanding: the fundamental truth which indeed lies at the heart of Jesus' power as 'king of Israel' is that the divine power which he uses for others he will not use for himself (not in the impotence supposed by the mockers, but in the moral and spiritual refusal to relinquish unconditional trust); but this makes no sense to those who are hostile to him. As for Abraham, 'power' with God to benefit others leads to a climax in which he cannot do for himself what he does for others except through embrace of that which symbolizes death for himself, so too for Jesus in a way that is consistent throughout his ministry.

Such reflections of course go well beyond Roshwald's and Levenson's accounts of Genesis 18 and Genesis 22. But the differences between the Jewish and the Christian accounts do not, I think, lie where they are sometimes thought to lie in terms of misreading or incomprehension. Rather, Jew and Christian alike are seeking to engage with substantive issues about God and humanity which are posed by the biblical text. Levenson, as a Jew (whose handling of the biblical text has a stronger exegetical base than Roshwald's), tends to develop the issues in relation to the implications of *torah* as enduringly normative (his observations in his first account cited above conclude a fascinating discussion of God's creative activity and Israel's worship). He might wish to develop the significance of Abraham's fear of God in relation to continuing corporate and individual Jewish observance of *torah* (in line with the clear implications of the story within its Hebrew canonical context). I, as a Christian, develop the issue in relation to Christ as the one in whom the will of God in *torah* is fulfilled in such a way that grasp of God's will, and its accessibility to Gentiles as well as Jews, is enduringly transformed through its realization in  Christ's death and resurrection (in line with the implications of the Christian canon as a whole). We are each concerned to engage with the realities of God and human life today. We each recognize the dialectics of exegesis, hermeneutics, and appropriation. We are each concerned with a faith and practice that is of significance for those other than its obvious adherents. We differ importantly in understanding, identity, and practices, but the differences are public and discussable. As such there always remain mutual possibilities of growth in understanding of God and fulfilment of human life.

# 5

## Genesis 22 and the hermeneutics of suspicion

The next step in our argument must be to reflect yet further upon Genesis 22. It is not enough solely to situate our exposition in relation to classic Christian concerns, from the New Testament to von Rad, and to note some similarities and differences with Jewish approaches. Other contexts too require attention.

The context with which I wish to engage is that of 'suspicion'. This takes many forms, one or two expressions of which were noted near the outset of the exposition of Genesis 22; in place of a paradigm of faithful response to the one true God, we find Abraham's response to a 'diabolical' deity being seen as 'insane'. Although this problem was already touched on towards the end of the exposition, more needs to be said, since the hermeneutics of suspicion is a major issue in contemporary biblical criticism. Reserve towards the story of Abraham comes not only from those who are alienated from Jewish and Christian faith, but also from those who locate themselves within, and wish to remain within, these faith traditions.

In general terms, a Christian theologian should not be quick to dismiss a hermeneutic of suspicion, for the prime reason that it represents a kind of secularized counterpart to the dogma of original sin. Indeed were it not for the decay of some of the classic disciplines of faith and theology in important strands of post-Reformation and post-Enlightenment thought, the rediscovery of the problems which suspicion touches on would not come as any great surprise. Suspicion touches on something that is basic within a Christian account of life, the recognition that there is nothing which cannot be abused and that humans have an enormous capacity for self-deception in the ways they try to rationalize and justify their greed, desires, and idolatries. The religious life is not exempt from this; rather it may be a prime exemplar of it. However, just as unremitting and unqualified emphasis on sin leads to a deficient understanding of the content of the Bible and Christian faith, so suspicion as prime hermeneutical key leads to a deficient understanding of biblical (and most other kinds of) interpretation.

The purpose of the present discussion is not to engage with the literature of suspicion in any extended way, but rather to offer a sampling of such positions with regard to Genesis 22, with a view to exploring a little the ways in which they may further, or may impede, the understanding of the biblical text and the role of its scholarly interpreters.

## Two feminist accounts of Genesis 22

### (1a) Phyllis Trible: preliminary exposition

I shall first consider two feminist accounts of Genesis 22 which are, I hope, reasonably representative of feminist concerns.[1]

First, Phyllis Trible and her essay 'Genesis 22: The Sacrifice of Sarah':[2] Trible is one of the most notable examples of a feminist biblical scholar who is suspicious of the patriarchalism of scripture and Christian tradition yet who wishes to remain within the Christian tradition; so her discussion of Genesis 22 is of particular interest. The approach of the essay is familiar from her earlier work, combining a rhetorical critical method with a feminist hermeneutic.

According to Trible, the central issue in the story is inappropriate relationship ('attachment') with Isaac on the part of both Abraham (in the specific wording of the text) and Sarah (in a possible inference from the text). From such attachment one needs to be delivered. She explains the theoretical basis for this in a note:

> This interpretation plays with three concepts: attachment, detachment, and nonattachment. The first two are interrelated, being positive and negative manifestations of an invalid mode-of-being in the world. This mode-of-being anchors existence in human relationships, rather than in God, with inevitable consequences of

---

1. Another characteristic feminist contribution to the study of Genesis 22 is Delaney 1989: 27–41. The essay has many interesting insights, but concludes with a speculative (and historically improbable) thesis that 'the story functions to establish the authority of the father', indeed that it 'functions to establish the authority of God the Father' and it 'legitimates the patriarchal way of life' (pp. 38, 39). Considerations of space and proportion within this chapter preclude detailed discussion of Delaney's arguments here.

2. Trible 1991. Trible says (n. 1) that the essay is an abridgment of a forthcoming study. In correspondence she has told me that the fuller study will not differ in substance from this essay.

problems and sufferings. Nonattachment is a transcendent way of knowing and thinking. It moves human beings beyond interpersonal entrapment to a realization of the divine. Thus it offers a spiritual perspective that allows one to be in the world but not of it. In the language of Genesis 22, nonattachment is the fear of God. It frees human beings one from another so that they can be one with another. In addition to scriptural foundations, this interpretation builds on Zen Buddhism and Metapsychiatry. (1991: 251)

In the light of this, Trible (pp. 178–9) interprets the story thus:

To attach one's self to another is to negate love through entrapment . . . To attach is to practice idolatry. In adoring Isaac, Abraham turns from God. The test, then, is an opportunity for understanding and healing. To relinquish attachment is to discover freedom. To give up human anxiety is to receive divine assurance. To disavow idolatry is to find God.

The fact that Abraham is able to undergo the test and display fear of God enables him to be delivered. But what about Sarah? Where is she in all this? Trible gives a new twist to the old question of Sarah's whereabouts and the possible impact of Abraham's action upon her. She focusses upon Sarah's attachment to Isaac as 'my son' (21:10), and her corresponding mal-treatment of Hagar and Ishmael, arguing that this portrays inappropriate relationship to Isaac as being as much a problem for Sarah as for Abraham (for whom, indeed, attachment is not a problem prior to Genesis 22):

Attachment is Sarah's problem. Nevertheless, Genesis 22 drops Sarah to insert Abraham. The switch defies the internal logic of the larger story. In view of the unique status of Sarah and her exclusive relationship to Isaac, she, not Abraham, ought to have been tested. The dynamic of the entire saga, from its genealogical preface on, requires that Sarah be featured in the climactic scene, that she learn the meaning of obedience to God, that she find liberation from possessiveness, that she free Isaac from maternal ties, and that she emerge a solitary individual, nonattached, the model of faithfulness . . . The story . . . fails to offer Sarah redemption and thereby perpetuates the conflict between her and Hagar . . . Patriarchy has denied Sarah her story, the opportunity for freedom and blessing. It has excluded her and glorified Abraham . . . If early on patriarchy casts out the woman in the gutter (Hagar), the time comes when it also dismisses the woman on a pedestal (Sarah). (pp. 188–9)

Thus the patriarchal assumptions of the story undermine its own positive meaning:

> By her absence from the narrative and her subsequent death, Sarah has
> been sacrificed by patriarchy to patriarchy. Thus this magnificent story
> of nonattachment stands in mortal danger of betraying itself. It fears
> not God but holds fast to an idol. If the story is to be redeemed, then
> the reader must restore Sarah to her rightful place. Such a
> hermeneutical move, wed to rhetorical analysis, would explode the
> entrenched bias to fulfill the internal logic of the story. And it would
> do even more: it would free divine revelation from patriarchy. (pp.
> 190–1)

And Trible (p. 191) concludes the essay with a homiletic and existential
flourish:

> To be faithful to the story no interpretation can become an idol. And so
> the essay ends with a disorienting homily. After we perceive the
> sacrifice of Sarah and move to free the narrative from patriarchy, after
> and only after all these things, will we hear God testing us: 'Take your
> interpretation of this story, your only interpretation, the one which
> you love, and sacrifice it on the mount of hermeneutics.' If we
> withhold not our cherished reading from God, then we too will come
> down from the mountain nonattached. In such an event, we and the
> story will merge. Interpretation will become appropriation. Testing
> and attachment will disappear, and the worship of God will be all in
> all.

Trible's essay is a remarkable *tour de force*. On the one hand, it has many elements of central and indisputable importance to scripture and Christian
tradition: first, the strong critique of idolatry, with the recognition that
even the closest and most important human relationships have the capacity to become idolatrous; secondly, the value of 'nonattachment' in enabling genuine relationships, where I take it that by 'nonattachment' she
means what in traditional Christian parlance in, say, Saint Teresa of Avila
in her *Way of Perfection*, chapters 8–11, is called religious 'detachment'
(Peers 1957: 37–48) – the transcending of self-seeking through finding in
God the true nature and meaning of love, which thereby enables truer
loving of one's fellow humans; thirdly, the sense that, for the believer, biblical interpretation is ultimately a matter of appropriation, in which the
biblical text becomes the medium for a transforming encounter with
God. On the other hand, she achieves the Christian feminist goals both of
making more visible the role of a woman who in the received tradition is
less visible and of showing (on her reading) that the patriarchy of the text
is at odds with its own real message, so that the scriptural message is
enhanced rather than diminished by the feminist critique.

### (1b) Phyllis Trible: analysis

Trible's interpretation raises many issues. Its basis, however, is an understanding of Abraham's relationship with Isaac (and Sarah's, in a different way) as being an 'attachment' which is idolatrous and from which he (and Sarah) needs to be freed. But while it is one thing to recognize that this may be a genuine issue in life, it is another to show that it is the issue at stake in this particular biblical text. If it is the issue, then the meaning of Abraham's sacrifice is changed. It is not that Isaac is the one who is dearest to Abraham, a gift from God in a relationship implicitly wholesome, and that to relinquish in sacrifice the one who is dearest is the test for Abraham. Rather, the relationship is skewed by Abraham's attachment, so the issue in the test is the healing of relationships between Abraham and Isaac and between Abraham and God. The story is no longer about Abraham giving God what is intrinsically good and valuable – a genuine sacrifice – but about Abraham needing healing from a faulty relationship.

What basis does this have within the biblical text? Since Trible herself notes that this problem of attachment, as she conceives it, does not characterize Abraham prior to Genesis 22, all the evidence must come from within the story itself. What then is the evidence? The obvious material depicting Abraham's relationship with Isaac comes in verse 2, on which she says:

> The object of the verb is not a simple word but heavy-laden language. It moves from the generic term of kinship, 'your son', through the exclusivity of relationship, 'your only one', through the intimacy of bonding, 'whom you love', to climax in the name that fulfills promise, the name of laughter and joy, the name *yishaq* (Isaac). Language accumulates attachments: 'your son, your only one, whom you love, Isaac'. (1991: 172)

The comments on the individual phrases are well put. Yet the inference drawn from all the phrases together is problematic. Why should this accumulation of language about Isaac express 'attachment' in the specifically negative sense with which Trible uses the term? That this is the textual basis for the interpretation becomes fully explicit in the further comments on verse 12:

> Fearer of God! To fear God is to worship God. The term 'fearer of God' embodies awe, terror, and devotion in the presence of *mysterium tremendum*. And the worship of God abolishes all idolatries, specifically now the idolatry of the son. 'You have not withheld your son, your only one, from me.' This interpersonal language takes the reader back to the beginning of the story, to the words, 'your son, your only one,

whom you love, Isaac'. The repetition underscores the issue to clarify the test. Abraham had formed an attachment to his son. Attachment threatened the obedience, the worship, the fear of God. Thus the test offers Abraham an opportunity for healing, an opportunity to free both himself and his son. (p. 178)

*Why* should the accumulation of terms of endearment towards Isaac be seen as unhealthy and idolatrous?[3] The fact that not all the phrases used are necessary to say that Abraham loves Isaac does, of course, open the way to a range of possible interpretations of their significance (as the tradition of Jewish exegesis well illustrates). But at least two considerations tell against Trible's supposition of a negative significance. First, there is no ambivalence in the terms used of Isaac: an 'only son' (*yaḥid*) is the regular Hebrew term for the prime object of a parent's love and hope;[4] and the verb for 'love' (*'ahav*) has none of the ambiguity of other verbs that could have been used, such as 'desire' (*ḥamad*).[5] Secondly, there is the consistent Hebrew understanding that sacrifice in the form of whole burnt offering (*'olah*) should involve that which is intrinsically good ('without blemish', *tamim*, Lev. 1:3). If Abraham is to relinquish idolatrous attachment to Isaac, such relinquishment would be of value, but it would not be a sacrifice as the Old Testament understands sacrifice.

To sum up: Trible's interpretation, for all its insights, raises acutely a problem similar to that which we have already noted in relation to von Rad; that is, the relationship between 'literal' and 'spiritual' senses. A good interpretation must be able to withstand the argued criticism that it is a misreading of the text. Trible's interpretation has strengths as 'spiritual' interpretation, for those to whom the insights of Christian feminism are important – though even so it rather too easily transposes

---

3. My initial response to Trible's exposition was to suppose that she uses the word 'attachment' equivocally. That is, the initial exposition of verse 2, where 'attachment' is unexplained and could have its general and regular meaning of affectionate bonding, can induce the reader to suppose that 'attachment' is an appropriate term for the relationship between Abraham and Isaac. Once accepted as appropriate, at a later stage 'attachment' is given its specialized, negative connotations. There would thus be a slide from 'attachment' in (apparently) a normal, positive sense to 'attachment' as a problem, a threat to obedience to God. In correspondence, however, Prof. Trible assured me that her usage of 'attachment' is consistent throughout the essay. Therefore my suggested shift in meaning is an interpretation inimical to the writer's intention and as such must be abandoned (though whether Trible's delay in explaining the specialized sense of 'attachment' – her usage of 'attachment', 'detachment', and 'nonattachment' is not spelt out at the outset, but only appears well into the essay in a footnote to the exposition of verse 12 – might encourage such a misreading remains a moot point).
4. The loss of such a son is therefore the ultimate grief, Jer. 6:26; Am. 8:10; cf. Zech. 12:10.
5. The connotations of *ḥamad* are easily negative because of its well-known use in the tenth commandment (Exod. 20:17; Deut. 5:21). But it can signify positive desire, as, for example, 'the mountain which God desired for his dwelling' (Ps. 68:17 (ET 16)).

human engagement with God into the healing of defective human relationships. But it is questionable as 'literal' interpretation, in that the wording of Genesis 22:2 does not sustain the notion of defective and idolatrous relationship that Trible finds there. The healing of defective relationships between parent and child is a valid concern, a problem of considerable contemporary significance. But it is not the concern of Genesis 22, and constructive contemporary engagement with the problem will not be furthered by supposing otherwise.

### (2) Bobbie Groth

To recognize something of the diversity of feminist interpretation – for many do not share Trible's priorities – we will consider a poem by Bobbie Groth, 'Isaac's Body', an unpublished manuscript of 1989 cited by W. Dow Edgerton (1992: ch. 4) in the course of a discussion of Genesis 22. Groth's poem is not a piece of scholarly writing, and is a good reminder of how often biblical interpretation may take forms other than that of the scholarly monograph and commentary. Edgerton (pp. 89–90) writes:

> Consider also the angle of vision of a contemporary poem by Bobbie Groth . . . In her poem also the scene is transformed. The three-day journey becomes an attempt to hide a terrible deed from the eyes of Isaac's mother. The altar of Moriah is transformed into a hospital bed upon which a young boy lies, a victim and survivor of his father's brutal incest. The talk of commitment, covenants, and God, are the lies and rationalizations of perpetual lust satisfying itself, excusing itself, and hiding the evidence of crime so the sacrifice may continue. The voice of Isaac's mother speaks:

> > But you forget that I
> >   really talk to God
> > and it has nothing to do
> >   with taking life
> >   to show love
> > It has to do
> >   with snatching boys' bodies
> >     off of hilltops
> >       and bringing them
> > to hospital rooms
> >   to get better
> > So they can hate me
> >   and I can love them back
> > and fight to undo
> >   your despicable covenants.

It never was the voice of God at all, the poem concludes. It was Satan's voice, the voice of Abraham's own lust, and he was too stupid to know the difference.

Groth introduces powerful contemporary images. Abraham as child abuser (one of the most heinous and emotive crimes in contemporary imagination) and ideological deceiver, who resorts to fine-sounding religious language precisely to conceal his abuse from others and so perpetuate it, but in his stupidity deceiving only himself. Isaac as both victim and survivor (primary terms in much feminist discourse). Sarah as one who brings victims to hospital (one of the most powerful contemporary symbols of a place for doing good) and shows unconditional love precisely in thankless opposition to religiously generated bigotry and cruelty; and who, in so far as it is any longer meaningful to speak of God, is the only one who actually knows God in her opposition to the religious establishment.

It is a fascinating passage. It conveys a profound alienation from Jewish and Christian traditions, expressed in a way which seems positively to invite a corresponding response of offence and alienation on the part of those for whom the traditions are living and life-giving. As such it captures well the polarization of attitudes to Jewish and Christian traditions of faith which regularly characterize a contemporary context. Yet if one analyses the passage it becomes clear that a simple focus on alienation and polarization may miss what is really going on.

In many ways the passage is a good example of using the religious tradition against the tradition: the intense moral passion, the depiction of unconditional love as characterizing the true healer, the opposing and unmasking of self-seeking in religious disguise are all elements prominent in movements of renewal in Jewish and Christian history; though here they appear to be directed not against an abuse of the religious tradition in order to revitalize it, but against the religious tradition itself in order to replace it. Sarah in the poem makes perhaps the central claim in Jewish and Christian traditions – to speak with God and to interpret God's mind truly – not so as to appropriate the religious tradition but to dismiss it.

The challenge for those within Jewish and Christian traditions is to recognize the validity of a protest against religious language and practice which too regularly and easily become a mask for self-serving and exploitative behaviour; and to recognize that a genuine response to such protest cannot be solely a matter of words and formulations but must be a demonstration in life of an integrity and self-giving that truly embodies those elements of the tradition which the critique has used against it. Such practical demonstration may involve painful reworking of the tradition where it reflects social and cultural assumptions of an earlier and different age; that is, the demonstration must be not only in interpersonal relationships but also in the reforming of those institutional procedures and laws which structure personal life.

The challenge for the alienated feminist is to recognize the extent of positive indebtedness to those traditions from which s/he feels alienated. It is easy to show a confident moral rationality, rather reminiscent of the eighteenth century, that some qualities of life and understanding are self-evidently correct; but the fragmentation of contemporary culture, and the corresponding fragmentation of feminist (as other) thought, make it ever less clear which patterns of thought and life, if any, are self-evidently correct and able to preserve human dignity from corrosive pressures within contemporary society. It may be that some qualities of life and understanding, inherited from Jewish and Christian faiths, cannot survive when those faiths are no longer practised and when their residual cultural influence is marginalized and privatized, and that therefore to seek in some way to renew the tradition, rather than abandon it, may be the best way of preserving valued priorities of life.

### Abraham as anti-hero

#### (1) Gunn and Fewell, and Davies: exposition

I would like next to consider two studies of Genesis 22 which form part of suspicious readings of the Abraham story as a whole and are sufficiently similar to be usefully treated together – that of David Gunn and Danna Fewell in their textbook *Narrative in the Hebrew Bible*,[6] and that of Philip Davies, 'Male Bonding: A Tale of Two Buddies'.[7]

Both accounts are so suspicious that the Abraham who emerges is no longer a model for Jewish and Christian faith even in modified form, but is rather a paradigm of self-preservation at the expense of others (Gunn and Fewell), the moral of whose story is: 'Do not trust a deity. He or she or it almost certainly does not trust you, and has no reason to tell you the truth' (Davies). Since this is a somewhat surprising construal of the

---

6. Gunn and Fewell 1993a: ch. 4. A very similarly worded account is also available in their more overtly ideological 1993b: ch. 2.

7. Davies 1995: 95–113. A version appeared in *Bible Review* 1995: 24–33, 44–5, and achieved some notoriety, to judge by the pages of correspondence in response in the following issue.

biblical text, it is important initially to clarify the assumptions which make such interpretation possible. There seem to me to be four.

First, one must discount the whole Jewish and Christian history of interpretation, which treats Abraham so positively, on the grounds that it prejudices one's reading of the text and inhibits fresh thinking. Davies is most explicit about this:

> Without the benefit of this long history of interpretation, how would *we* read the story of Abraham? Since very few of us can pretend we know nothing about Abraham before we read his story, we must make an effort to resist seeing what we think we need to see. That requires very detailed attention to the text itself. The following is a reading that presumes nothing about the values of the author of the story (except that it was an ancient Judaean) and takes Abraham, his deity and his world to be projections of that author's creativity.[8]

Secondly, as an intensification of the first point, one must effectively discount the rest of the Hebrew scriptures. The story of Abraham must be considered in its own right. Neither Gunn and Fewell nor Davies make this a point of principle, but in practice their readings have no cross-references to usage of terms or religio-cultural assumptions elsewhere in the Hebrew scriptures.[9] The point is to clear the decks of all possible prejudice in favour of a positive portrayal of Abraham, so that the Abraham story in Genesis may engage us as readers genuinely open to the text.

Thirdly, whereas Jewish and Christian tradition has privileged those portions of the Abraham story where Abraham at least appears to be a model of faith and/or faithfulness, and has considered those stories in which he deceives Pharaoh and Abimelech about Sarah (Gen. 12:10–20; 20:1–18) and allows Hagar to be maltreated (16:1–6) as lapses and inconsistencies in character, Gunn and Fewell and Davies reverse this. They privilege the stories of Abraham's questionable behaviour as providing the real key to Abraham's character – 'the actions of Abram in Egypt are powerful clues to his personality, and they suggest a scheming and selfish character' (Davies 1995: 100) – and they portray Abraham as a consistent character,

---

8. 1995: 96. This is a recurrent theme in Davies' book: 'In the case of Jewish and Christian readings, the question to be asked is whether the reader can tell the difference between what the text says (or might say) and what the Jewish and Christian interpretative traditions have decided that it says (or should say). If the text (and this might be true to an extent of any text) becomes a prisoner of its own reception, by what strategies can the text be continually liberated?' (1995: 12–13, cf. 14, 54–5).

9. There is a partial exception in Davies' passing reference to Numbers 14:20–3 (p. 97) and to Moses' exclusion of Ammonites and Moabites from the congregation of Israel (p. 103).

with the consequence that stories that might appear to portray him more positively do not in fact do so:

> While some commentators, in trying to reconcile Genesis 22 with the preceding episodes, have suggested that, in Genesis 22, the man of unfaith has reached a pinnacle of ultimate faith, *a reading attentive to consistency of character* might conclude otherwise. Abraham is a man who has shown that he has no problem sacrificing members of his family. (Gunn and Fewell 1993a: 98; my italics)
>
> This story [sc. Genesis 22] has to be understood in a completely different way [sc. from conventional interpretation] if we want to understand the motivation of *the characters we have come to know*. (Davies 1995: 110; my italics)

Fourthly, the reading strategy depends on utilizing gaps and silences in the text in such a way that they support the portrayal of Abraham being advocated. For if one ceases to assume that Abraham is to be viewed positively, then gaps and silences are amenable to suspicious construal.

When the Abraham narrative is read with these assumptions, Genesis 22 as a story of unfaith becomes less remarkable. Gunn and Fewell see it as the final outworking of Abraham's self-seeking at the expense of others, in which all that is finally revealed is his craven nature:

> Suppose, however, that God is well aware of Abraham's tendency to forfeit his family to danger and uncertainty. What if the test is really designed to see just how far Abraham will go? To begin with, we might ask, what is the unspoken alternative? If Abraham refuses to do this thing, what will happen to him? Disobedience results in punishment. Might not Abraham hear in the silence a threat, an unstated 'or else . . .'? Abraham, as we have seen, is rather sensitive when it comes to his personal safety.
>
> How far will Abraham go when self-preservation is at issue? Perhaps God needs to see if there is ever a point where Abraham is willing to sacrifice himself rather than his family. He has sacrificed the other members of his household; will he go so far as to sacrifice this son of promise? Will he go so far as to implicate himself in the violence?
>
> What might we have heard from an exemplary Abraham? 'Take me! I am old. The boy has his whole life in front of him.' Or might we have even heard the Abraham of old (cf. Gen. 18:25): 'Far be it from you to expect such a thing . . .' . . . But . . . this Abraham risks nothing for this innocent boy.
>
> Instead, we get nothing but silent obedience. . . . Abraham makes every effort to go through with the sacrifice of his son. Only God's intervention keeps him from murder. Here we have a rather sudden

revelation of character: God is not willing to have the boy killed. But Abraham is. . . .

God's response to Abraham is impossible to decipher. 'Now I know that you fear God.' For most commentators, this spells triumph for Abraham: he reveres God for God's sake. Tone, however, is an elusive thing, and 'fear' can mean more than reverence. God could be saying that, at the very least, Abraham has shown that he fears God, indeed for his very life. He may not have much backbone or compassion, but at least he fears God. Or perhaps, God is saying, 'Now I know that you fear God as much as you do other human beings. You have given in to your fear of me in the same way that you have given in to your fear of others – the Egyptians (ch. 12), the men of Gerar (ch. 20), even Sarah (chs. 16 and 21).'

Abraham, ironically, names the place 'YHWH will see' . . . But what has YHWH actually seen? On the mountain, YHWH sees a man who fears, a man in need of grace . . . Whether or not Abraham has passed the test, we do not know. We fear not. (1993a: 98–100)

Davies sees the story as the climactic illustration of a relationship between Abraham and YHWH which is all a matter of manipulation and bluff, a politics of male mistrust:

Now Yhwh wants to 'test' Abraham, truly enough, but not in the sense of taxing his obedience, because he knows that Abraham's obedience threshold is very low. The test is of a different kind. He wants Abraham to have to show some positive feeling towards Isaac, to take emotional possession of his appointed heir, and to ask for something on Isaac's behalf; to protest, to finally admit defeat . . .

Abraham's behaviour does not necessarily indicate blind obedience. There is a game of bluff going on, of course, because Yhwh does not want the son he has bestowed on Abraham, the Abraham he has chosen, to die. That death would shatter Yhwh's own plans. But Abraham knows this is a bluff, and he intends to call it. The weakness of the god's position is that he cares about Isaac more than Abraham does. It is Yhwh, not Abraham, who says that Isaac is the son whom Abraham loves. Abraham has never confessed such feelings. Even so, Yhwh knows that Abraham cannot go ahead. Yet equally, Abraham knows that Yhwh will not let it happen (he has only to remember that even Ishmael was rescued). The only thing to be resolved is: who will blink first? . . .

Yhwh is the one who backs down. He tells Abraham to stop, not the reverse. Abraham has successfully called the bluff and won the contest. But what can Yhwh do? Deities are not supposed to lose, or at least to be seen to lose. He must save face by playing his favourite card, saying in effect, 'because you have done this, you will indeed have what I promised you anyway'. He must pretend that this episode was a test Abraham had to pass in order to get his promise fulfilled. He and Abraham know better, but at least the impression has been created that the deity is in charge. And that impression has largely worked: most commentators misread accordingly. (1995: 110–12)

## (2) Gunn and Fewell, and Davies: analysis

How should these suspicious readings be evaluated? Rather as with Groth's poem, one might rightly or wrongly suppose that they deliberately aim to affront and offend those who reverence the God of whom scripture speaks. But here the important questions are, Are they right? Can anything be learnt from them? This is best approached through a consideration of the first three of their four underlying assumptions (since the treatment of gaps and silences, while important, will almost entirely depend on assumptions about the course of the story as a whole).

First, the history of interpretation: the more or less unanimously positive assessment of Abraham by Jews and Christians since the formation of the Hebrew scriptures *rightly* creates a strong initial presumption in its favour. To be sure, the interpretative tradition *might* be mistaken. But nothing less than a rigorous, detailed, and persuasive exegesis could legitimately begin to make an alternative case. It is not as though it were merely a point of detail or a solitary difficult text, but an extended narrative sequence, with a famous dramatic climax in Genesis 22. Moreover, whatever difference modern historical insights may have made to an understanding of the genre of the Abraham narrative and the kind of history that may underlie it, they have made no difference whatever to an understanding of the general tenor of the stories as they now stand.[10]

If the history of interpretation is to be seen as a history of misinterpretation, can we find any evidence of a time when ancient Judaeans did not thus misinterpret the story? In so far as Abraham is mentioned in Hebrew scripture outside Genesis, it is always positively. We noted at the outset the depiction of Abraham as 'friend of God' (Isa. 41:8; 2 Chron. 20:7). What, moreover, is likely to have been the kind of understanding held by those editors who incorporated the stories of Abraham with the stories of Israel within the Pentateuch? Are they not likely to have seen Abraham as in some way exemplary of the kind of relationship with God that the *torah* as a whole promotes (as argued above)? If so, then presumably the history

---

10. The Abraham material has thus not been reconstrued in the way that messianic passages have been reconstrued.

of misreading must go behind the whole canonical history of the text. Perhaps everyone since its original author(s) has misread it. Again, this *might* be so. But the claim to be the first to have seen what all others have missed is increasingly bold, as is the corresponding claim that some 'ancient Judaean' managed to write in such a way that all fellow 'ancient Judaeans' entirely misconstrued his/her work and adopted it as their scripture through giving it a sense diametrically opposed to that which it really had. Such boldness needs an exegetical quality of corresponding rigour and persuasiveness.

It is at this point that the exclusion of appeal to the rest of the Hebrew scriptures (the second assumption) seems increasingly curious. It is one thing not to prejudge one text in the light of another. It is another thing not to practise the fundamental principle of interpretation that the meaning of words and concepts in an ancient text written in an ancient language is best discerned by looking at other instances of those words and concepts within related literature, preferably within the same cultural context. So when Gunn and Fewell say of the divine pronouncement of Abraham's fear of God in Genesis 22:12 that it is 'impossible to decipher' one wonders if they have tried very hard. Have they consulted a concordance and considered the extensive uses of 'fear of God/YHWH' within Hebrew scripture? Have they considered how poorly attested is their own proposed meaning of craven fear, and how well attested is a positive moral and spiritual sense? Likewise, have they and Davies considered the usages of 'test' in Hebrew scripture, and its consistent linkage with notions of obedience to God's will and human growth to moral and spiritual maturity? And if they have, why have they not explained why none of this extensive, and sometimes exactly parallel, usage is applicable in Genesis 22? Davies' refusal to assume more about the author than that the person was an 'ancient Judaean', which presumably is meant to depict an attitude of mental openness freed from debilitating preconceptions, is in fact an excuse for inventing an implausible freak who used the Hebrew language to mean what he wanted it to mean, rather in the manner of Humpty Dumpty.

The one strong point that Gunn and Fewell and Davies have is their focus on the apparently weak and self-serving actions of Abraham in Genesis 12:10–20; 16:1–6; 20:1–18. It is a useful reminder that the biblical portrayal of Abraham is much less straightforward than some hagiography might suggest. In particular, the similar stories in Genesis 12:10–20 and 20:1–18 are puzzling stories to modern readers, not least because they portray God's commitment to Abraham in a way that lacks the critical moral edge which other biblical material has given to doctrines of election in their traditional form, with the principle that much is expected of those to whom much is given.[11] But even if it is correct that Abraham is self-serving in these stories, it does not follow that he is so elsewhere. The consistency of Abraham's character which Gunn and Fewell and Davies assume (their third assumption) is no more than an assumption. It is a possible heuristic model, but one which needs convincing exegesis to sustain it when some texts point in a different direction. It is particularly surprising that Gunn and Fewell should advocate such a flat understanding of Abraham's character in a textbook on Hebrew narrative, when one of the most striking results of recent study has been a renewed appreciation of the subtlety and frequent indeterminacy of character portrayal in Hebrew narrative.

To conclude: these suspicious readings are reminders of the fragility of narrative depictions of trust and obedience in the face of conceptual mis-understanding and highly charged ideological critiques. If interpreters do not understand the dynamics implicit in divine testing and human fear of God as Hebrew scripture portrays it in its key passages, and insist on importing their own agenda, then they are likely to misconstrue everything in the narrative in so far as it relates to these key points. Neither Gunn and Fewell nor Davies appear able to conceive anything more likely with regard to Abraham than the satan's second accusation of Job, that the paradigmatic righteous person is really self-seeking, and ruthless about it too, at others' expense. Granted that at certain moments in the wider narrative Abraham does appear to be self-seeking at others' expense, it is dismaying when interpreters cannot see that the story of God's testing and Abraham's fear of God in Genesis 22 is rebutting any such construal of a relationship with God. Thus, to use again the traditional categories, these readings of Gunn and Fewell and Davies fail comprehensively as 'literal' interpretation. Whether their 'spiritual' interpretation, that is their suspicious portrayal of Abraham in the mode of a (post)modern anti-hero, will be considered sufficiently compelling to sustain itself without an exegetical basis seems, to me at any rate, unlikely;[12] though others, who esteem anti-heroes more highly, may find more of value in them.

11. Characteristic of Hebrew prophecy is Amos 3:2, 'You only have I known of all the families of the earth; therefore I will punish you for all your iniquities.'
12. Davies says with regard to an assessment of his interpretations: 'If you ask yourself whether my interpretations are unorthodox or extreme, or even offensive, then ask by what canons you are making that judgment. What do I not like and why? Ask instead whether the arguments are well conducted, whether the ideas stimulate thought, whether the engagement gives enjoyment, and, of course, whether I clearly misread the written words' (1995: 55). Let the reader decide.

## Genesis 22 as manipulative religious propaganda?

If the initial point about the potential significance of hermeneutics of suspicion is to be taken seriously, it does not suffice to show, on primarily exegetical grounds, the inadequacies of the accounts above. Rather, I need to attempt my own suspicious reading of Genesis 22, one which builds on the exegetical foundations laid, and so is not open to rebuttal on the simple ground of exegetical inadequacy. Only then can the issues which suspicion raises be appropriately engaged with. What follows is a preliminary attempt to do this with one kind of suspicion.

The interpretation in chapter 3 did not just try to elucidate the meaning of Genesis 22 as a paradigmatic narrative portrayal within the Old Testament of the primary Hebrew category for appropriate human response to God, the 'fear of God', in relation to the important concepts of divine testing, seeing/providing, and blessing. It also sought to point out the wider resonances and associations that have become associated with that portrayal: on the one hand, 'Sinai', that is God's gift of *torah* to Israel, representing definitive insight into the nature of God and his will for Israel; on the other hand, 'Zion', the place chosen by God to be the focus of God's presence on earth within the temple built by Solomon, the place where God's people are to gather in worship.

This synthesis of 'Sinai' and 'Zion' is not peculiar to Genesis 22 but in fact represents the canonical shape of the Old Testament more generally. For the book of Deuteronomy gives definitive expression to the exclusive nature of the relationship between God and Israel which is given content by *torah*, and requires that the relationship be given symbolic enactment in a place prescribed by God – a place which could at an early stage be Shechem but which definitively becomes Jerusalem in the book of Kings. Thus, among other things, Genesis 22 presents *in nuce* what Deuteronomy and the deuteronomistic history – not to mention the Chronicler's history, many of the prophets, and many of the psalmists – present *in extenso*: Israel's fulfilment of *torah* through obedient sacrificial worship in the Jerusalem temple. Genesis 22 is thus a hermeneutical key to the Hebrew scripture.

What is one to make of this? One move is to point out that such a harmonious consensus does not fully represent the realities of Israel's history where the nature of *torah* and the significance of Jerusalem were contested. To be sure, the Old Testament itself explicitly recognizes that the role of Jerusalem was contested. But it presents it in such a way that in the mind of the reader there should be no real contest, because Jeroboam's establishment of Bethel and Dan were idolatrous acts of apostasy akin to Israel's paradigmatic apostasy with the golden calf at Sinai, while God's choice of Jerusalem is rooted in the faithful response to God of Israel's ancestor Abraham.[13] The Old Testament presents a one-sided, and at times anachronistic, account of disputes over Jerusalem. It has thus been one of the strengths of modern reconstructions of the history of Israel and its religion to show that history as characterized by a far greater complexity than the present shape of the Old Testament would suggest.

This, among other things, raises the question of the status of the present shape of Old Testament history. Apart from its use as a source to reconstruct a history different from itself, what is it in itself? Is it (to put it crudely) other than religious propaganda on behalf of the Jerusalem establishment, related to particular moments in Israel's history, perhaps the reform of Josiah and/or the struggle to reestablish Jerusalem after the exile? And even as the expression of a Jerusalemite perspective, is it other than the work of a small, non-representative, scribal elite, whose claims to privilege have been foisted on others even within their own constituency?

Specifically, is Genesis 22 an example of the Jerusalem establishment validating itself through the appropriation of the prestigious figure of Abraham (and thereby invalidating any rival sanctuary)? Is it not implying that valid, God-ordained sacrificial worship as specified in *torah* takes place in Jerusalem (and not elsewhere)? Does it not convey the message that appropriate human response to God, the 'fear of God', can best be shown by those who follow the example of Abraham in coming to Jerusalem (and thereby bringing money and resources to the Jerusalem establishment)? Does not Abraham's unquestioning obedience to God imply that true worshippers should be similarly unquestioning (and thereby should not challenge the privileged Jerusalem establishment)? Does not the focus on Abraham and the absence of Sarah imply a religious system where all significant action is a male preserve (leaving women invisible and powerless)? Is not therefore Genesis 22 a fine example of religious propaganda and ideology, which is interesting as a document of ancient religious history but cannot, and should not, have any further significance for a person in the modern world?

It will be obvious to the reader of this book that the final conclusion is not one which I hold, and so I will outline one possible response. But a

---

13. David also is a foundational figure in 2 Samuel 24.

suspicious reading must be taken seriously, lest it be supposed that a Christian appropriation of Israel's literature as Old Testament scripture is undertaken in ignorance of the kinds of consideration that are often urged against it. Moreover, since a responsible historical awareness must allow that the answers to the above questions may be in some sense affirmative – they are all possible, and not necessarily invalid, implications of the text – such questions can help a Christian use of scripture be aware of some of its own possible implications.

### Limitations of suspicious interpretation of Genesis 22

With regard to a narrative such as Genesis 22, there are three particular limitations to thoroughgoing suspicion.[14] One is a reluctance to enter into the narrative world in its own right and to take the irreducibility of the narrative with full seriousness. The irreducibility of the narrative is not just a point about literary genre, true of any narrative – that it cannot be transposed into another idiom or genre without loss. It is also a point about narrative as the vehicle of moral and theological discourse, in which certain moral and theological concerns are explored and conveyed precisely through their embodiment in narrative. Because a suspicious reading tends to see the narrative as a disguise for something else, it can be difficult to take seriously the issues of the narrative as genuine issues in their own right.

In the story of Genesis 22 the crucial thing is the relationship of a human being with God in an extreme situation of human relinquishment and divine provision, where the language and imagery readily become a metaphor for a multiplicity of situations, the more so when the story resonates with its wider canonical context (as the history of interpretation indicates). If the story is *really* about unquestioning obedience to a self-serving Jerusalemite male religious hierarchy, then this simply undercuts the imaginative world of the narrative, except in so far as one can think of ingenious ways in which it could be put to self-serving uses by the hierarchy. But this is a reductive approach to the text, in which one is unlikely to take seriously the question whether the fear of God, as displayed by Abraham, is indeed an appropriate human response to God, which may be promoted in paradoxical ways by God himself. If one knows in advance of each rereading what the text really means, it will

---

14. Of course, a more qualified suspicion requires greater nuance in evaluation.

only ever convey what is already known; the ability of the text to surprise, disturb, or challenge is safely neutralized (as also, of course, in many reading strategies other than the suspicious). The suspicion can become a mirror image of the very complacency it set out to challenge.

A second consequence, which follows from the first, is that thoroughgoing suspicion lacks adequate criteria for assessing in what way the content of the story might, in some important sense, be true. Or rather, there is a tendency to judge it primarily by two criteria: the 'historical' ('It never really happened like that anyway'), and the 'socio-political' ('What happens in the story makes no difference to what really matters'). The first wholly excludes moral and theological, not to mention imaginative, criteria; and easily adopts an oversimple understanding of the complex relationships between text and the living of the 'fear of God' in ancient Israel/Judah which has given rise to the text. The second tends to restrict significant criteria to those which in one way or another relate to often hidden structures of power and money and gender, which preserve themselves and manipulate others the more successfully the more they are hidden. Thus to focus on Abraham's act of obedience and God's blessing at a place given the pious-sounding name 'YHWH sees', diverts attention from struggles over money and power within the Jerusalem priesthood and the use of a story about Abraham's piety to validate Jerusalem against its rivals.

The difficulty here is not just that such struggles are inevitably to some extent the product of the modern interpreter's imagination, compensating for exiguous hard evidence with generous extrapolations from the interpreter's own understanding of ecclesiastical politics to show what 'must have been' the case (the perennial problem of interpreters discovering their own face at the bottom of the well). Even more important is a prejudgement of precisely the crucial issue of 'what really matters'. It is one thing to criticize those who stress a narrowly defined personal piety at the expense of any critical understanding of, or engagement with, the social, economic, and political dimensions of institutional, not least religious, life. It is another thing to undervalue the realities of personal encounter with the living God or to dismiss its foundational nature for human existence. Because by its nature much suspicion is concerned with 'structural' questions about language and social role,[15] it may be insensitive to those dimensions of human life such as loyalty or trust which are

---

15. Suspicions about self-deception in relation to God on a personal level tend to operate on a more psychological basis, which requires separate discussion.

either 'on the surface' or, in so far as they touch the depths of human persons, may remain largely oblique to the discourses of social power.

A third limitation is that a suspicious reading of the text tends to have difficulty with doing justice to the processes of recontextualization, and in particular the metaphorical reconstrual of religious language, which are present within the canonical text. The further the content of the text moves from its original setting, the less plausible at least some suspicions become. We have already noted this phenomenon with reference to the construal of child sacrifice as a metaphor. Further, one might reflect upon the logic of the various ways in which Genesis 22 characteristically functions in Jewish and Christian contexts *post 70 AD* and the destruction of the temple in Jerusalem. Most obviously, for Christians (and differently within rabbinic Judaism) worship in the Jerusalem temple ceases to be significant in the same ways as once it was. This is not just for the historical reason of the destruction of the temple. More decisive for a Christian view is the understanding, encapsulated (as we will see) within the narrative of Matthew's Gospel, that Jesus replaces the temple as the unique and privileged place of encounter between God and humanity. This means, among other things, that Jerusalem goes the way of child sacrifice and retains its significance primarily as a symbol. It is symbolic of many things, but in Christian thought it especially symbolizes the Church, to which the Old Testament language of God's election and judgment is often transferred. The geographical location of the place God chooses for acceptable worship, where 'God sees/provides', is no longer capable of any straightforward definition – in terms of the biblical text, the symbolic language of Moriah and 'YHWH sees' is more or less detached from its particular realization within Jerusalem and seen as open to realization within any number of other contexts where God is truly worshipped. It is not that geographical locations no longer have any significance – for the histories of Rome, Constantinople, Canterbury, Geneva, and the many places of Christian pilgrimage (including Jerusalem!) would tell against any such simplification – but that any one place does not, and cannot, have the kind of significance that Jerusalem has within the Old Testament. To be sure, the Church is in no way immune to, but rather requires, suspicious critique (and, as already noted, much of the suspicious critique formulated as historical hypothesis is a projection of contemporary suspicions). The point is that when Christians appropriate the Old Testament in the light of Christ an understanding of the biblical text may be transformed in subtle and far-reaching ways. What to the unsympathetic may appear an ever-shifting evasiveness (and can at times be such) may be a searching attempt to penetrate the significance of symbols in such a way as to enable continuity in the midst of change. In any case, the evaluation of such processes cannot meaningfully be carried out in isolation from consideration of the actual ways of living which they promote.

In short, the question of 'God', and what it means to speak responsibly of God in relation to the interpretation of the Bible, is too difficult and demanding an issue to be easily resolved by transposition into the categories of ideological suspicion (however salutary these may be against idolatrous and self-deceiving tendencies). The moral passion of the suspicious critique can become as one-sided and inadequate to human life as the position it is meant to challenge. Yet one responsibility of the biblical interpreter is at least to imagine in a disciplined way, and convey to others, what it might mean for the fear of God to have the kind of importance that Hebrew scripture attributes to it; and for the Christian theologian there are further questions as to the appropriation of such an imagining within the realities of contemporary life.

## Conclusion

From the perspective of interpreting Genesis 22 as scripture, one primary critical norm in assessing the story is that which it itself offers, that is the fear of God, as explained and displayed within the text. To the charge that religious people act self-seekingly, as the satan said of Job, and as Abraham himself apparently displays on occasion, the answer is that *this* is what true religion entails: a trusting obedience of God which means relinquishing to God that which is most precious (sacrifice Isaac, the beloved son); a self-dispossession of that on which one's identity and hopes are most deeply based (sacrifice Isaac, the long-awaited bearer of God's promise and Abraham's hopes for the future); a recognition that response to God may be as costly, or even more costly, at the end of one's life as it was earlier on (Abraham must relinquish his future as once he relinquished his past); a recognition that the outcome of obedience is unknown and cannot be predicted in advance (a test is not 'only' a test, but is a real test); and a recognition that the religious community to which one belongs and which tells this as one of its foundation stories can only become complacent at the expense of the essence of its identity.

To say all this is not to deny the institutional realities of the Jerusalem temple as underlying the present form of Genesis 22. It is rather to say that, to the extent that the institutional forms of a religious community, whose purpose is to enable and preserve openness and responsiveness to God ('fear of God'), become devoted to maintaining their own existence at the expense of the very qualities they exist to foster, they deserve no less than the full critical impact of their own identifying charter.

→ The exegetical ~~potel~~ of suspicion
. if ~~well~~ understood as the suspicion
inherent in the story, & not
in our story (the reader/int.)

# 6

# Jesus in Matthew's Gospel as Son of God

Hitherto we have considered the portrayal of Abraham in Genesis 22. We have sought to establish a rigorous exegetical basis for interpretation, in the light of which we have reflected on some of the possible strategies for appropriating the ancient text in a contemporary context. In this chapter we will consider how the substantive issues of human life in relation to God as raised in Genesis 22 are raised in the New Testament also – an exercise quite distinct from studying the specific New Testament usage of Genesis 22. That is, how do divine testing, providing, and blessing relate to appropriate human response to God when they are focussed in Jesus Christ? In the light of a study of Old and New Testaments together we will then be best placed to consider what the implications of the biblical text for today might be.

The exegetical basis within the New Testament will be a study of Jesus as Son of God, as this is portrayed in Matthew's Gospel. There are four reasons for this focus upon Matthew's Gospel.

First, a focus upon one specific gospel takes seriously the genre of gospel as a coherent portrayal of Jesus. The four evangelists each offer their own construal of Jesus, all four of which have been received as authoritative for Christian faith and theology. The concern here is not to address the differences between, or interrelationship of, these portrayals, but solely to grasp the contours of one, the one which introduces the New Testament as a canonical collection (as Genesis introduces the Old Testament as a canonical collection).

Secondly, the pattern of divine testing and faithful human response, which is central to Genesis 22, is also, we shall argue, central to Matthew's Gospel (in a way that is not quite the case with the other three canonical gospels). This makes possible reflection on the interrelationship between key passages in Old and New which is responsive to the content of the biblical text itself.

Thirdly, the language of Jesus as Son to God as Father, although less prominent in Matthew than in John, occurs at arguably all the key moments in the gospel story: baptism (3:17), testing (4:3, 6), response to rejection (11:25–7), Peter's confession (16:16), transfiguration (17:5), Gethsemane (26:39, 42), trial (26:63), crucifixion (27:40, 43, 54), great commission (28:19). Interestingly, it is only in three passages (11:25–7; 24:36; 28:19) that the text speaks of Father and Son in conjunction. But the terms Father and Son are correlative and imply each other, even if only one is used. The consistent appearance of the terminology at key moments, some of which are explicitly probing the nature and implications of Jesus' sonship (4:3, 6; 16:16ff.; 26:63; 27:40, 43, 54), suggests that a way of reading Matthew's Gospel as a whole is as an interpretation of the meaning of sonship – what does it mean for Jesus to be Son to God as Father? And, by extension, what might it mean for those who follow Jesus to be children to God as Father?[1] A study of this particular issue in these particular passages will mean that many important Matthean themes, such as 'kingdom of heaven' or 'righteousness', will not be discussed, and there is of course a danger of misconstruing the chosen passages if they are isolated from their wider context. I hope that the selectivity will not in fact distort, but rather that the specificity of the thesis will allow certain central implications of the passages in question to emerge with greater clarity.

Fourthly, the structure and content of Matthew's portrayal of Jesus' sonship offers, as I will suggest at the end of the chapter, a significant conceptual linkage with Pauline theology. This will further our concern to draw out wider resonances within the Christian canon whose significance is less appreciated than might be.

### Method and approach in relation to current debate

Some brief preliminary points of method. It is impossible to read recent scholarly study of Matthew without being aware of at least two major debates, which might for simplicity be termed 'tradition and redaction'

---

1. There are obvious dangers in such discussion of unconsciously slipping into anachronism, too easily merging the meaning of sonship in the world of Jesus with contemporary understandings and concerns. The balance between faithful and creative appropriation and finding one's own face at the bottom of the well is a fine one. For a succinct account of the meaning of sonship in Jesus' world, see Harvey 1982: 159ff. Harvey suggests that three primary characteristics of sonship are obedience to, learning from, and agency in acting on behalf of, a father.

and 'again the historical Jesus', so I wish briefly to situate the present discussion in relation to them.

First, there is discussion as to the extent to which many texts in Matthew should be interpreted in the light of antecedent Jewish texts, of which Matthew is seen to be a midrashic[2] reworking in the light of Christ. This tends to be part of a wider interest in questions of tradition and redaction, that is, how far Matthew's terms and concepts were derived from existing material and how far they were coined by him. This extends beyond those passages where Matthew cites Hebrew scripture, to those where it may be argued that the content was influential even without explicit citation.

For example, Matthew's conclusion, 28:16–20, has no scriptural citation. On the one hand, Jane Schaberg (1982: 32, 319ff.) argues not just that the depiction of the Ancient of Days giving authority to one like a son of man in Daniel 7:14 LXX is the 'source' of Matthew's depiction of Jesus' receipt of authority from God in Matthew 28:18 (and 11:27), but that the theologically important formula 'in the name of the Father, the Son and the Holy Spirit' developed out of a pre-Matthean midrash on Daniel 7, where there is also triadic language concerning the Ancient of Days, the one like a son of man, and the angels. On the other hand, Dale Allison (1993: 262–6, 218–33), while accepting Schaberg's thesis of the derivation of the depiction of 'authority' in Matthew 28:18 from Daniel 7:14 LXX, finds that other elements in Matthew 28:16–20 have Mosaic background and associations in passages such as Joshua 1:1–9 LXX and Jeremiah 1:1–10 (while Matthew 11:27 derives not from Daniel but from a christological reworking of three Moses texts, Exod. 33:11–23; Num. 12:1–8; Deut. 34:9–12).

There is much to be gained from these studies. But while it may seem odd for an advocate of interpretation of Christian scripture as a whole to be less than enthusiastic about studies which focus on possible intertextual linkages, I think there are important limits to their value, at least in the ways in which they are commonly conceived. First, one cannot be other than largely agnostic on the historical question of what traditions were not only known by Matthew but also deliberately utilized by him (with the likely exception of Mark, and of course Jewish scripture in general terms). We simply do not know. The data collected by Schaberg and Allison to formulate a putative tradition-history of religious thought

---

2. I use this word in its most general sense to denote a process of contemporary actualizing and appropriation of existing texts through the writing of new texts.

may, however, be useful in other ways in terms of possible reading strategies, where one can see resonances between Matthew and earlier Jewish texts which may be interpretatively interesting irrespective of whether or not Matthew intended allusion to them. Secondly, it is important to read Matthew's narrative as meaningful in its own right. This is not to deny Matthew's rootedness in Jewish tradition, nor to deny the value of a knowledge of such tradition for interpreting Matthew (not least since Matthew himself so regularly refers to it). It is rather to insist on taking with full seriousness the intrinsic logic of Matthew's portrayal of Jesus. To be sure, all kinds of factors from beyond the text may be significant for its interpretation, and what may be found to be interpretatively important cannot be predicted in advance. But there is a fine line between, on the one hand, recognizing Matthew as deeply rooted in, and liable to be misinterpreted in the absence of good knowledge of, Jewish tradition and, on the other hand, construing Matthew as some kind of cryptogram or palimpsest whose interpretation tends to depend on the ingenious production of extraneous material.

A second debate is the 'Third Quest for the Historical Jesus'; the most recent contribution to it that I have read is N. T. Wright, *Jesus and the Victory of God* (1996). This debate is the contemporary manifestation of what has been perhaps the most fundamental and enduring debate of modern biblical scholarship. Wright illuminates much of the synoptic gospels. The conceptual apparatus which, as an historian, he brings to the text escapes many of the anachronistic assumptions which too often are brought to bear, such as an antithesis between 'politics' and 'religion' or a separation of Jesus' words from Jesus' actions or the assumption that apocalyptic language was meant to refer to the end of the world. As a result, he is able to offer a more-persuasive-than-most overall picture of Jesus' ministry which fits coherently into a Jewish first-century context. Moreover, Wright robustly claims for the ministry of Jesus much gospel material which it has become conventional to ascribe to the early Church.

Although my present discussion is indebted to insights from this debate, it will advance a different kind of argument, for three reasons. First, when any gospel is read according to the canons of modern historiography with reference to 'the historical Jesus', greater or lesser amounts of the text are necessarily discounted, for the gospels were written according to different canons. In particular, those portions of text which may be vital for the structure and purpose of the gospel as a whole may be among those most problematic for modern historiography. I shall argue that Matthew's portrayal of Jesus' ministry is crucially structured by the baptism and testing in the desert at the beginning (3:13–4:11) and Jesus' resurrection appearance to his disciples at the end (28:16–20). One needs to work to an agenda other than 'questing for the historical Jesus' as commonly conceived in order to do full justice to such passages.[3]

Secondly, while the gospels remain indispensable for reconstructions of Jesus' earthly ministry, they themselves may to a greater or lesser extent refocus the nature of the issues confronted by Jesus (a process most obvious in John). Even if, for example, Wright's account of Jesus' messiahship is granted in its entirety, it does not follow that messiahship has quite that role in Matthew's portrayal. The term 'Son of God' could, in a first-century Jewish context, be no more than a term for a Davidic king, effectively synonymous with 'messiah'. As Wright puts it: 'We must stress that in the first century the regular Jewish meaning of this title had nothing to do with an incipient trinitarianism; it referred to the king as *Israel's representative*. Israel was the son of YHWH: the king who would come to take her destiny on himself would share this title' (1996: 486–6). But in the following discussion I will suggest that 'Son of God' within Matthew means rather more than this, is preferred to 'messiah' (though often used in conjunction), and is in some sense incipiently trinitarian (though this of course must not beg the question as to what is meant by 'trinitarian'). In order to follow through Matthew's meaning, our quest will be oblique to the historical Jesus quest.

Thirdly, however much one may reasonably try to distinguish between 'event' and 'interpretation' within Matthew's Gospel, it remains the case that for historic Christian faith it is the combination of these – the 'event' of Jesus as 'interpreted' by the gospel – that is authoritative for Christian faith.[4] This is not to deny the value of historical reconstructions of Jesus' ministry, and of trying to trace the development of thought and content from Jesus to gospel text. Rather it is to observe that the relationship between Christian faith and the text of the New Testament is multifaceted, and that reconstructive work 'behind' the text should not be allowed to displace the significance of the form of the gospel material in its own right.

---

3. There are, of course, a growing number of studies of historiography and narrative which are seeking to reconceptualize the ways in which narrative conveys what may be recognized as historical truth (e.g. Watson 1997: 33–69).

4. Of course, the very conceptualization of the material in the categories of 'event' and 'interpretation' may beg important questions and may sometimes be too easily subsumed within a kind of positivism.

There is, of course, far more that could be said about the nature and purpose of the gospel material and the problems of interpreting it well. But that debate must be continued elsewhere. I would like, therefore, rather summarily to conclude this prolegomenon with an observation (made in a different context) by Donald MacKinnon which sharply brings together the questions of christology and appropriate interpretation of gospel narrative. It suggests the kind of interpretative concern which this chapter (whether successfully or unsuccessfully) seeks to embody. MacKinnon (1986: 181) writes:

> It is a manifest weakness of much traditional Christology that it has evacuated the mystery of God's self-incarnation of so much that must take time, that must be endowed with the most pervasive forms of human experience, its successiveness, its fragmentariness, above all its ineluctable choices, fraught equally inevitably with tragic consequence. It is a paradox that in a narrative, in which in the form in which we have received it, the mythological, the typological, even the contrived framework seem to take charge, we have in fact a standing protest against failure to take seriously the sheer concreteness of God's self-incarnating.

### Starting at the end: Matthew 28:16–20 as a key to the gospel

How best should the portrayal of Jesus in Matthew be approached?[5] I propose to use the revelation of Christ after Easter in Matthew 28:16–20 as a kind of heuristic key to interpreting the gospel as a whole. This is, of course, nothing new in principle. As Otto Michel put it in a well-known article:

> There is no need to dwell at length on the importance of this closing composition of Matthew [sc. Matt. 28:18–20] for the Gospel as a whole. It is sufficient to say that the whole Gospel was written under the theological premise of Matt. 28:18–20 ... In a way the conclusion goes back to the start and teaches us to understand the whole Gospel, the story of Jesus, 'from behind'. *Matt. 28:18–20 is the key to the understanding of the whole book.*[6]

This is similar in principle to our study of the Emmaus story where, although the focus was on the story in its own right, it became clear that

---

5. A standard treatment of the topic is Kingsbury 1975: ch. 2. Although I have learned from Kingsbury's treatment, my understanding of the text diverges considerably from his.
6. Michel 1983: 35. The question of whether Matthew's conclusion is indeed an interpretative key, rather than more simply a summary, is still debated (see Stanton 1992: 345), but does not materially affect the present thesis.

the story functions as a kind of hermeneutical key to the gospel as a whole.

To read the gospel in this way is not to flatten the dynamics of its portrayal of Jesus, nor to obscure the real and important differences between a pre-Easter context and a post-Easter context. It is to take with full seriousness the perspective from which Matthew composed the gospel and which is implicitly that of the 'ideal' reader (and also, of course, the historic stance of the Christian Church when reading Matthew as its scripture). If there is something at the end which somehow 'makes sense' of what precedes, then, if we wish to understand Matthew's Gospel, we are most likely to make progress if we follow the lead we are given.

How then should the final scene of the gospel be used as a key to interpreting the whole? Although there are resonances with many episodes within the gospel, there are particular resonances with the one other story where Jesus is situated on a mountain (*oros*) and the issue is that of universal power and authority (*exousia*) and possible submission (*proskunesis*) to it.[7] That is, there is an obvious correlation between the closing scene of the gospel and the third temptation of Jesus (Matt. 4:8–10). It is a correlation that has often been noted by interpreters. As Allison (1993: 171) puts it:

> What Jesus gains from God the Father in Matt. 28:16–20 he earlier, in 4:8–10, refused to accept from the tempter. Thus the kingdoms of the world become his, but only in time, and only from God.

Or as Ulrich Luz puts it:

> He who, on the mountain, rejected the devil's offer of world domination (4:8–10) and chose the path of obedience, will for this very reason, again on a mountain, be granted all the power in heaven and on earth at the end of his chosen path of obedience (28:16–20).[8]

Although Allison and Luz briefly note the linkage between what Jesus refuses and what he receives, they do not as such focus upon the issue. Interestingly, in their brief comments about the linkage between the two scenes Allison focusses solely upon the divine gift ('only in time, and only from God'), while Luz focusses primarily upon what Jesus himself has to do ('chosen path of obedience'). This suggests that Matthew's portrayal of Jesus may be open to reading in terms of the possible relationship

---

7. It is a little surprising that Matthew 4:8–9 does not contain the word *exousia* ('authority'), although it does appear in Luke 4:6 and may have been in the evangelists' *Vorlage* ('Q'). Nonetheless, the conceptual linkage remains clear. There is a not dissimilar surprise in Matthew 12:27//Luke 11:20 where, in the light of Luke's interest in the Spirit elsewhere, one would have expected Luke to have 'Spirit of God' and Matthew 'finger of God', rather than vice versa.     8. 1995: 37. Lange 1974: 92 and n. 187 gives other references to this linkage.

between divine initiative and appropriate human action, an issue we have already seen to be fundamental to both the Emmaus story and also Genesis 22.

Since Matthew in this way links the final scene of the gospel with the opening story of Jesus' ministry, our initial observation that the gospel may be read as a construal of Jesus' sonship may be reformulated into a specific question with which to read the gospel: How must Jesus as Son of God live, such that at the end of his earthly life God gives him the dominion which he refuses to take?

### The authority of the risen Jesus: Matthew 28:16–20

#### (1) Setting the context, verses 16–17

One preliminary thing to note about Matthew 28:16–20 is the sense it gives to seeing the risen Jesus. The preparatory announcements to the women by both the angel and Jesus lay great emphasis upon Galilee as the place of seeing Jesus (28:7, 10). Yet when the disciples go to Galilee and see Jesus (v. 16), the account is remarkably brief. First, there is no reference at all to the appearance of Jesus, despite the account of the dazzling appearance of the angel at the tomb (28:3); a transformed appearance of Jesus is in no way an issue, and the implication is that, if anything, his appearance is no different from what it was during his earthly ministry. Secondly, the disciples' vision is in no way climactic in itself, but is mentioned as a preliminary to reverent obeisance and the words of Jesus. This suggests that what the vision of the risen Jesus means and entails is less a matter of seeing someone with the eyes than it is a matter of a responsive openness to what is specified in verses 18–20.[9]

A further preliminary is the famous difficulty of 'doubting' (*distazo*, v. 17b), which has brought forth numerous suggestions as to its possible significance here and is generally considered a puzzle. Much of the problem lies in a likely misconstrual of the Greek. The almost universal assumption is that 'doubting' is an alternative to reverent prostration,[10] that is, that some reverently prostrated themselves while others doubted.[11] But there is nothing either in the Greek or in the context to warrant this.

9. There are analogies with Genesis 22, where the language of divine seeing and being seen (vv. 8, 14) does not coincide with any actual vision of God (vv. 11–12), but is linked with Abraham's responsiveness to the divine voice and his seeing of the ram which enables the symbolic fulfilment of his 'fear of God' in worship for himself and for his descendants.
10. For this sense of *proskuneo*, see Matthew 28:9. The traditional rendering 'worship' is not inappropriate but I am inclined to think that worship as such is not the issue in 28:17.
11. So, most recently, Davies and Allison 1997: 681–2. An important exception is Giblin 1975, which constructively analyses Matthean usage in an argument similar to mine.

The subject of *edistasan*, that is *hoi de*, is not distinguished from the subject of *prosekunesan*. If distinctions within a group were intended ('some reverently prostrated themselves, while others . . .') Greek would naturally use either *men* and *de* (i.e. *hoi men prosekunesan, hoi de edistasan*) or *tis* (i.e. *prosekunesan, tines de edistasan*).[12] Further, as a clause at the end of the sentence, the construction with *hoi de* as subject is simply awkward. Nor does Jesus in his following words make any reference to two categories of disciples in different states, but addresses the disciples as a whole. All these problems are caused by the assumption that *hoi de edistasan* is meant to introduce a subgroup within the disciples, which then becomes puzzling precisely because of the lack of further reference to it. The problems are resolved by dispensing with the assumption. That is, the sense of the text is that *distazo* characterizes the response of all the disciples.[13] Moreover, the Greek reads better and the overall sense is improved if one repunctuates the sentence with a full stop after *prosekunesan*. *Hoi de* would be a natural subject for a new sentence, resumptive of the *hoi de hendeka* with which the previous sentence begins, and *hoi de edistasan* should be followed by a comma as it leads into what follows.

Thus one should translate: 'and when they saw him they reverently prostrated themselves. But they were hesitant, and Jesus came up and said to them . . .'

Why then the depiction of the disciples by *distazo*? The only other use of *distazo* in the New Testament is Matthew 14:31, where it is part of Jesus' rebuke to Peter for his failure to respond consistently in his walking on the water to Jesus. The rendering 'doubt' is probably due to its juxtaposition in 14:31 with 'little faith' (*oligopistos*) and the traditional Christian polarity of 'faith' and 'doubt'; but it is unhelpful in either 14:31 or 28:17 because it is likely to imply too much. The sense of *distazo* in each text is that of hesitancy and uncertainty.

The likely reason why Matthew should depict the disciples thus in 28:17–18 is that seeing the risen Jesus and responding in reverent prostration leaves the disciples not knowing what is the meaning and significance

---

12. One possible parallel usage is Matthew 26:67. Blass, Debrunner and Funk 1961: §250 includes this under a discussion of *men* and *de*: '26:67 (only *hoi de* "but others"), 28:17 (ditto; in these two places no differentiation is indicated at the beginning of the sentence, but with the appearance of the *hoi de* it becomes evident that what was said first did not apply to all)'.

The parallel between 26:67 and 28:17 is, however, imperfect. The *hoi de edistasan* in 28:17, if a continuation of the preceding sentence, is preceded by a subject which already includes *hoi de*, namely *hoi de hendeka*. But because of the way it introduces what follows, *hoi de errapisan* in 26:67 might be seen as the beginning of a new sentence, analogous to our proposal for *hoi de edistasan* in 28:17.

13. One might compare the characterization of the disciples as a whole as 'of little faith' (*oligopistoi*, Matt. 6:30; 8:26; 16:8).

of what is happening. They have been told that they will see Jesus, and they do, and they respond appropriately. But what does it mean? What follows from such an encounter with Jesus? They are uncertain, which introduces a hesitancy into their otherwise appropriate response. It is this that Jesus then addresses and resolves in the words that follow. The use of *distazo* with reference to the disciples prepares for the definitive interpretation that follows in which Jesus resolves the uncertainty otherwise inherent in his appearance to the disciples.

### (2) The meaning of Jesus' 'authority', verse 18

The opening words of Jesus, 'All "authority" (*exousia*) in heaven and on earth has been given to me', forms the basis upon which the following command to make disciples, baptize, and teach is based. The interpretation of these words in recent debate has focused extensively, but somewhat inconclusively, on questions of genre and relationship to Daniel 7:14 LXX where the Ancient of Days gives *exousia* to one like a son of man.[14] For present purposes the discussion of two issues will suffice. First, what is the meaning of *exousia*? Secondly, how does what Jesus says of himself now relate to what had already been the case during his earthly ministry?

The term *exousia* is difficult to define precisely. Not least of the difficulties is the ease with which we may introduce a distinction between authority in a formal or moral sense (*auctoritas*) and power whereby things are done (*potestas, dunamis*). Although this is a valid distinction, it is probably not helpful within a Matthean context. *Exousia* may be a broader term than *dunamis*, but it is inclusive of *dunamis*, not separable from it. For in all the uses of *exousia* with reference to Jesus prior to 28:18 the context refers to the transformative impact of Jesus upon people.[15] The centurion's reference to himself as also someone 'under authority' (*hupo exousian*) is explicated by the fact that what he says is carried out (8:9), and Jesus' gift of *exousia pneumaton akatharton* to the disciples is the power to cast out unclean spirits (10:1). Jesus' authority should be understood as powerful.

What does Jesus' *exousia* imply? For Jesus to say 'authority in heaven and on earth has been given to me' would not in itself be particularly remarkable. Although during the earthly ministry of Jesus within the gospel his *exousia* is linked to his being Son, the fact of such *exousia* would not, within a Jewish context, be unprecedented. For one could regard the holding of *exousia* in heaven and on earth as tantamount to the classic

---

14. *kai edothe auto exousia . . . kai he exousia autou exousia aionios.*
15. Matthew 7:29; 8:9; 9:6, 8; 10:1; 21:23 (2×); 21:24, 27.

depiction of a prophet in Luke 24:19 as one 'powerful in word and deed before God and all the people'. The display of *exousia* in the heavenly and earthly realms is precisely the role of Moses and other great figures in Jewish scripture. What distinguishes the claim of Jesus in 28:18 is *pasa*, 'all'.[16]

Within the immediate context some form of 'all', *pas*, is repeated three times. The injunction to teach all that Jesus had commanded[17] envisages the enduring significance of the content of Jesus' earthly ministry. The commission to make disciples of all nations envisages a mission without spatial limit, while the promise to be present for all days envisages a mission without temporal limit. So the primary sense of 'all authority' is similar; that which God has given Jesus has been given fully and without limit.

Yet it is difficult to know precisely how to construe this 'all'.[18] One can easily envisage alternatives by contrast with which it would receive its meaning. It could, for example, be set against alternative human claims to exercise spiritual power – such power is to be found supremely in Jesus. But although this might be an issue in other contexts, it is not an issue within this Matthean context. Within Matthew, the likely concern is a contrast with Jesus' earthly ministry – while previously he had *exousia*, now he has *pasa exousia*.

On the one hand, the baptism of Jesus, with the descent of the Spirit and the divine address to Jesus as Son, marks the beginning of Jesus' ministry and his exercise of authority in word and act. Moreover, during his ministry Jesus can say 'All things have been given to me by my Father' (11:27). On the other hand, the resurrection of Jesus marks a decisive act of God in response to the death of Jesus (*edothe*, v. 18, complements *egerthe*, vv. 6, 7) and introduces something new and unprecedented. In his earthly ministry Jesus has authority, as the risen one he has all authority. How should the difference between these be understood?

The difficult christological issues here can best be understood through reflection on the nature of inter-personal relationship. In general terms, living in relatedness with another necessitates continuous responsiveness in one form or another. True relationship is always susceptible of

16. The important parallel in Dan. 7:14 LXX does not use 'all', but the context there hardly envisages restrictions on the *exousia* which is bestowed.
17. The use of *entellomai* rather than *didasko* is revealing. Jesus' words are now *entolai*, commandments, analogous to God's words to Israel at Sinai.
18. One difficulty is posed by the use of anarthrous *pas* elsewhere as a Matthean idiom in contexts where it would be unwise to attach too much significance to it (Matt. 3:15; 5:11; 23:27, 35; 24:22). It is the context of Matthew 28:18 which makes it appropriate to give weight to *pas*.

development and growth as a potentially expanding and deepening real-ity (though, conversely, it may stagnate and decay), and such growth in relationship need in no way imply deficiency or inadequacy in the antece-dent relating (though often that would be the case) but rather unrealized potential which needs time and situation to unfold. More specifically, one of the prime biblical idioms for expressing a growing and deepening rela-tionship with God is 'testing' (whose general dynamics have already been considered in relation to Genesis 22). It is in the light of this biblical con-ceptuality and terminology that the movement within the life of Jesus may best be understood.

The need to take testing seriously may be illuminated by an alternative account from Karl Barth (1961b). In the course of an exposition of Mat-thew 28:16–20 Barth (pp. 62–3) addresses the question we are discussing and says:

> That all authority has been 'given' to him must however not be interpreted to mean that he received it only in his resurrection. Such an assumption is refuted by a number of very clear texts in the Gospels where the affirmation made in verse 18 undeniably refers to Jesus before his death. 'All things have been delivered to me by my Father' (Mt. 11:27) [Barth then revealingly moves away from a Matthean context and cites Jn 3:35; 13:3; 17:2] ... *exousia* is given to the man Jesus as divine authority can alone be given to a human creature. Only when man prays for it, believes in God, is obedient to Him, is it given as free grace. Because God's free grace is eternal, authority is given everlastingly; potentially in God's design to create and save the world, actually in the incarnation of the Word ... By forgiving sins and accomplishing signs and miracles, Jesus made at least a partly visible use of his authority long before his resurrection. There was never a time when he was devoid of it. His 'emptying himself' (Phil. 2:7) was nothing but the hiddenness of his majesty, caused by human blindness. What he achieved in the state of utmost weakness, his death upon the cross, was truly a manifestation of his might ... In the Resurrection, however, Jesus reveals himself to the disciples as the one who held, holds, and will hold all authority, a fact that had hitherto been hidden from the disciples as well as from the world.

Barth clearly recognizes that there is both continuity and difference between a pre-Easter and post-Easter context ('not ... only in his resurrec-tion', 'at least a partly visible use of his authority long before his resurrec-tion'). But the only difference he allows for is one of *visibility* – what is hidden during the earthly life is revealed in the resurrection. This is indeed an important element (though the question of visibility even in the resurrection context is still not straightforward), but it does not suffice to explain Matthew's sequence. Barth's account of the relationship between human and divine ('only when man prays . . . is it given as free grace. Because God's free grace is eternal, authority is given everlastingly') is couched in very general terms, and entirely lacks any sense of a growing, deepening relationship between Father and Son. Or, to revert to the biblical idiom, what Barth lacks is any sense of testing as integral to the relationship between Father and Son. Yet it is testing, which was so central to Abraham's engagement with God in Genesis 22, which is also (as we will see) central to Jesus' relationship as Son to God as Father in Matthew's Gospel.

To be sure, some of the problems of depicting a relationship which is always fully sustained, and yet which is also capable of genuine growth and development, are clear in historic christological debates as they reflect upon the gospel texts. On the one hand, it is problematic to talk of Jesus' sonship being given to him at a particular moment (whether baptism or resurrection) if this is taken to imply that he did not have it already; for even the baptism is clearly continuing a relationship with God which is already in place (though its precise nature prior to the baptism is unspecified, beyond the fact that Jesus' very birth is ascribed to the same Spirit as descends at his baptism, 1:18, 20); and the pronouncement of Jesus as Son at the baptism need no more imply the beginning of that sonship than does the similar pronouncement at the transfiguration (17:5). On the other hand, it is problematic to speak of Jesus' sonship as given in such a way that his sonship undermines the human integrity of the story, and so diminishes its moral and theological seriousness; and there may be a danger that if the appearance of the risen Jesus becomes the perspective from which the earthly ministry of Jesus is understood, the sonship of Jesus in his earthly ministry could be denied its own integrity.

Our present concern is not to do justice to the New Testament material as a whole – in which the Hebrews portrayal of Jesus as Son being 'perfected' (*teleioo*, passive) through suffering and testing without ever falling away from God (2:10, 18; 4:15; 5:7–9; 7:28) would be an important witness to set beside Matthew, and the Johannine portrayal of Jesus which lacks testing would also need to be taken seriously; nor is it to engage in a sustained way with the classic formulations of christology. Rather I wish to do justice to the Matthean portrayal of Jesus, without premature conflation with Johannine or other perspectives, while still suggesting that the Matthean portrayal may in its own way be pointing towards that which classic trinitarian theology seeks to articulate.

So, in Matthew's account, Jesus deepens his relationship with his Father by the continuing appropriation, in differing situations, of the existing givenness of his sonship, especially through faithful response to testing. As Jesus' sonship is a living reality in which he grows during his ministry and supremely in his passion, so Jesus' authority is likewise open to growth, for it is a corollary of his sonship. Thus it may become intelligible that Jesus in his resurrection is given fully and definitively that which was already truly his during his earthly life.

### (3) The consequences of Jesus' authority, verses 19–20

On the basis of Jesus' unlimited authority and power, the command to make disciples, baptize, and teach is given. The baptismal formula (v. 19) is important for our discussion because of its christological language.

The baptismal formula is perhaps most striking in that it does not say 'baptizing them in my name' (*eis to onoma mou*).[19] For that would seem to be the obvious corollary of verse 18: if all authority is given to Jesus, then people should be baptized in his name. It is presumably this inherent logic of the focal position of Jesus within Christian faith (whether or not expressed as in v. 18) that led to the early Christian practice of baptism solely in the name of Jesus as attested in Acts (Ac. 2:38; 8:16; 10:48; 19:5) and implied by Paul (1 Cor. 1:13, 15). What we have in Matthew 28:19 is not designed to relativize the central significance of Jesus – the context of verse 18 makes this clear – but rather to clarify what it means that Jesus should be of such prime significance. Jesus is not significant on his own, and in no way displaces the one God. Rather, the one to whom all authority is given, is given it in his capacity as Son to God as Father in a relationship mediated by the Spirit.

It is well known that the language of spirit/Holy Spirit[20] is rare in all the gospel accounts of the ministry of Jesus, probably primarily because such language comes into its own after Easter in accordance with

19. Bultmann (1963: 151) links Matthew 28:19 with other synoptic texts which refer to Jesus' name (*onoma*, Mk 9:37, 41; Matt. 7:22; 18:20) and speculates about an original reading *eis to onoma mou* (though in a context other than its present Matthean context).

20. It is difficult to know whether to say 'spirit', 'Spirit', 'the spirit', 'the Spirit'. To be sure, to capitalize and make definite as 'the Spirit' implicitly relates the text to a Christian trinitarian frame of reference, which is not Matthew's own context. Any decision depends ultimately on one's assessment of the heuristic value of Christian theology in developing the intrinsic implications of the gospel text.

the differing modes in which the disciples encounter God through Jesus and the differing ways in which this encounter is understood. It is striking, therefore, how the ministry of Jesus according to Matthew is framed by reference to the Spirit in specific conjunction with the language of Father and/or Son. At the baptism of Jesus the heavens, symbolically the realm of God (cf. Matt. 6:9–10), are opened and the Spirit of God (*pneuma theou*, anarthrous) descends on Jesus; there is also a voice from the divine realm which says 'This is my Son.' The descent of the Spirit from the divine realm prior to the voice symbolizes a context within which the pronouncement of Jesus as Son takes its form and meaning. It is therefore in accord with this when the baptismal formula at the conclusion of the gospel adds reference to the Spirit when speaking of the Father and the Son; the relationship between Father and Son is somehow intimately associated with Spirit.

Of course, Matthew's Gospel is not trinitarian in the sense that the credal formulations of the fourth and fifth centuries understood and defined 'trinity'. On the one hand Matthew shows no interest in probing the implications of the relationship between Son and Father other than in terms of unlimited mutuality, unconditional trust and obedience, and the exercise of authority as a consequence of this. On the other hand, the closing words of Jesus about his enduring presence with his disciples neither mention the Holy Spirit in this context, as does Paul and later mainstream Christian thought, nor offer any further indication of how the presence of Jesus relates to the presence of God than was given in the use of the fulfilment of the Immanuel prophecy with reference to Jesus as 'God with us' at the outset of the gospel (1:22–3; cf. 18:20). Nonetheless, Matthew depicts the mysterious reality of the relationship between Jesus as Son and God as Father in terms whose implications it is the interpreter's task to probe and explore.

In the light of this understanding of the conclusion to Matthew's Gospel, we shall now consider the portrayal of Jesus' sonship during his earthly ministry as that which makes such a conclusion possible.

### The designation and testing of Jesus as Son: Matthew 3:13–4:11

#### (1) Setting the context

When Jesus is baptized, the divine voice speaks to him (3:17) in language fully comprehensible in its own right, yet also resonant with scriptural overtones. The term 'my son' is found on God's lips with reference both to

Israel (Exod. 4:22–3) and to the Davidic king, who came to be understood as the messiah (Ps. 2:7). The phrase 'beloved son' is used by God of Isaac in relation to Abraham in Genesis 22 (vv. 2, 12, Heb. *yaḥid,* LXX *agapetos*). 'In whom I take delight' is said by YHWH of his servant (Isa. 42:1). Which of these, and other, resonances the gospel writer intended to convey is impossible to determine and not of primary importance. The significant point is that the language resonates so richly with things said by God of people within Israel's scripture; that Jesus should be God's beloved son is not, within the context of Israel, something startling. To be sure, the particular combination of terms used of Jesus is unprecedented, but that is likely to be the case with any creative use of scripture. The significant point may be less that this language marks Jesus out as one who is somehow unique than that it locates Jesus fully within the context of Israel's encounter with God as attested in scripture. It is the nature and possibilities of this already given encounter which is to be probed and appropriated by Jesus in his ministry as Son.

The testing of Jesus takes place immediately after his baptism and is to be understood as an essential corollary to it.[21] If Jesus is Son to God, as God has just declared, then what follows from this? The 'if' of 'if you are Son' is the if not of uncertain possibility, but of definition and analysis. What is *meant* by the designation of Jesus as Son? This is the issue which explicitly introduces the first two tests (4:3, 6), and is a key to the subsequent gospel narrative as a whole, as becomes clear from the recurrence of testing in relation to Jesus as Son at other key moments in the story up to and including the crucifixion (and, as already noted, from the links between 4:8–10 and 28:16–20).[22]

Jesus' engagement with God is also evident in his fasting, which is an action of self-denial in order to grapple with basic issues about God and himself at a deeper, more genuine because more costly, level. Prayer as such is not specified, but it does not need to be, for such a self-denying engagement with God is the essence of prayer. It would be a mistake to see

---

**21.** Significant recent studies of the temptation narrative have tended to focus on its putative meaning within Q, to the exclusion of its meaning in its present context in Matthew and Luke (e.g. Kloppenborg 1987: 246–62, Tuckett 1992: 479–507). A suggestive study of the story within its canonical context is Farrer 1965.

**22.** This is consonant with the significance of testing stories in the wider Graeco-Roman context. As Kloppenborg comments, 'Temptation stories are pregnant with meaning for the material which surrounds them. The testing story so to speak projects a "heroic career" for which it will serve as an explanation or anticipatory confirmation. It is not related simply for the parenetic and paradigmatic value which it might possess (however important that may be), but because it serves to explain or make intelligible other parts of the hero's "story" or to legitimate and guarantee the reliability of his teachings or the revelations which have been entrusted to him' (1987: 261).

Jesus' handling of his testing as any less an act of prayer than his address to God in Gethsemane, even though only the latter uses the verb *proseuchomai* (Matt. 26:39, 41, 42, 44).

As with God's words at the baptism, the resonances of the testing with the story of Israel in scripture are many and obvious. The wilderness is where Israel was for forty years, during which time God led, tested, and taught Israel, not least through making them hunger (Deut. 8:1–5).[23] Moses at Sinai fasts before God for 'forty days and forty nights' (Deut. 9:9, 11, 18, 25).[24] The primary import of these resonances may not be simply a typology of the superiority of Jesus (faithful where Israel failed; one greater than Moses). This is indeed part of the significance of the story for the reader who approaches it within a total biblical context. But if one focusses on what these resonances might mean specifically at the outset of Jesus' ministry, when the typology of superiority cannot yet be taken for granted, the point may be rather a typology of similarity; that kind of encounter with God which lies at the heart of Israel's story is what is taken up in the story of Jesus, and this sets the context where the meaning of a true relationship with God may be realized; and there are paradigmatic implications for followers of Jesus also.[25]

It may also be appropriate to sound a cautionary note about reading the testing story too directly in terms of Jesus' messiahship,[26] although this is obviously an important christological category within Matthew as a whole. There are two reasons for this. First, the nature of the specific tests which Jesus faces are sometimes skewed by being too readily assimilated to assumptions about what the testing of a messianic vocation would be likely to involve. Secondly, although there are clear messianic overtones in the royal imagery of the infancy narrative, subsequent to the infancy narrative the specific issue of Jesus as 'the Christ' is not intro-

---

23. The rare *limagkoneo* in Deuteronomy 8:3 LXX has no verbal resonances with the gospel text.
24. The wording 'and forty nights', peculiar to Matthew, particularly evokes this sojourn of Moses on Sinai in Deuteronomy's account.
25. Both Kloppenborg and Tuckett (see n. 21) opt for an interpretation of the story in which the behaviour of Jesus is paradigmatic for others (as also advocated by Bultmann and many others). Interestingly, Kloppenborg comments that 'the usual objection to this kind of interpretation is that the temptations are vastly disproportionate to what an ordinary believer would ever expect. This, however, overlooks the fact that equally fantastic (and contrived) stories are told of various Jewish and Christian heroes' (1987: 248). Perhaps it would be more accurate to say that while the precise form in which the issues are raised might be unusual for 'an ordinary believer', the issues themselves (when understood for what they are) are neither fantastic nor contrived and are likely to characterize any genuine attempt to live a life of faith and integrity.
26. So e.g. Jeremias 1972: 123; Wright 1996: 536–7.

duced until later – first, through John the Baptist's question from prison (11:2ff.) and then through Jesus' question to his disciples at Caesarea Philippi (16:13ff.). Although Jesus as Son and Jesus as the Christ are linked at Caesarea Philippi, they are not so linked here. The issue of Jesus' sonship in the testing may be in some sense a prior issue, not only in narrative sequence but even in intrinsic significance, to that of messiahship. Jesus' sonship at the baptism is specified not by terms that suggest the particular role of being messiah, but by terms that express God's delight in the one who is Son – 'beloved, in whom I delight'. It is sonship in this sense that the testing explores – if Jesus being Son to God means on God's part that God loves and delights in him, what does it mean on Jesus' part? What is the appropriate response to a knowledge of God's love and delight and what may be expected to follow from it? It is the construal of sonship to God, rather than messiahship as such (inseparable though these ultimately are), that is the concern of the testing story.

### (2) The three tests

The first test, to turn stones into bread, follows directly from the statement of Jesus' hunger after fasting for forty days and forty nights. If Jesus is hungry, then should not his hunger be met? It is Jesus' own needs that are at stake; it is not a matter of providing food for others, as he does later in his ministry. In other words, the issue is not what Jesus may do for others (i.e. messiahship), but what relationship with God means for himself (i.e. sonship). Although it would be artificial to separate sonship from messiahship (especially if this was aligned with a sharp distinction between the 'person' of Jesus and his 'work'), the nature of Matthew's presentation appears to be that Jesus' role as messiah, which focusses especially on what he does for Israel, is rooted in Jesus' engagement with God as Son.

If Jesus is Son to God, then he is in a position to be a channel for divine power; and indeed in his ministry Jesus will exercise this power for others, both to feed and to heal. The question is whether he should exercise this power for himself, even to meet a legitimate need of hunger. The danger in this is that as soon as the divine power is used for himself, then it may become a means to his own ends. A relationship of mutuality and trust could be reduced, albeit subtly, to a means of self-gratification.

Although circumstances are different, the issue is not in essence different from that which the satan raises with respect to Job, 'Does Job fear God for naught?' (Job 1:9). Is relationship with God at heart a matter of deriving benefits from God? Israel's scripture has already given a clear, if demanding, answer to this. It is this that Jesus must appropriate for himself as Son, for being Son to God cannot involve less than the fear of God shown by Job and Abraham. So Jesus appeals to a fundamental tenet of Israel's scripture (Deut. 8:3), where human life is defined in a richly nonreductive way: beyond the necessary meeting of regular mundane needs, what truly constitutes human life is attention and obedience to God. The creative word of divine power which will meet Jesus' needs is not a new word of his own but that word which has already been given normative shape in Israel's scriptures, which calls human life into true relationship with God.

The second test is that if Jesus is Son to God, then he should be able to throw himself off the temple with impunity. Although this is regularly construed in terms of Jesus performing a miracle either for its own sake or to prove something to other people (on the assumption that the temple area is likely to be crowded with people, so that any miraculous action there would be sure to have spectators), the issue is given its particular shape by the satan's citation of scripture. If Jesus appeals to the word of God in scripture as the basis for not using divine power for himself, what then should he make of those passages in scripture which promise God's protection to those who trust in God? The promise of God's blessing and protection is a recurrent theme in Israel's scripture, and Psalm 91 is a good representative instance. The point of the test will be missed if it is assumed that the satan must be somehow twisting the meaning of the biblical text and so misusing it. Psalm 91 represents something genuinely characteristic of Israel's scripture, and it is the plain meaning of scripture with which Jesus has to wrestle.

Psalm 91 entirely focusses on God's protection of the person who trusts in God. Assurance after assurance is given to the one who lives close to God, and these assurances include: 'For he will give his angels charge of you to guard you in all your ways; on their hands they will bear you up, lest you dash your foot against a stone' (vv. 11–12). The few words which are omitted in the satan's citation ('to guard you in all your ways') make no difference to the sense. If this is God's promise to the one who trusts in him, then it must apply to the one who is Son to God.

The symbolism of placement in 'the holy city' and the temple is that this is the place where God is specially present, the place above all others where one can be confident that God will be encountered and will not let his promises fail. Wherever precisely the 'pinnacle' (*pterugion*) of the tem-

ple is, the significance of the term is that it envisages a high point from
which a clear fall would be possible in the presence of God in the temple.
Although the imagery of Psalm 91:12 of 'bearing up' (*airo*) naturally links
with that of stumbling or slipping as metaphorical for help in time of
trouble,[27] the unusual wording of 'dashing one's foot against a stone'
could readily suggest not just stumbling but falling to the ground from a
height. Jesus is thus encouraged to act to claim God's promised protection
in its apparent plain sense, in the holy place where God is specially present. If human life is constituted by the words of God, what follows from
these particular words?

Jesus' response is that to use Psalm 91 thus and throw himself off the
temple would constitute 'testing' God, which is prohibited in scripture.[28]
What does this mean? The point can hardly be that God does not protect
the one who trusts in him, for to deny that would be a fundamental denial
of Israel's scripture. The point must therefore be to do with what such a
promise really means. For Jesus to throw himself off the pinnacle of the
temple would be to take an initiative that sought to force God to enact the
terms of his promise. But that would be to take a rigid and limited view of
divine promises, as though the real significance of a promise was to be
able to respond to it with 'You've said it and so you must do it.' The language of divine promise (or warning) is always relational, seeking to
evoke appropriate response from the one addressed. It therefore becomes
illegitimate to invoke a divine promise if the person invoking it is not
relating appropriately to God. The promise of protection in Psalm 91 is to
evoke and enhance trust in God. An act of trying to force God to keep his
promise would, by its very nature, not be an act of trust; it would be, in
the terminology of the text, an act of testing. If trust is truly to be trust, its
logic requires that the one trusted be allowed to act without constraint on
the point at issue. God's promise of protection, therefore, does not constitute an exception to the initial point that the power of God should not be
channelled for selfish purposes. God must be trusted to enact his promise
in his way.

The third test, the offer of the glory of universal dominion at the cost

---

27. E.g. Isa. 63:9; Ps. 35:15; 37:31; 38:17 (ET 16).

28. Israel's scripture demonstrates a consistent asymmetry, in that while it is right that God
should test (*nissah*, LXX *peirazo*) Israel (as in Exod. 16), Israel should not test (*nissah*, LXX
*peirazo*) God (as in Exod. 17:1–7) – with the sole exception that a certain testing of God may
be permissible (Jdg. 6:39, *nissah*, LXX *peirazo*), even encouraged (Mal. 3:10, *baḥan*, LXX
changes imagery with *episkeptomai*), if it is an action that represents genuine relational
engagement with God.

of doing obeisance to the satan, again probes possible implications of Jesus' sonship. The desire for power and glory is a deep human desire. And in the context of Jesus discerning the nature of his sonship through engagement with the will of God as expressed in Israel's scripture, there are specific resonances to a picture of universal dominion. For scripture offers such dominion. In Psalm 2 the pronouncement of royal sonship (2:7) is followed by the offer of universal dominion (2:8). God's promise to Abraham depicts Abraham as the model of blessing to which all others aspire, and a dimension of this blessing is dominion over others (Gen. 22:17; 27:29; Num. 23–4). In the book of Isaiah other nations find the true God through submission to Israel (e.g. Isa. 45:14–25; 49:22–6). Daniel 7 depicts a human figure ('one like a son of man') whose humanity contrasts with the bestial character of other great kingdoms, and who represents the saints of the Most High to whom everlasting dominion over all the earth is given. The underlying assumption is that Israel's God is the one true God of all the earth, and that universal dominion is therefore his. Since God exercises his power and authority through those who are called by him to serve him, that is, Israel as a whole and Israel's human representative (king, son of man) in particular, then this expectation naturally devolves on Jesus as Son.

What then is the nature of the test? It is not 'Gain power by forsaking God', for that would be too easy. For any observant Jew an overt choice between the worship of the one God, so fundamental to Israel's faith, and worship of the satan would hardly be a contest. It would be an instinctive reflex to adhere to God. The issue, therefore, is the deeper one of what is entailed by worshipping the one God. It is the word 'alone' (*mono*) which provides the key. This addition which Jesus makes to the text of Deuteronomy 6:13 (which admittedly no more than makes explicit what is clearly implicit within Deuteronomy), clarifies that it is the nature of the exclusive commitment to God which is the issue. The test has sharpness if its meaning is not 'Turn from YHWH and worship the satan' but 'Worship YHWH and the satan as well', that is, 'Within allegiance to YHWH, recognize another conflicting allegiance also.' What confronts Jesus is the prospect of trying to obtain the glory that is indeed promised by God by means of compromising his loyalty to God.

The test is thus a form of the familiar conflict between end and means. This conflict is most commonly formulated in purely moral terms – can a (supposedly and hoped-for) good outcome justify an (apparently) limited resort to doubtfully moral or clearly immoral actions? For Jesus, as for the scriptural witness he is interpreting, the moral issue is inseparable from the religious, relational issue of stance towards God. The implications for Jesus will be spelt out more fully in the developing gospel narrative. In the present context, one might paraphrase the text: desire for power and acclaim, even that which is promised by God to those who are faithful to him, is idolatrous and conflicts with the fundamental requirement of faith to allow God to be the supreme value in human life. In the categories of the gospel, the end of receiving dominion and glory from God can only be received by the means of uncompromising loyalty to God – a means which for Jesus, and for those who follow him, will soon be shown to be the way of the cross.

The third test is thus congruent with the previous two tests. If Jesus being Son means that he is obedient to God in such a way that he will not seek to use God's power for his own ends, and if God's promises of protection cannot be invoked in such a way as to undermine the trust which they are meant to enhance, then the promised gift of dominion cannot be attained by any means other than that which intrinsically leads to it, which is unswerving allegiance to the giver. This sets the context for the ministry of Jesus as a whole – and for the climax of the gospel where Jesus is given that which here he declines.

### The mutual knowledge of Son and Father: Matthew 11:25–30

> At that time Jesus declared, 'I thank you, Father, Lord of heaven and
> earth, that you have hidden these things from the wise and
> understanding and revealed them to babes; yea, Father, for such was
> your gracious will. All things have been delivered to me by my Father;
> and no one recognizes the Son except the Father, and no one
> recognizes the Father except the Son and any one to whom the Son
> wishes to give revelation.' (Matt. 11:25–7)

Within the body of the gospel, this is the main passage prior to the conclusion where the text speaks both of Jesus as Son and God as Father and of the unrestricted authority of Jesus.[29] The context is that of the problematic nature of response to God's revelation in both Jesus and John the Baptist, a key issue whose treatment here in Matthew 11 appropriately

---

29. The christological issues here are well known in the context of the Johannine portrayal of Jesus. Since the language that Jesus uses in Matthew 11:27 is characteristic of the Johannine portrayal of Jesus (e.g. Jn 1:18; 14:6), there are striking affinities between the Matthean and Johannine portrayals (although the language is not characteristic of Matthew as it is of John).

follows the extensive discourse on mission to the disciples in Matthew 10. The whole of Matthew 11 looks at different dimensions of the dynamics of response to a message from God (and so is a counterpart to the focus on the dynamics of response to Jesus' parabolic teaching in Matthew 13).

Initially the uncertainties of John the Baptist himself about Jesus are voiced and responded to (11:2–6). This leads into Jesus speaking about John and his significance (11:7–15) in a way that leads on to a wry reflection on the paradoxical difficulties in gaining a positive response from people – no matter that Jesus' style and John's are so different, whichever way they handle themselves people still cavil and find fault (11:16–19a). Jesus sums up with an epigram (11:19b) whose point seems to be that, just as prophets are discerned by their fruits (7:15–20), so wisdom (sc. the rightness of what John and Jesus say and do) is to be discerned by that which comes out of it, that is, moral and spiritual reality can be discerned by publicly accessible criteria if people will only see it. Within this context of reaffirming a classic biblical criterion for spiritual discernment, Jesus then rhetorically reproaches some of the Galilean towns where his ministry had been exercised for their failure to respond to him: there had been sufficient evidence of divine power at work for even the notorious recipients of God's judgment within Israel's scripture to have responded positively (11:20–4). Yet if those who have regularly encountered Jesus have not responded, this raises in acute form questions about the nature of God's communication in and through Jesus.[30]

Jesus first speaks a prayer of thanksgiving to God as his Father of sovereign power for confounding human expectations by revealing to 'simple' people what is concealed from the 'wise and understanding' (v. 25). This is hardly a dismissal of wisdom as such, but rather an ironic representation of those who aspire to, or claim, such status while lacking its reality. Such ironic characterization of supposed human wisdom is already expressed within Israel's scripture by both Isaiah and Jeremiah (Isa. 29:13–14; Jer. 8:8–13), and Jesus' words resonate strongly with those of Isaiah.[31] His affirmation of such as the Father's will (v. 26) shows that he fully accepts the consequences of defective human wisdom, which is nothing less than the widespread non-recognition, and apparent failure, of his ministry.

30. Luke presents the same unit (Lk. 10:21–2) also within the context of response to mission, though within the context of the joyful return of the seventy-two (10:17–20); and he follows it with the positive emphasis that longed-for revelation is indeed given to the disciples – though the fact that this is said to the disciples in private (10:23a) suggests that only they will appreciate its significance.
31. Isaiah 29:14 LXX contains the same word pair, *sophoi, sunetoi*, as in Matthew 11:25.

Jesus' strong emphasis on divine initiative in hiding and revealing ('Lord of heaven and earth', 'you hid', 'you revealed', 'your will') may make the divine action sound arbitrary. Yet the preceding verses have emphasized the problematics of human responsiveness (11:16–19) and in particular lack of repentance (*metanoia*, 11:20–4). God's will is in some way related to human attitude, for the simple receive what is withheld from the wise. The depiction of simple and wise as a contrasting pair is in line with characteristic biblical idiom (e.g. Lk. 1:52–3), where the positive and negative terms within the pair always depict human qualities in relation to the action of God. In general terms, the language of revelation is characteristically portrayed in moral and relational categories (and there are obvious affinities with the implications of the Emmaus story).

The novelty within the context of Matthew's Gospel is that a principle about divine revelation and human response, already familiar within prophetic literature, is related specifically to the person of Jesus (v. 27). These words of Jesus in verse 27 (which appear no longer to be a prayer to the Father) consist of two elements. First, a general statement about Jesus as the trusted recipient of what his Father has, who faces no limit in what he may receive from his Father. The logic is one which grows out of Jesus' faithfulness when tested. If Jesus' sonship means unqualified trust in God, its corollary, now made explicit, is that God as his Father withholds nothing from him. The logic of 'all things have been given to me' may perhaps best be understood as that of the relationship with God in prayer which is in principle open to any believer: 'whatever (*panta hosa*) you ask in prayer trustingly (*pisteuontes*), you will receive' (Matt. 21:22) – though the distinction between what is peculiar to Jesus as Son and what may characterize others also is particularly difficult in this context. The 'all' is not open to precise definition because its purpose is to specify the absence of limitation in relationship with God as Father. Further, the point is not that 'all things' have been given already in such a way that they cannot and will not be given further and again in the future. Rather, a relationship has been established without limitations on either side, a relationship characterized by trust on the part of the Son and giving on the part of the Father, a relationship which can continue to grow as long as it remains true to itself.

The second element in Jesus' words links his relationship with the Father to the specific contextual issue of lack of response to his message. Recognition of Jesus as Son (in the sense already established) is only possible within the context of his mutual relationship with his Father. This sense of mutual knowledge is recognizable within Israel's scripture in terms of YHWH and Israel (e.g. Deut. 4:32–40). What is unprecedented is its focus within Jesus as Son. The only one who truly knows how Jesus as Son relates to God as Father and what this relationship means is God the Father. Conversely, the only one who truly knows what it means to relate to God as Father is the one who relates as Son, that is Jesus. If the essence of relationship is the process of relating then by the nature of things the relationship cannot be appreciated from outside; the one who does not share the relationship cannot understand its nature. It is the counterpart to the principle that relationship with God is discernible in publicly accessible moral conduct and influence (11:16–24), a principle that stresses that something about a relationship can be known from the outside. This text stresses that the essence of a relationship can only be known from the inside. The two emphases complement each other.

Yet although the mutuality of the relationship between Son and Father is in one sense exclusive to Son and Father, it is not exclusive in the sense of being closed or inaccessible to all others. Access to the relationship is possible, but only when it is mediated by the one who is in a position (and has the necessary *exousia*) to make it accessible. This, according to Matthew, is the basic premise of Jesus' ministry. Jesus seeks to enable others to enter into the relationship with God as Father which he himself enjoys; his role as Son is to reveal his Father.

The actual language used – 'no one recognizes the Father except the Son and anyone to whom the Son wishes to give revelation' – describes the Son's initiative in the same absolute terms as the Father's initiative has just been described (vv. 25–6). Any arbitrariness that this prerogative might suggest is immediately countered by the invitation of Jesus which follows (vv. 28–30). The invitation is addressed to 'all' (*pantes*), yet not all without qualification, as though the lack of response to Jesus' mission was irrelevant. Rather, it is addressed to all who seek rest, a rest which is expressed in terms of exchanging one burden or yoke for another, that of Jesus.[32] If Jesus as Son gives access to relationship with God as Father, then what is said about Jesus in verses 29–30 gives content to what is entailed in the relationship. The two key terms *praüs* and *tapeinos*, both significant elsewhere in Matthew's portrayal of Jesus and the way of living he commends (Matt. 5:5; 18:4; 21:5; 23:12), are both difficult to capture in

---

32. There are well known resonances between the language here and other texts in which wisdom personified speaks, and likewise the imagery of a yoke is familiar in a Jewish context from the idiom of the yoke of *torah* as that which the faithful take upon themselves. These resonances add to the momentous nature of Jesus' summons.

English because of the complex (and often pejorative) resonances of 'humble', 'meek', 'gentle', and associated terms. Their point is that they are terms which depict those qualities that make true relationship possible – the refusal to impose upon and constrain another, and the willingness to define identity through engagement with God (as in Deuteronomy 8:2–3), through the kind of lifestyle already associated in Jewish tradition with *torah* and wisdom.

Jesus is not simply inviting people to take up a yoke which is easier than any other, but is also saying what it is about that yoke which makes it thus – the finding of rest is consequent upon learning from Jesus this particular quality of being and relating (cf. Betz 1967: 23). For this is what characterizes the relationship between God as Father and Jesus as Son, and it is only in so far as people are open to this kind of reality, and willing to appropriate it for themselves, that they will respond positively to Jesus and his mission.

### Peter's confession: Matthew 16:13–28

The primary focus in the episode is on Jesus as the Christ (16:16). This is clear not only from a synoptic comparison with Mark and Luke, where only 'Christ' and not 'Son' is used (Mk 8:29; Lk. 9:20), but also from Matthew's own account in which silence about Jesus as the Christ is enjoined on the disciples (16:20). However, the qualification within Peter's words of 'the Christ' with 'the Son of the living God', together with corresponding words from Jesus about 'my Father' in the following verse, means that what is said about Jesus as messiah is directly correlated with the portrayal of Jesus as Son; the meaning of 'Son', already to some extent explicated, is to be allowed to inform the interpretation of 'the Christ'.

Peter's recognition that Jesus is 'the Christ, the Son of the living God' uses language of such resonance that it can legitimately mean different things according to the context within which it is set. If the primary context were that of first-century Jewish expectations informed by scripture and tradition, 'son' and 'the christ' might be interchangeable messianic terms. Within the present gospel context, where the language of Father and Son has already taken on fresh dimensions of meaning, the terminology readily assumes a more specific sense. This is further suggested by Jesus' response to Peter (16:17) which not only makes the point that true insight is a gift, but does so in language reminiscent of 11:27. To be sure, here the point is that the Father has revealed the Son rather than that the

Son has revealed the Father, but the underlying logic is similar: the mutual relationship of Father and Son is such that access to it can only be given from within – but access is given.

Peter's recognition of Jesus is constitutive for Jesus' community (16:18–19). Then Jesus begins to interpret his role to the disciples (16:21ff.).[33] The prediction of Jesus' death and resurrection introduces something new into the story. The costly nature of Jesus' obedience to God as God's Son has already been made clear not only in the testing (4:1–11) but also in Jesus' transformation of widespread rejection into a matter of thanksgiving and opportunity (11:25–30). But now it is stipulated that Jesus' discernment of his Father's will ('it is necessary', *dei*) means death in Jerusalem. The question of how Jesus knows this is not raised. Rather, the question is what such a vocation means for Jesus himself and for others. The logic of the text is in many ways similar to that of the baptism and testing. In each context a designation and role is given to Jesus, directly or indirectly from God as Father (3:17, 16:16–17), and immediately there is a probing of the meaning of the term; 'Christ' receives an interpretative scrutiny similar to that of 'Son'.

The episode of Peter's confession of Jesus as 'the Christ' may also be read as a testing (*peirasmos*) analogous to that in 4:1–11. This is suggested initially by Jesus' striking address to Peter, 'Get back, satan' (*hupage satana*, 16:23), as said previously to the satan (4:10), but this construal emerges also from the total content. For there is an obvious sense in which Jesus is being tested in that he has to reject a less demanding understanding of his vocation, even when it is urged upon him by his chief disciple. Additionally, however, the episode is a test of Peter. His being named Peter and being identified as the rock on which Jesus' church will be built immediately leads to a scrutiny as to what this means for him; the meaning of 'Peter', as of 'Christ' and 'Son' is probed. In this first test Peter fails, because his understanding is faulty – he does not think the thoughts of God (v. 23). This rebuke makes sense in the light of 4:1–11 where the mind of God is discerned through an engagement with scripture which rejects some of the possible construals of the text. It is worth noting, moreover, that even though there is an implicit critique of first-century Jewish mes-

---

33. There is a textual problem in verse 21, and the likely reading is 'Jesus Christ'. The sudden change from 'the Christ' as title and role in 16:16, 20 to proper name in 16:21, coupled with the usual Matthean idiom of referring to Jesus simply as Jesus, has led many commentators to doubt its originality. But the use of *christos* as name here, as is common elsewhere in the New Testament, reminds the reader that what was a moment of revelatory insight for Peter has indeed become foundational for the church.

sianic expectations, the critique is hardly limited to that. Peter's problem is not that he thinks too Jewishly (*ta ton Ioudaion, ta tou Ioudaismou*), that is, that his thoughts are too set in a particular religious context, but that he thinks too humanly (*ta ton anthropon*), in the sense of understanding human well-being with insufficient openness to the radical demand of the will of God as discerned by Jesus.

What this means is that testing of Jesus in his role as the Christ is ultimately inseparable from testing of his followers in recognition of him in that role. It is thus no surprise when the text continues with a definition of discipleship which makes the predicted destiny of Jesus in death and resurrection a metaphorical paradigm for the discipleship and life of others also (16:24–8).

Finally, within Jesus' challenging call to discipleship (16:24–8), we should not overlook another explicit linkage with the initial testing of Jesus – the possibility of gaining the whole world but losing oneself in the process (v. 26), which was, in essence, Jesus' third test (4:8–10).[34] For the disciple, as for Jesus, to try to attain God's promised gifts in a way that undermines the very nature of those gifts is the extreme of folly. Implicit also in the linkage between 16:26 and 4:8–10 is a characteristic biblical understanding: to compromise allegiance to the one God is tantamount to losing oneself – a principle which rests upon the positive assumption that it is only in obedient relation to the one God that humanity is enabled to become its true self.

### Gethsemane: Matthew 26:36–56

At the heart of the Gethsemane episode lies the prayer of Jesus. Its context is set by the awareness which Jesus shows that his death is going to take place during the Passover – a recurrent motif in one form or another during the narrative which precedes.[35] Jesus announces to his disciples that he is going to a specified place to pray (v. 36), and he takes with him the three disciples whom he had taken with him at the time of the transfiguration (v. 37; cf. 17:1). Jesus' reasons for taking the three disciples are not given, but two are implied. First, that in a time of extreme anguish, Jesus wants their companionship and support, so that they share the time with him (v. 38). Secondly, they need for their own sakes to pray, for the crisis which is coming will affect them all (vv. 40–1; cf. vv. 31–5).

---

34. I am grateful to Elizabeth Raine for pointing this out to me.
35. 26:2, 12, 18, 21, 24, 28, 29, 31, 32.

Jesus' initial words to his disciples speak of overwhelming grief (*perilupos estin he psuche mou*), an anguish so extreme that it threatens to extinguish life itself (*heos thanatou*). No reason is given as to why this should be so, but the natural implication is Jesus' anticipation of what lies ahead. There are various possible responses to such anguish. One would be to seek alleviation through time-honoured means – either to distract oneself through conversation and activity with friends (the three disciples), or to seek some narcotic drink to dull the sensibilities.[36] Jesus' response is to request the company of his friends, so that they and he should devote themselves to engaging with his Father in prayer.

Jesus' distress is evident in his action of falling on his face which introduces his prayer.[37] The content of Jesus' prayer is specified twice (vv. 39, 42). There is a movement between the two, inasmuch as the first prayer formulates the possibility that the cup might be removed, even while seeking that it should be the Father's will, rather than his, which should be done. The second prayer recognizes that there is no alternative to his drinking the cup, and so solely seeks that this, the Father's will, should be done. How should this be understood?

First, the whole sequence again resonates with the story of the testing (4:1–11). A verbal and conceptual linkage is clear in the shared usage of *peirazo/peirasmos* (4:1, 26:41). If Gethsemane is less explicitly an exploration of the meaning of Jesus' sonship than is the testing in the desert, the centrality of Jesus' prayer to God as 'my Father' still makes the passage an appropriate focus for the meaning of Jesus as Son to God as Father. In both stories Jesus is alone (in effect, in Gethsemane), and has to work through for himself without human support the meaning of his vocation as Son. In each situation Jesus embraces his Father's will through scripture. Admittedly, there is no explicit scripture quotation by Jesus in Gethsemane, yet the substance of Jesus' prayer, with the appropriation of the Father's will as his own, is readily recognizable within scripture, the closest wording perhaps being that of the psalmist (Ps. 40:7–8), but the general pattern being widely discernible. Indeed, it would be difficult for Jesus to say something so basic to relationship with God without there being deep resonances between his words and Israel's scripture. Further,

36. The alleviation of the pain of those dying was recognized as a Jewish religious duty, on the basis of Proverbs 31:6–7. This may be the point of the offer of wine to Jesus on the cross (Mk 15:23), though probably not in Matthew's version (27:34) where the drink is mixed with gall, not myrrh (cf. Brown 1994: 940–4).

37. If it were a regular act of prostration in the presence of God, the Greek would more likely have *prosekunesen*, either in place of *epesen epi prosopon*, or perhaps in addition to it (cf. 2 Sam. 9:6; 1 Cor. 14:25).

in each story Jesus discounts the possibility of using divine power in a miraculous way to ease his situation. Although this is not explicit in the account of Jesus' prayer, during the arrest Jesus rhetorically raises (only to dismiss) the possibility of his asking for, and being granted, a massive army of angels from his Father (26:53); if the promise of angelic help was not to be utilized in the desert, neither is it to be utilized now. It is this disparity between Jesus' use of power to help others and his refusal to use it to help himself which becomes a focus for mockery during the crucifixion – 'others he saved, himself he cannot save' (27:42). Its recurrence in Matthew's portrayal must make it a defining characteristic of Jesus' sonship.

Secondly, Jesus' praying displays a process of coming to acceptance of his Father's will.[38] Initially he expresses a hope, a longing, that, for all that he has spoken clearly about his coming death and prepared accordingly, there may yet exist some alternative (26:39). This has no formal basis in terms of his life and ministry (as Jesus puts it in the Johannine counterpart to this narrative, 'but it was because of this that I came to this hour', Jn 12:27), but the logic is that of a lingering hope that a particular course of events, whose appalling climactic sequence has not yet begun (as it will with his arrest) is not yet foreclosed; the responsiveness of God to prayer, as attested in scripture and Jesus' own teaching, may offer the possibility of a reconfiguration of events. It is not a 'serious' hope, in terms of there being any likelihood of an alternative course of events; but it is still a real hope. If it is illogical, it is an illogic native to the human mind.

Alongside this, however, Jesus recognizes that his lingering hope for an alternative course of events could become an alternative to obedience to God. The hope is not in itself wrong, but in this context it becomes a moment of testing, a moment of choice between obedience and faithlessness. So in the second prayer (26:42), when Jesus accepts that the lingering hope for another way must be relinquished, he still needs so to appropriate his Father's will that it becomes fully his own (for a grudging or reluctant acceptance would be tantamount to no acceptance), so that his enacting of his Father's will is as truly his own action as it is his Father's.

In this context, Jesus uses the very words which he taught his disciples to pray, 'your will be done' (*genetheto to thelema sou*, 6:10; 26:42), and shows the nature of such a prayer. 'Your will be done' is a way of putting things

---

38. Gethsemane differs from the testing in the desert in that it shows something of the process whereby Jesus came unreservedly to embrace his Father's will, and so is imaginatively more engaging than the desert testing which shows only the conclusions reached.

into God's hands which sets the praying person free – but it is the freedom not of disengagement ('You do it, it is no longer my responsibility') but of acceptance and appropriation ('What I most want is what you want'). In relational terms, the prayer is not a shrug but an embrace.

Thirdly, the will of the Father is symbolized by 'this cup'. What does 'this cup' mean? The difficulty is that although it is comprehensible as a metaphor on its own terms, there are uses of 'cup' elsewhere in Old and New Testament which naturally encourage attempts to 'explain' its meaning.[39] Perhaps the best guide to its meaning is that provided by the clearest parallel usage, the account of the request of the sons of Zebedee, relayed through their mother, for positions of primacy and power in Jesus' kingdom (Matt. 20:20–8).[40] To this request Jesus initially replies, quite simply, that they do not know what they are talking about. To ask such a question shows a fundamental failure even to begin to understand Jesus' ministry. But Jesus turns the matter around by asking them 'Can you drink the cup which I am going to drink?', a question whose import in context seems to be 'Can you do what I am going to do?' To this they reply 'Yes'. Whether they understand what they are saying yes to is doubtful, but it is at least an expression of willingness to be a follower of Jesus. To this Jesus makes a reply (v. 23) which might be paraphrased thus:

> Very well, that is indeed what you will do. What can be done humanly for the sake of the kingdom is what must be done; as I do it, so shall you. But the giving of positions within the kingdom is a gift of God the Father. All that humans can do is to live in obedience to God in such a way that they become able to receive the gift of God, as and when God gives it.[41]

This is then followed by a redefinition of the terms 'great' and 'first' in terms of being a servant or slave to those from whom such honorific terms are sought; familiar patterns and priorities are wholly inverted. And this is then related to Jesus' own pattern of life in terms of his service, which includes the very giving of his life.

Here both 'drinking the cup' and the giving of life are spoken of by Jesus. The context and content, however, are revealing and reticent in the

---

39. For an overview of interpretative options, see Brown 1994: 168ff.

40. Matthew's tacit commentary on the significance of this episode is the reappearance of the mother of the sons of Zebedee, who asks the uncomprehending question (20:20–1), at the crucifixion and death of Jesus (27:56), where the meaning of what they were talking about is finally made clear.

41. This is analogous to advance knowledge of the day and hour of the coming of the son of man, a knowledge which is simply not given to humans, not even the one who is Son to the Father (24:36). All that humans can do is to watch actively for the coming, so as to be ready when it happens.

same kind of way as are Jesus' words after Peter's confession: the confident exposition of a consistent kind of paradox about human life and priorities, related to and embodied in the life of Jesus. But no explanation is given as to why death is involved, or what death means for Jesus himself, except that it is consistent with the paradoxical pattern as a whole. What 'this cup' means in Gethsemane, beyond this, one may not be able to say.

Finally, one may ask why Jesus shrinks from the cup if his awareness of his coming death is combined with an anticipation of being raised on the third day. Put crudely, should not confidence in resurrection remove the sting of death? Two points may be worth making. On the one hand, resurrection does not cancel out death. The termination of existence in this world remains final. Although the risen Jesus is able to reveal himself to the disciples and give them to know not only that he is risen but also what it means that he is risen (28:18–20), he does not resume life in this world. And although the resurrection is portrayed in the New Testament as an action of God analogous to that of creation, in itself it is not described and remains wholly hidden from human sight and grasp (none of the canonical gospels even attempts to describe the resurrection of Jesus).

On the other hand, we do not know what construal of his death was in the mind of Jesus, for Matthew has not told us (beyond the conversation in 20:20–8 and the interpretative words at the last supper, 26:26–9).[42] It is natural to look ahead to his cry of dereliction from the cross (27:46) and see this as representing an abyss of separation from his Father which he was anticipating in Gethsemane, an abyss which was part of 'a great struggle with Evil, the great trial that preceded the coming of the kingdom' (Brown 1994: 218). One can then try to probe further what that abyss might entail. This may be right. But since it is hard enough anyway to understand a mutual and unlimited relationship between Jesus as Son and God as Father, it is even harder to know what might constitute an unprecedented extremity within that relationship. This is essentially for the reason given in 11:27 – the interior depths of the relationship between Son and Father are inaccessible to those who do not participate. In so far as faith in Jesus, through the medium of the gospel, gives access to the relationship of Son to Father, some understanding may become possible. But the task may ultimately produce silence.

---

42. Arguments that Jesus in his earthly ministry conceived his vocation in terms of martyr theology and key passages from Israel's scripture (Wright 1996: ch. 12), even if they be granted in their entirety, cannot fully answer the question of the interpretation of Matthew's portrayal of Jesus.

### The trial before Caiaphas: Matthew 26:57–75

The trial scene is not easy to interpret if one is looking for legal procedure and substance, for Matthew's concern focusses on two contrasts: that between Jesus and Peter, in the outworking of the testing of Gethsemane; and that between Jesus and the religious leaders who, with patent lack of integrity, start by struggling to find any coherent case against Jesus that will serve their purpose (vv. 59–61), and end by treating Jesus with a brutality and contempt that will be matched by the Roman soldiers (vv. 67–8).

The key moment is the solemn adjuration by the high priest to Jesus to say 'if you are the Christ the Son of God' (v. 63). The wording is identical to that of Peter's confession.[43] Ironically, what Peter was able to say freely in response to a question from Jesus, and for which he was told that he had been favoured with an insight from Jesus' heavenly Father, the high priest sees as needing to be compelled from the lips of Jesus. In terms of understanding Jesus it is of course useless, for in a context where manipulation has replaced genuine relating, there would be no possibility of the high priest actually understanding what the words mean; for revelation is a gift not given in such circumstances (cf. 11:25–7). The question serves as a pretext for pre-resolved action, in which the term 'Christ' represents something that can become a kind of formal charge in the trial before Pilate.

When Jesus responds affirmatively but non-committally (cf. *su eipas*, 26:25, *su legeis*, 27:11), because the words on the high priest's lips are empty of real meaning, and then appeals to the Danielic vision of the son of man, his point may be primarily to comment on the lack of integrity of the proceedings by contrast with a famous depiction of divine justice. At any rate, the high priest, who shows no interest in genuinely understanding Jesus, is unlikely in context to understand the words in any way other than as a criticism of his own conduct. His response, to tear his clothes and proclaim blasphemy, need not imply that Jesus has in fact transgressed religious legal propriety.[44] Rather it is a deliberate manipulation of everyone else present.[45] When the chief priest proclaims blasphemy, dispenses rhetorically with the need for other witnesses and says to the

43. The only difference is the omission of the conventional epithet 'living' with reference to God.

44. Wright comments that the charge of blasphemy 'is the hardest to understand historically' (1996: 526). Although he then proceeds to offer an intelligible, if somewhat complex, account (1996: 550–2, 643–4), he never raises the possibility that the charge might be understood as rhetorical manipulation, as suggested here.

45. For a similar construal of the high priest's actions, in a historical reconstruction of Jesus' trial based on Mark, see Sanders 1993: 271.

rest of the gathering 'See now, you have heard the blasphemy. What do you think?' then there can be no possible doubt in the minds of those present how they are expected to respond. Whether or not the chief priest is speaking the truth is beside the point. The gathering came together for the purpose of condemning Jesus, and this is now the moment when the chief priest makes clear that they must do so. So they do: 'He is guilty of death.'

The trial scene is thus an ironic counterpart to Peter's confession. The key term 'Son of God' is again used in conjunction with 'the Christ', but what it might mean that Jesus should be 'the Christ, the Son of God' is not the concern of those holding the trial; their concern is not to understand the words but to use them for their own purposes. Their religious position might qualify them as wise, but theirs is the wisdom from which insight into Jesus is withheld, because their abusive and manipulative behaviour are the very things that make it impossible for them to receive such insight.

### The crucifixion: Matthew 27:31–56

The meaning of the crucifixion of Jesus is depicted by Matthew through a variety of means, central among which are two particular narrative units which specifically explicate the sonship of Jesus. First, the extended account of mockery of Jesus at the cross (27:38–44), and secondly the reaction to the death of Jesus (27:51–4).

The formal charge for which Jesus is crucified, which is appended to his cross, is that he is 'the king of the Jews' (27:36). This is the issue in his trial before Pilate (27:11), and becomes the object of abusive and brutal mockery by Pilate's soldiers (27:27–30). For the reader of the gospel, the scene now and following is one of manifold irony. The reader knows that Jesus is indeed the Christ, the king of the Jews. The soldiers use the words as a taunt, not least because they interpret kingship in a conventional sense – the one who wears fine clothes and a crown, holds a sceptre which symbolizes his power, and receives homage from his subjects. Jesus, a condemned criminal, already lacerated by the scourge and shortly to be given the execution fit for slaves, is so far from this condition of kingship, that to the soldiers the title is ludicrous, fit only to receive the kind of treatment reserved for scum.

The irony continues in the positioning of the two who are crucified with Jesus, 'one at his right and one at his left' (27:38). For this is the language which speaks of the positions of the two favourites of a king, who sit at either hand of their master, the positions requested by the mother of the sons of Zebedee for her sons (20:21, 23). The king of the Jews is crucified with his subjects before him – two armed robbers.

Then begins the stream of explicit abusive taunts (*eblasphemoun*).[46] Initially, the passers-by voice the ludicrous-sounding claim ascribed to Jesus at his trial about destroying the temple and building it in three days (26:61). Let the one who would perform such a great miracle perform the much smaller one of saving himself. If Jesus is Son to God (the wording is identical to that in 4:3, 6 – the satan is reappearing on the lips of the passers-by), then he should exercise God's power on his own behalf to rescue himself. This rescue should take the simple form of descent from the cross. Deliverance from a helpless, lingering death would give real content to divine sonship.

Then the religious authorities raise a similar series of taunts. First, they note the obvious discrepancy between Jesus' public ministry with his effect upon other people and his present situation. That power should be restricted in the very situation where its exercise would seem to be most natural calls in question the reality of such power – 'Others he saved, himself he cannot save' (the mocking 'he cannot', *ou dunatai*, displacing recognition of Jesus' underlying choice, 'he will not', *ou thelei*).

Secondly, they invoke the mocking *titulus*, and ascribe to the title 'king of Israel'[47] content and expectations similar to that which the passers-by gave to Jesus as 'Son of God'. An act of power, demonstrated in descent from the cross, would serve not just to save himself but also to evoke a response of faith from Israel's religious leaders. If the reality of an act of power (*dunamis*) or a sign from God (*semeion*) is shown supremely in its evoking the transformed response of repentance (*metanoia*) in people (Matt. 11:21; 12:39–41), then that is what Jesus could now achieve: the descent of Jesus from the cross would transform the religious leaders' response to Jesus, and they would recognize him as Israel's king.[48] The goal of Jesus' ministry could be realized by this one act (as a gesture of homage to the satan could have achieved glory and dominion).

Thirdly, they invoke the hallowed principle within Israel's scripture, that God delivers those who trust in him – the principle of Psalm 91,

---

46. For the usage and implications of *blasphemeo*, see Brown 1994: 522, 986.
47. The religious leaders naturally refer to themselves as 'Israel', while it is the Romans who call them 'the Jews'.
48. It is notable that Matthew does not use the title *ho christos*, even though this is present in the other synoptics (Mk 15:32; Lk. 23:35). If any weight is attached to this, it supports our contention that 'Son' is the prime category in Matthew, into whose meaning and significance 'Christ' is subsumed.

though here ironically cited from Psalm 22. If this applies to the believer in general, how much more must it apply to one who claims a special relationship with God. If the claim is not realized, it will show how baseless it is. If someone says 'It is of God that I am Son',[49] then let it be God who demonstrates the reality and mutuality of the claim by showing reciprocal care – 'Let him deliver now *if* he wants him.' Divine sonship should be given content by obvious reciprocal divine action. The fact that the wording of their taunt evokes a psalm about a righteous person suffering (Ps. 22:9 (ET 8)), a recognized theme in Israel's literature (cf. Wisd. 2:17–18), ironically escapes the notice of these religious leaders in their glee.

Finally, the armed robbers scorn Jesus in a similar way (27:44). Everyone present thus takes a similar view of Jesus' situation in relation to the kind of status ascribed to him. Although the title 'king of the Jews/Israel' is used, the key term is clearly 'Son of God', the term with which the scorn both begins and ends. Both uses of the term in this context are, not surprisingly, peculiar to Matthew's account of the crucifixion, for they belong to his distinctive portrayal of what it means for Jesus to be Son to God as Father.

After Jesus dies Matthew records an astonishing sequence of portents. First, the temple curtain is torn in two (v. 51a). In the context of the mockery of Jesus with regard to his supposed claim to destroy and rebuild the temple (v. 40), it is likely that this in some way represents the fulfilment of at least the first part of the claim. The point would not be that some new kind of access is given to the presence of God within the temple (although the imagery in itself could sustain such a meaning, and it is a construal which could be suggested by the tent, sanctuary, and priest imagery of the writer to the Hebrews, esp. Heb. 10:19). Rather, the temple ceases to be the unique and privileged place of God's presence, for it is somewhere else that that presence is now to be found.

The portents that follow (vv. 51b-53) are peculiar to Matthew's account and, like the preceding references to Jesus as Son, are eloquent of Matthew's understanding of the death of Jesus. Initially the earth is shaken and rocks are split. The shaking and splitting of that which is most solid is symbolic of a divine action that transcends and overturns usual categories of human understanding and experience, as at the angel's coming to reveal the resurrection (28:2). Within this general context tombs are opened and many saints are raised: the death of Jesus is that which gives life to the dead, especially the faithful dead. The saints who are

---

49. This rendering seeks to capture the emphasis of the Greek where *theou* precedes *huios*.

raised do not, however, leave their tombs and appear publicly until 'after his resurrection': the death of Jesus must be complemented by his resurrection for its full significance to be enacted and to become apparent. In so far as there is significance in the fact that 'many bodies' (*polla somata*) are raised, and they appear to 'many' (*pollois*), it is likely to be similar to that of the 'many' (*polloi*) for whom Jesus came to give his life (20:28) – the effect of Jesus' death is wide-ranging but not to be quantified more precisely.

These portents are witnessed not only by the centurion, the officer on duty, but also by the other soldiers on duty with him (v. 54a; cf. v. 36). Their response is that of great fear – here clearly not an Abraham's developed fear of God, but rather awe and terror at that which is overwhelming and breaks all known bounds. Characteristically, however, attention is drawn to the content of what they say. That which was disbelievingly scorned by the onlookers at the crucifixion is now confirmed by those who have no intrinsic stake in the matter – 'Truly, this man was God's Son.'[50] At this climactic moment it is recognition of the sonship of Jesus to which all the portents of divine action and resurrection point. Through Matthew's stretching of his narrative conventions to their limit, the kingship of Jesus, the death of Jesus, new life for many dead, and resurrection are all drawn into the confession of Jesus as Son of God.

### Matthew's Gospel and Philippians 2:5–11

Our study of key passages about Jesus as Son to God as Father has brought us back to the conclusion of the gospel, where we began (for the next passage about Son and Father is 28:16–20). Rather than recapitulate what was said at the outset, I propose a different kind of reflection on the significance of Matthew's portrayal of Jesus as Son in the light of its concluding episode. To do this we will turn to Paul. The concern will be not a history of ideas (did Matthew know Paul, or vice versa, or is there a common tradition utilized by both?) but will rather be conceptual, exploring possible ways of rethinking some well-known interpretative issues.

It is often noted that there are similarities between the exaltation of Jesus at the conclusion of Matthew's Gospel (Matt. 28:18–20) and the exaltation in the dense quasi-poetic account of Christ of which Paul makes use in Philippians 2:6–11; a similarity often depicted in terms of analogies with the ancient practice of enthronement (Michel 1983). I am unaware,

---

50. The Greek is difficult to translate for two reasons. First, both *theou* and *huios* are anarthrous. Secondly, it is unclear whether *theou huios* is subject or predicate.

however, of any scholar who has attempted to explore this similarity in any depth.[51] So I offer some preliminary suggestions here.

First, there is a similar narrative structure in the presentation of Jesus. Jesus' ministry in Matthew is framed by his declining of a dominion that would compromise his obedience to God, and his final receiving of full dominion from God, and this gives content to his being Son (*huios*). In Philippians 2:5–11 it is the self-emptying of Jesus and the consequent exaltation by God that is the focal point of the passage, and it is this which gives content to the Christian confession of Jesus Christ as Lord (*kurios*). This could suggest, among other things, that the meaning of Jesus as Son in Matthew is not ultimately very different from the meaning of Jesus as Lord in Paul.

Secondly, the recognition of Jesus' significance is inseparable from that of God as his Father. We noted the pattern in Matthew 28:18–20 where the full authority of Jesus led to baptism not in his name alone but in the name of a God identified as Father to Jesus as Son and in relation to the Spirit, in language akin to that at the outset of Jesus' ministry at his baptism. Similarly, in Philippians 2:9–11, the exaltation of Jesus, the bestowal of a supreme name upon him, and the confession of Jesus as Lord is all directed to a perhaps surprising goal – to the glory of God the Father. It is striking because it could so easily have been otherwise. The sentence beginning in verse 9 could have ended with the confession 'that Jesus Christ is Lord'; or, if extended, then extended solely 'to the glory of God'. Yet in fact all that is bestowed on Jesus is 'to the glory of God the Father' (*eis doxan theou patros*, anarthrous). Although the passage has not mentioned the sonship of Jesus, it relates the significance of Jesus as Lord to the worship of God as God is known in relation to Jesus, that is as Father.[52] The pattern of understanding is strikingly akin to that of Matthew 28:18–20.

Thirdly, the content of Philippians 2:6–8 resonates strongly with the portrayal of Jesus' ministry in Matthew, especially the formative baptism and testing in Matthew 3:13–4:11 (although, of course, it also resonates with other possible scenarios, such as the pre-existent Christ becoming human, or Jesus as antitype to Adam). Not using God for his

---

51. Recent discussions of the relationship between Matthew and Paul tend to concentrate on familiar issues of 'faith and works' and do not address this particular subject (Mohrlang 1984; Luz 1995: 146–53).

52. Although at the beginning and end of the letter Paul speaks of God as Father in relation to Christians (*pater hemon*, 1:2; 4:20), this can hardly be understood in terms other than those of Romans 8, especially 8:14–17, 29 (cf. Gal. 4:4–7), where the sonship of Christians is derivative from the sonship of Christ.

own advantage (*harpagmos*),[53] but self-emptying (*heauton ekenosen*), self-humbling (*etapeinosen heauton*), and obedience without limit, that is not just obedience up to and including death (*hupekoos mechri thanatou*), but death of a uniquely repugnant and shameful kind in crucifixion (*thanatou de staurou*).[54] These categories of Philippians 2 could well describe the Matthean portrayal of Jesus' sonship in the testing after his baptism, at Peter's confession, in Gethsemane, at the trial, and at the crucifixion; a portrayal summed up perhaps most acutely in the incomprehending mockery of Jesus' refusal (understood as inability) to use divine power to help himself, 'others he saved, himself he cannot save'.[55]

Fourthly, Philippians 2:5–11 presents the same difficulty as Matthew in any attempts to draw a sharp line between what is unique to Jesus and what is open to all Christians. On the one hand, each account of Jesus has a clear sense of singularity and finality – only Jesus has done this, and only he has been raised by God to an exalted position where his identity and God's identity are inextricably intertwined. On the other hand, Jesus is a living pattern to which believers must be conformed, a conformity upon which no limits or qualifications are placed.

Finally, the relationship between human and divine action in both Philippians 2:6–11 and Matthew shows a similar paradoxical tension. In Philippians 2:6–8 the subject of all the verbs, the initiator of action, is Christ; in 2:9–11 the subject and active agent is God. This corresponds to the pattern of the gospel where for the most part Jesus is the active agent (though in his passion he gives himself to be acted upon by other people), but after his death he is acted upon by God in that he is raised (*egerthe*, 28:6) and given (*edothe*, 28:18) unlimited authority. Such a pattern might seem to imply not only that God is responsive to human self-giving but

53. I follow Wright's account of *harpagmos* as meaning something to be used to one's own advantage (1991: esp. 78–9, 83, 97).
54. Hengel 1977 remains a valuable guide to the significance of crucifixion in its ancient context.
55. There may be further resonances between Philippians and Matthew if 'being equal with God' (*to einai isa theo*) in Philippians 2:6 is set alongside its one close parallel in the New Testament, John 5:18, where Jesus' calling God his own Father is said by the narrator, interpreting those hostile to Jesus, to be 'making himself equal with God' (*ison to theo*); that is, the language of 'equality with God', whatever its precise connotations (on which see Meeks 1990) – which are of course likely to be much looser in the New Testament context than later dogmatic construals of the equality of the Son with the Father – is associated by John with Jesus as Son to God as Father, a relationship whose meaning is profoundly formulated in John 5:19ff. This raises the possibility of interpreting Philippians 2:6–7 as a depiction of the way of living chosen by Jesus in his ministry, analogous to Matthew's portrayal of Jesus' response to being the Son in whom God delights, as pronounced at the baptism.

also that God's action is subsequent to human action, such that the transformative action of God, which those who seek to be conformed to Christ look for, lies solely in the future, after death. Yet Paul's immediate application of this pattern of Christ's action followed by God's action (2:6–11) is to the Philippians' present action within which God is already the primary agent (2:12–13; the verbal and conceptual linkage is that of obedience (*hupakouo*, v. 12, *hupekoos*, v. 8)). And this corresponds to the gospel pattern in which God's gift to Jesus after his death is the continuation and fulfilment of that which had already been given to him in his life (esp. Matt. 11:27). The interweaving of human and divine action and of present and future displays a characteristic Christian understanding both that what God gives after death is continuous with the reality already lived in this life and that self-giving human action in obedience to God is action in which God himself is fully involved.

### Conclusion: Matthew's portrayal of Jesus as Son of God

This chapter has centred around two questions: What does it mean for Jesus to be Son to God as Father? What needs to happen so that what Jesus declines from the satan at the outset he receives from his Father at the conclusion? Matthew's narrative so presents the life of Jesus that these two questions are different facets of one reality.

For Jesus to be Son means living in constant trust and obedience towards God as his Father. A full flowering of this relationship at the beginning of Jesus' ministry is not incompatible with its receiving new definition and depth in the course of his ministry. Various situations become moments of testing when fresh response is necessary for the relationship to be maintained and deepened. The satan speaks not only in the desert at the outset of Jesus' ministry; he also speaks through the lips of Peter at the turning point of Jesus' ministry at Caesarea Philippi. And he speaks through those present at the crucifixion as Jesus dies. The possibility, the temptation, for Jesus to misconstrue his sonship and use God's power for his own advantage, remains to the very end.

One fundamental issue within this is Jesus' need to remain receptive to God giving that dominion which it would be natural to strive to take. This receptiveness to divine gift is not a matter of inaction but rather of attentive obedience to the divine will. The fact that God gives without limit to Jesus as Son does not mean that all is given at once without regard to the significance of continuing obedience and a corresponding growing capacity to receive. The logic of the story is that it is only Jesus' sustained obedience, continuing to death, 'even death on a cross', that enables him to be given, and to receive, the unrestricted powerful authority which is his in the resurrection and which is the basis for his commissioning of his disciples to spread the truth that they have encountered in Jesus.

In this we see also what is the nature of the power that God gives to Jesus – that it is not the power of coercing but the power to renounce coercion, the power of channelling God's power to others for their wellbeing (which may of course regularly take challenging and even abrasive form) while refusing to take advantage of it for oneself, the power of living human life in an unqualified trust and obedience to God which will endure anything rather than deny that trust. These qualities in Jesus are not a form of weakness, to encourage timidity and fear and so in effect to leave the ruthless and the unscrupulous with a clear field. Rather, the way of Jesus is a confrontation with evil and the abuse of power in its starkest forms, which displays a divine and human reality greater than evil and abuse. Caesar was still upon his throne after Easter, as before, and Judaea was still an unwilling province of the Roman Empire after Easter, as before. Yet Jesus embodies and enacts a reconstrual of what it means to be human and what it means to understand and relate to God, which is definitively affirmed by God in the resurrection. In so far as other people too become willing to appropriate such a pattern for themselves, then the nature of human reality changes and is transformed in accordance with the purposes of God. When life and priorities are thus reconfigured, Caesar on his throne is no longer the same power that he was.

Finally, to put the above point in a different way, although Matthew makes clear in many ways the singularity of Jesus, he also assumes that much which characterizes Jesus as Son can, and should, also characterize those who through him are enabled to be children to God as Father (e.g. 5:43–8; 6:7–9; 12:46–50; 16:24–8). One basic implication of this, in general conceptual terms, is that Matthew's theology and christology entail also anthropology. Or, in the terms of classic patristic theology, the confession of the divinity of the Son is inseparable from confession of the possible divinization of other humans through the Son. In short, our understanding of Jesus and God and our understanding of ourselves are different dimensions of one reality.

# 7

# Summary and prospect

Our final task is twofold. On the one hand, it is necessary to give a summary account of my thesis as a whole, to draw together the threads of the previous argument, and to show how the exegesis of Genesis 22 and Matthew's Gospel illustrates the wider thesis about biblical interpretation in relation to faith in God, as focussed in Jesus Christ. On the other hand, I will offer some preliminary heuristic suggestions as to one way to take debate further, with reference to how one important issue within this thesis – the theme of testing – might relate to a wider engagement of Christian faith with contemporary contexts of life where God and faith are not (apparently) on the agenda.

## Summary

### (1) Biblical interpretation and the problem of 'letter' and 'spirit'

In general terms, the issues posed by the interpretation of the Old Testament in relation to Christ, as discussed in the context of the Emmaus story (chapter 2), have many significant analogies to the question of the interpretation of the Bible as a whole in relation to the question of God within the context of a rule of faith (chapter 1). The same kinds of anxieties about misreading through historical anachronism and/or misuse through interpretative imperialism constantly recur in both contexts. Yet although these are real and recurrent dangers for Christian interpretation, they are not its necessary corollaries, being signs rather of the malfunctioning of a living tradition.

We have argued that to read the Old Testament in the light of Christ is not to introduce into the text something that is not really there (references to Jesus or a suffering messiah), but rather to read the text in a particular kind of way, with reference to the construal of the significance of the text by the New Testament witness to Christ. In terms of our extended case study, the task for the contemporary interpreter is not to replicate the specific use made of the Old Testament by the New, as if Christian interpretation of Genesis 22 must proceed on the basis of Hebrews 11:17–19 or James 2:18–24 or Romans 8:32. These will naturally inform any Christian approach to the text. But the Christian interpreter need not seek somehow to return to or repristinate the ancient world (except in disciplined historical imagination), but rather to ask what it might mean for people today to understand and in some way appropriate that reality of God and human life to which scripture is a unique and privileged witness. The task is to consider the significance of the Christian canon as a whole (a task not possible for any of the writers within the canon), which in this study means an engagement with the substantive issues raised by Genesis 22 as these are raised also in the New Testament, specifically in Matthew's Gospel and Philippians 2:1–13.

Specifically it is our thesis that Jesus' divine sonship in relation to Abraham's fear of God is a good example of the principle which, according to Matthew, Jesus himself enunciates near the outset of the Sermon on the Mount: 'Do not think that I have come to destroy the law or the prophets; I have not come to destroy but to fulfil' (5:17). Jesus continues and extends the understanding of God and humanity already present within Israel's scripture. This does not, of course, constitute all that there is to be said on the issue of the relationship between Jesus and Israel, or between New Testament and Old Testament. But it does constitute a real affinity and continuity, and it is indicative of one important way in which the Old Testament might continue to be significant within a Christian context as a true witness to the nature of God and humanity.

We find in Genesis 22 a story with many elements which suggest its function as a hermeneutic key to the Hebrew scriptures as a whole, a kind of mature distillation of the heart of Hebrew religion,[1] which probes the nature of the Hebrew understanding of what Christians call 'faith'. The story, in many ways paradigmatic of an Old Testament construal of God and humanity, specifically constitutes and interprets Israel's sacrificial worship in Jerusalem. It functions in this way not least because of a move

---

1. One story cannot, of course, say everything. For example, the Old Testament needs other stories, and another context, to indicate the complementary definitional truth of repentance: that 'the sacrifices of God are a broken spirit' (Ps. 51:19 (ET 17)).

to metaphor and a recontextualization within Israel's understanding of God with regard to Abraham's readiness to sacrifice his son; and Jerusalem itself is depicted symbolically. The wider resonances of 'fear of God' represent other key dimensions within that story of Israel which as a narrative Genesis 22 now presupposes and introduces. The nature of life is to be learned in terms of responsiveness to God (especially in Deuteronomy 8), and entails enduring in relationship when its fruitfulness relates to no obvious self-interest. Indeed, the divine test of Abraham is unanticipated within the Genesis narrative, and it serves no obvious purpose other than to complicate what had just seemed to become clear (Abraham having Isaac as heir), indeed to call all that had preceded into question. Yet the text's portrayal of God's providing and God's blessing as both setting the context for, and being confirmed and enhanced by, Abraham's 'fearing' response to God's testing, clearly depicts the enduring fruitfulness of that which at the time could appear fruitless. The text thus depicts an intrinsic interplay between divine initiative and human responsiveness which can only be understood, and realized, in that actual process of human living which the narrative portrayal of Genesis 22 represents.

Within the New Testament, Jesus' life as 'Son of God' as portrayed by Matthew has a significance in many ways analogous to that of 'fear of God' as exemplified by Abraham. For Jesus to be Son of God involves remaining and growing within a relationship of trust to God as Father which is consistently moral in that it entails (among other things, but at its heart) a steady refusal to try to use or manipulate God for his own benefit or protection, even as he exercises God's power on behalf of others in fulfilment of the hope for a messiah. The relationship with the Father is developed in the face of a recurrent process of testing in which the satan, in one guise or another, continues to offer other, seemingly attractive but less demanding, construals of being Son of God, and Jesus must constantly renew his adherence to his Father's will until in his death and resurrection he is able to receive that promised universal dominion (the mark of the messiah) which can only be received in this way.

There are thus obvious parallels between the issues of 'faith' raised by both Genesis 22 and Matthew's Gospel (though as soon as one spells them out in summary and abstract form one risks flattening out, and so losing, the contours and depths of the narratives which give the content). Both depict a God who calls at the beginning and who responds with definitive gift at the end. Both depict a radical displacement of human self-seeking in order to grow in a true relationship with God. Both depict a trust in

God which involves genuine willingness to relinquish that which is humanly most valued in situations where compromise or refusal would seem natural. Both depict relationship with God by particular categories which are open to other people also in so far as they are willing to embody and enact the kind of dynamics which those categories entail. Both are foundation stories for communities whose identity is defined by the content of the story.

Yet it is not only between Genesis 22 and Matthew's Gospel that there are clear affinities. For the structure of Matthew's portrayal of Jesus is so similar to Paul's depiction in Philippians 2:5–11, that one can readily use the terms of the latter to describe the former. When one asks how it is in Matthew's Gospel that Jesus receives at the end what he would not take at the beginning, we see someone for whom relationship with God as Father is not a matter of using God for his own advantage (*harpagmos*), but of unreserved self-emptying (*kenosis*) in obedience to death, even death by crucifixion, in response to which God highly exalts him and bestows on him unlimited sovereignty (he is the one to whom every knee should bow) in conjunction with the name above all other names, which, for Matthew, is that Jesus is the Son through whom, in relation with the Spirit, God as Father is known.

One of the underlying issues here is that which I have identified, in line with a historic Christian distinction, as the relationship between 'literal' and 'spiritual' meaning, though I have not considered these complex hermeneutical notions in their own right, but have simply made use of them (there are, of course, various other ways of articulating some kind of distinction between understanding on one level what the words of the biblical text say and mean, and understanding at a deeper level that of which they speak; this latter is often depicted as the *res* or *Sache* of the text).[2] This age-old distinction was given a new form in the modern context of biblical study establishing itself as an independent discipline, in which it was often argued (in effect, though it was not usually formulated this way) that post-biblical theological dogmas and pieties represented a 'spiritual' reading which threatened the integrity of the 'letter' and so needed to be excluded, just as within the Bible the 'spiritual' insights of the classically central texts (e.g. Deuteronomy, Isaiah 40–55, Paul, John) should not be imposed upon other texts. Despite the obvious force of such a distinction in some contexts, I have argued that such a way of construing the issue is

2. For valuable historical survey and contemporary reflections on this issue, see Childs 1992: 30–51, 80–90.

of limited value. The issue is not that one can only preserve the integrity of the biblical 'letter' by excluding the later-biblical or post-biblical 'spirit', but rather that one must examine which of the many later-biblical and post-biblical formulations and insights genuinely enable the reader better to penetrate and grasp the meaning and significance of any particular text, and which fail to do this. The exegesis of Genesis 22 and Matthew's Gospel has sought to show how the 'letter' of these texts may be fully respected through use of standard scholarly methods, while the bringing together of the texts of Old and New Testament and the contextualization of the whole within a rule of faith has sought not to subvert the exegesis but rather to enable the exegesis to open up the fuller implications, that is, the 'spirit', of the text.

My account of the relationship between the story of Abraham and the story of Jesus may be set alongside the important work of von Rad,[3] with which my own account has important continuities and on which I build in at least three ways: a concern to engage the question of God in and through the biblical text; a corresponding locating of the Hebrew text within the context of Christian faith and theology; an understanding of the primary analogy or typology as that of Abraham with Christ and, through Christ, with subsequent believers.[4] The differences, I think, are that I seek to develop more fully the implications of the key concepts of Genesis 22 within a Hebrew frame of reference; and by selective detailed working with the gospel text I try to show how Israel's normative account of God and humanity is presupposed and taken further in Matthew's portrayal of Jesus, so that the divine testing of Abraham is recapitulated and extended in Jesus. Jesus thus more clearly 'fulfils' existing scripture; and a Christian reading of the Old Testament can appropriate Israel's witness to God in the light of Christ and Christian faith while still paying full attention to, and learning from, the particular and distinctive character of Israel's witness – thereby holding together 'spirit' and 'letter'.

There are also, of course, important discontinuities between the stories of Abraham and Jesus. Abraham's sacrifice symbolically establishes the significance of the Jerusalem temple as the place of encounter between God and Israel, while the death of Jesus symbolically removes that significance from the temple and relocates it in the person of Jesus

---

3. Vischer's theory and practice had attractive features, but seemed prematurely to shortcircuit the task, and so will not be considered further.

4. I deliberately leave to the side the classic typology of Isaac and Christ; it will always remain a possible reading, not without real value, but it is limited in its ability to penetrate the text either of Genesis or of the gospels.

himself (and the corresponding presupposition of *torah* is likewise recon-strued). Abraham's true response to God leads to a promise of Israel's dominion over its enemies, while Jesus' true response to God redefines what such dominion might mean. But while such transformation of the categories within Genesis 22 leads to the full affirmation of some features of the text and a more qualified stance towards others, which can either be left as reminders of historical difference or else reinterpreted (so that, for example, the dominion over enemies within Genesis 22 be understood in moral and spiritual, rather than military and political, terms), this latter move would be in continuity with the move towards metaphor already present within the Genesis text. Thus, for all the clear recognition of his-torical difference which remains possible, the very notion of the 'literal' meaning of the text becomes highly complex, depending on the wider context within which it is read.

The issue of 'spirit' and 'letter' is posed rather differently by suspicious approaches to the text. Here there can be a tendency, like many classic 'spiritual' readings, either to sit relatively light to the 'letter' of the text through interest in the wider linguistic and structural assumptions which the text supposedly makes, or to focus on the 'letter' precisely as the point of entrance to the underlying structural assumptions. But the object is no longer (except perhaps sometimes in qualified form) the appropriation of the substance of the text but rather the unmasking, and thereby disabling, of the text's more or less malign implications. After considering examples which, on analysis, skewed the 'letter' of the text in favour of the 'spiritual significance' which was sought in (and imposed upon) it, and so in their own way replicated a classic failing to which bib-lical interpretation is prone, we offered a suspicious reading in which the 'letter' and 'spirit' would hold together; for such a suspicious reading may give an important critical self-awareness in terms of what proposals for living in accordance with the biblical text should, and should not, in practice involve.

That discussion was directed solely to Genesis 22 and in no way to Matthew's Gospel. But it would not be difficult to replicate a similar argu-ment in relation to that gospel, the broad outlines of which may be quickly sketched. Indeed, of all the gospels Matthew is perhaps most quickly open to suspicion. On the one hand, it depicts 'all authority in heaven and on earth' being given to the risen Jesus (28:18); on the other hand, it is human beings who are called on to implement the conse-quences of that authority (28:19–20). And when this latter point is set alongside Matthew's account of Peter's confession of Jesus as the Christ, where Christ's community (*ekklesia*) is founded upon Peter as upon a rock, a community which holds 'the keys of the kingdom of heaven' and whose binding and loosing upon earth is in some way definitive for heaven also (16:15–19), the potential implications for *human* authority are enormous.[5] When the actual ways in which these implications have all too often been understood and enacted in human history are considered, suspicious critics may be happy to rest their case. Even if it be granted that the history of the Church is not solely a history of power seeking and manipulation, it cannot be denied that power seeking and manipulation feature with distressing regularity and prominence. Might it not be preferable, therefore, to do away altogether with any religious grounding of manipulatively authoritarian behaviour?

The trouble, of course, is that what this criticism proposes is almost precisely what Matthew's Gospel is seeking to do – so to redefine authority and power around the life, death, and resurrection of Jesus that the kind of self-seeking and grasping for power and security which can so easily characterize the human and religious quest is ruled out as utterly inadmissible, a kind of basic category mistake: to suppose that life-transforming engagement with the true God, the Father of Jesus, is a matter of palpable gain or self-promotion at the expense of others simply shows that people do not know what they are talking about, for the reality lies in the obedient giving of self in the service of God and others.

My proposal, therefore, is not to deny or blunt the sharp point of suspicion, but to reiterate with regard to Matthew's Gospel what was argued

5. It is not possible here to engage with the enormous debate over the meaning of the Petrine foundation of the Church. However, I cannot forebear to quote from Barth's discussion of Christian ministry and witness in relation to Matthew 28:18–20; 16:18–19; John 20:23. Specifically with reference to 'binding and loosing' he says: 'The solemn connexion with the founding of the community in which it occurs in Mt.16:19 and Jn. 20:23 . . . makes it probable that primarily and properly it is to be referred to the function of the community in and in relation to the world. If so, it speaks of that which, as the community is at work, either takes place or does not take place in the world and among men, including the members of the community itself. If everything is in order and its work is well done, there must be a great opening, permitting and releasing, i.e., the promise and reception of the forgiveness of sins. If its work is not done or done badly, then contrary to its task the community closes the kingdom of heaven and excludes men from it instead of pointing them to the door which is open to all. It holds where it should release. The remission which is the content of its witness is kept from men. Was it and is it not a strangely perverted mode of interpretation to think that the community may actually be commissioned to choose this negative alternative, using some standard (but which?) either to open on the one side or to close on the other, either to proclaim forgiveness or to withhold it, and thinking that this dual action is even given heavenly sanction? Unless it neglects or corrupts its ministry, can it possibly use the keys of the kingdom of heaven committed to it to close the kingdom to men?' (1962: 861).

with relation to Genesis 22, that the best defence against succumbing is to take with full seriousness the integrity of the biblical text on its own terms: that is, to find the 'spiritual meaning' precisely in the 'literal sense'. The basic reason is that the gospel's own criteria for evaluating human life and talk about God are more searching than alternatives; and that while one should take seriously wide-ranging social, political, and economic dimensions and implications of the text, nonetheless to transpose the text's own categories into such other categories is to diminish it and evade its most important challenge.

### (2) Biblical interpretation within the context of a trinitarian rule of faith

We argued at the outset for the importance of contextualizing biblical interpretation within a rule of faith if the question of God is to be able to be approached in any way adequately. We may now reflect a little more fully upon what is, and is not, entailed by such a context, in development of the preceding remarks about 'letter' and 'spirit'.

When Matthew's portrayal of Jesus is set within the context of a trinitarian rule of faith, this is not (or should not be) remote speculation about metaphysics, or alien imposition upon the first-century Jewish humanity of Jesus (an imposition from which biblical scholars need regularly to liberate Jesus). Rather, what is at stake is an account of the nature of God that is inseparable from the particularity and specificity of Israel's account of human nature in relation to God. As already emphasized, the interrelatedness of accounts of God with accounts of humanity is fundamental to the biblical witness of both Old and New Testaments: what we believe about God is inseparable from what we believe about ourselves (and vice versa). Where Christians part company from Jews is in the affirmation that these beliefs find their truest form in the Jesus to whom the New Testament bears witness. The human transformation, which Jews and Christians agree that confession of the one God entails, is for Christian faith supremely given content and shape by Jesus more than by *torah* (although much of *torah* remains foundational). And an understanding of God is reformulated so as to incorporate Jesus and the Holy Spirit, so that it becomes (in one way or another) trinitarian.

In general terms, the doctrines of Trinity and Incarnation are an attempt to formulate a kind of context of understanding of the Bible as a whole, where the scriptures of Israel lead on to the apostolic witness to the person of Jesus Christ, who is taken to represent the decisive self-revelation and action of Israel's God. The doctrine of the Trinity is rooted in a primary, and uncontroversial, dimension of Israel's scriptures, that the God of Israel is best understood in relational terms. Within the Old Testament, these relational terms are always in the context of God's dealings with his creation, primarily human beings (and the absence of classic mythology – stories about the divine realm in its own right – is a striking corollary of the Old Testament's austere refusal to speak of God other than in engagement with the created order). Within the New Testament, relationships between God and people are mediated by, and focussed in, the person of Jesus in a way that is without precedent within Israel's scriptures, despite significant analogies in prophetic texts. What the doctrines of Trinity and Incarnation do is to extend a relational account of God to God's very identity, in terms of the relationship between Father and Son and Holy Spirit.

The ramifications of historic and renewed contemporary debate about understanding the Trinity obviously lie beyond our present scope. However, the kind of approach I am trying to articulate needs at this stage only a short restatement of a classic trinitarian understanding. To state a complex matter briefly: over time, two specific terms became central to patristic theology and spirituality in regard to the Trinity: first, *kenosis*, and secondly, *perichoresis*. *Kenosis*, 'self-emptying', rooted in the terminology of Philippians 2:7, attempts to express what it means for Jesus as Son of God to be a human being in a life culminating in crucifixion. *Perichoresis*, 'interpenetration', attempts to express the relationship between Father, Son, and Spirit, and to say what must be the case if the relationship between Father and Son, as exemplified within the gospels, is an enduring reality in the being of God. Both terms were developed in attempts to spell out the implications of the New Testament. And both terms were seen (with qualifications) as applicable as well to humanity as to God – for in Jesus, in significant respects, what is true of God is true of humanity, and what is true of humanity is also true of God. One can thus re-express *kenosis* and *perichoresis* by saying that they are accounts of the nature of God which are also, in effect, accounts of what it means for humanity to become truly itself, for such becoming is realized through transformation by the Spirit into the likeness of God. 'Self-emptying', the process of learning to live by trust in the Father, is an essential corollary to 'interpenetration', the process of having one's being defined through relationship to God and to others, such that relationship in love becomes the essence of one's being.[6]

How does this relate to the specifics of biblical interpretation? First, in general terms, to read the Bible in the light of a trinitarian rule of faith – or, alternatively expressed, in the light of Christ, for it is in Christ that the trinitarian understanding of God and humanity is displayed and focussed – is not a matter of imposing anachronisms on the biblical text. It is not an exercise in scouring the Old Testament for covert or oblique references to Jesus or the Trinity (making much, for example, of divine self-reference with a plural form in Genesis 1:26; Isaiah 6:8), or of making the writers of the New Testament hold a christology which approximates ever more closely to Nicene or Chalcedonian definitions. Rather, it is to contextualize the Bible within a continuing attempt to realize that of which it speaks and so to bring a certain kind of concern to bear on the reading of the text. This concern is focussed in a particular understanding of God and humanity, which is used heuristically in reciprocal interchange between text and reader.

More specifically, the linkage between the *kenosis* of Philippians 2 and the *kenosis* of an orthodox Christian understanding of God is not dependent on the supposition that Philippians 2 depicts the incarnation of the pre-existent Christ (which it may, or may not, do). The incarnation affirms that what characterizes Jesus in his life, death, and resurrection characterizes God, indeed that it is definitive of God's very being. The trinitarian corollary of this is that Jesus' relationship to God as Son to Father is an enduring reality within God, to which the Spirit gives access. My thesis is that the biblical passages studied express an understanding of God and humanity in which identity, integrity, and growth in relationship revolve around the paradoxes of a certain kind of self-giving (*kenosis*) to enable life in profound interrelationship (*perichoresis*). On the one hand, the biblical text gives content to human life in relation to God, while on the other hand a contemporary attempt to live faithfully likewise gives content, and the interplay between the two enables genuine human growth and transformation.

We have seen how in Genesis 22 the dynamics of Abraham's relation-

---

6. This discussion has tended to emphasize the potential continuity between Abraham and Jesus and the life of faith today, and has not as such focussed on those senses in which Christians understand Jesus as having been and done that which no one else can be or do, that is, the nature and meaning of incarnation and atonement. But the purpose of the discussion is not to deny such uniqueness, but rather to reestablish a context within which such uniqueness might be an important issue with which to engage.

ship with God are given content by the particular terms 'fear of God', 'test', 'see/provide', and 'bless' in relation to the offering of Isaac, and these terms and concepts were set as fully as possible within their Old Testament context of meaning. Likewise the portrayal of Jesus in Matthew's Gospel was explicated by working with the narrative context and development of the gospel, in terms of what the text as a first-century text means. The dialectical relationship between exegesis of these texts and an understanding of God and humanity in terms of *kenosis* and *perichoresis* works in various ways. It was my own intellectual and experiential grasp (such as it is) of this Christian understanding which enabled my discussion of the biblical text to engage in some way with those realities of which the text speaks, for it is a presupposition which suggests a particular kind of questioning of the text and is open to a particular kind of pattern of things – though this pre-understanding itself arises out of prolonged engagement with the biblical text, and the learning of the appropriate intellectual and moral disciplines of interpretation. On the assumption that the trinitarian account of God and humanity represents an ultimate truth, I have sought to articulate how the biblical writers themselves understood and expressed the dynamics of relationship with God; not (I hope) prematurely conforming the text to some procrustean pattern, but rather respecting the particularities of the Genesis and Matthean texts while being enabled to see something of the profundity of the ways in which they articulate paradigms of human life in relationship with God.

If the context of a rule of faith thus enables better penetration into the content of the biblical text, the biblical text should also challenge the adequacy of the various ways in which that rule of faith is articulated and practised (which brings us back in a different way to the legitimate concerns of suspicious readings of the text). In general terms, Abraham's self-dispossession in obedience to God and Jesus' refusal to use God's power to his own advantage both should disqualify any use of the rule of faith (in power seeking or manipulative or coercive ways) which undercuts that which the rule of faith represents in the first place; the Church cannot be permitted to try to sustain itself by those very means which Jesus renounced and upon whose renunciation the value of the Church's life is predicated. This, to be sure, will rarely be straightforward, both because of the inherent complexities of life and human nature, and because the Christian faith does require a certain kind of insistence that certain things (including a particular and public configuration of texts and life and thought) be maintained for potentially true speech about God and humanity to be possible. Such an insistence can easily be heard to be (and can easily become) a denial of the integrity and value of other contexts and perspectives, rather than the maintaining of a wider and deeper reality through participation in which other contexts can maintain their particularity and integrity and yet be transformatively enriched.

In terms of possible implications of the biblical text for an understanding of God, a trinitarian theology must remember always to keep the Old Testament and gospel narratives in the foreground. Trinitarian theology always tends to locate in eternity that which was achieved in time. The appearance of Jesus on earth in his life, death, and resurrection is a new thing within history (however much the way is prepared within Israel), yet because that which Jesus is and does accomplishes and realizes a supreme truth about human life and God, and that supreme truth is understood to be definitive of God, then what God is in Jesus is reasoned to characterize God as he has been and as he will be. This process is already visible within John's Gospel, where the events of the passion come to characterize the ministry of Jesus as a whole, and where the Logos who becomes flesh in Jesus is present with God 'in the beginning'. Yet the Synoptic Gospels resolutely focus on the achievement in time. At a climactic moment in Luke's Gospel, where Jesus, returned from the realm of the dead, could make definitive pronouncement about the nature of God and a world beyond this one, the focus is wholly and solely upon that which Israel already has in its scripture in relation to the known person of Jesus as suffering messiah. Within Matthew's Gospel, Jesus must appropriate ever more deeply the givenness of his sonship through faithfulness when tested, and the cost of not using God's power for himself grows greater until it culminates in dereliction while being put to death. Both the Lukan and the Matthean accounts presuppose and intensify a pattern of true relationship found already in Abraham and in the Old Testament more generally. The tensions between time and eternity within trinitarian understanding are part of the mystery of God, where the theologian's task is not to dissolve the tensions but to depict them faithfully. The contribution of this study is to redescribe some of the dimensions of the definitive achievement in time as the primary articulation and realization of that which one believes to be true in eternity.

Secondly, a trinitarian theology which keeps the Old Testament and gospel narratives in the foreground will not articulate an account of God which disengages God from demanding and paradoxical relationality. Accounts of God as 'suffering' have been widely articulated in recent years, as a way of trying to speak about God that does not detach God from the realities and extremities of life, yet it is a form of speaking about God that the Bible itself does not adopt (except perhaps incidentally). That is not necessarily a fault, for 'suffering' may in certain ways capture something integral to the biblical picture. Nonetheless, the Bible's own preferred term for speaking of the engaged God is 'love' (*ḥesed*, *agape*) and related terms (grace, faithfulness, etc.), and one of the continuing theological tasks is to clarify the meaning of these terms and to remove misunderstandings, not least through taking seriously the narrative form in which the moral and theological content is regularly depicted. Attention to the narrative portrayal of the nature and development of the 'love' between God and Abraham in Genesis 22, and between Father and Son within Matthew's Gospel, is therefore an element in the continuing task of articulating a trinitarian understanding of God and humanity (for although Genesis 22 does not use *ḥesed* to characterize God, nor does Matthew characterize God with *agape*, the question is whether the gracious and demanding portrayals of God in these contexts respectively may not appropriately be depicted by these summative concepts).

### (3) The question of God in relation to the human

One of the basic issues at the outset of our discussion was the question of God, where we noted both the importance of the issue and the way in which it is regularly marginalized or elided in biblical study because of a fundamental intellectual and cultural shift which has characterized the growth of modernity. Although it is not possible here in any way to trace or analyse the nature of the shift, I hope one general observation may be permitted. This concerns the change in content attributed to 'God', which may perhaps be summed up in Pope's famous lines: 'Know then thyself, presume not God to scan; the proper study of mankind is Man.' This assumes a concept of God which would have been baffling to most biblical writers (possibly excepting Qoheleth) and to most theologians from the second to the sixteenth centuries. For them, knowing oneself and knowing God would not have been alternatives (the former implicitly attainable, the latter speculative and inconclusive), but rather interrelated facets of the one task of growing into human maturity in which God is the foundation for true human potential. Once God is understood as a speculative (and, in other contexts, heteronomously threatening) accessory to autonomous human life, it is hardly surprising if the question of God recedes from the public agenda.

The bafflement which Pope's lines would have generated can be well illustrated from our exegesis in chapters 2, 3, and 6. In these various texts a recurrent issue is the way in which the biblical writers juxtapose and interrelate divine action and human action. In the Emmaus story, the divine action of withholding and giving sight is not conceived arbitrarily but in relation to human engagement with the meaning of scripture and the sharing of a meal. Perception of the risen Jesus is an action of God correlated with particular kinds of human actions (classically understood as means of grace). In Genesis 22 God's testing enables Abraham to become that which the Old Testament holds out as the moral and spiritual goal for humanity in general and Israel in particular. The affirmation about divine action, that God sees/provides, only becomes definitive when Abraham embodies appropriate human response to God, and likewise the divine action of blessing is renewed and integrated with Abraham's obedience on this basis. In Matthew's Gospel it is the divine initiative which calls Jesus Son which constitutes the context for the continuing appropriation by Jesus of the true meaning of his sonship in response to continued testing. It is the unreserved responsiveness of Jesus to his Father which enables Jesus to receive the gifts of God, supremely the unlimited divine power which can only be received by the one who has learned to embody its true meaning. Within this overall portrayal, there is the recurrent sense that what God the Father and Jesus the Son give to others is both a matter of their initiative and a matter of appropriate human attitude and action – the simple receive what is withheld from the wise, so that what is withheld from an abusive high priest is given (in differing ways) to Peter and the centurion.

What is striking in all this is both the profound reciprocity of divine and human action, and the way in which divine action enables human life to grow to its fullest potential. In other words, these biblical texts all consistently illustrate the general axiom about the interrelatedness of meaningful speech about God with protocols of human responsiveness, in which God is neither heteronomous threat to human integrity nor arbitrary speculation but rather that summoning and challenging presence and power who is foundational to true humanity.

### Prospect: a suggestion about divine testing, human growth, and life today

Finally, some brief and tentative remarks about possible relationships between the kind of Christian interpretation of the Bible I have been exploring and other contexts of life and thought. I will base these on the concept of divine testing, which plays such a central role in both Genesis 22 and Matthew's Gospel.

There are obvious ways in which the exegetical discussion thus far could be extended. There is, for example, a well-known problem about the role of the satan in relation to God which I have passed over. In English terminology, it is to do with the differences between 'tempting' and 'testing'. In exegetical terms the problem may be described thus. In the Hebrew text of the Old Testament God is regularly the subject of the verb 'test' (*nissah*). Within the LXX the Greek verb *peirazo* is consistently used to render Hebrew *nissah*, so that regularly in the LXX God is the subject of *peirazo*.[7] Yet in the Greek of the New Testament God is never the subject of *peirazo*. If a subject of *peirazo* is specified, it is always the satan,[8] who may indeed explicitly be called *ho peirazon*, 'the tempter'.[9] To be sure, there is a sense that the satan is somehow subordinate to God's overarching power, as in the story of Job, for Jesus is led to *peirasmos* (testing/temptation) in the desert by the same Spirit who descends at his baptism.[10] However, the letter of James explicitly denies that *peirasmos* can ever be ascribed to God or that God can ever be the subject of the verb *peirazo*, that is, God never 'tempts'. Since there is no New Testament usage that differs from this, despite regular use of *peirazo* and associated forms, it may be that James, instead of being idiosyncratic, is making explicit what elsewhere in the New Testament is implicit. The problem may thus be neatly formulated by setting Genesis 22:1 LXX alongside James 1:13:

> Genesis 22:1 LXX, *ho theos epeirazen ton Abraam*
> James 1:13,     *ho gar theos ... peirazei ... oudena*

How is this conflict, a well-known problem in commentaries down the ages, to be understood?

This problem of vocabulary is in fact the terminological tip of a conceptual and existential iceberg. To state a complex matter briefly: the issue which is highlighted by the New Testament usage of *peirazo* is the paradoxical reality of evil in relation to a good and sovereign God and the moral and spiritual choices of human beings. The divine will for human growth and development, as set out in the Old Testament, is presupposed in the New Testament. But the New Testament sees that God's will for human growth, in itself intrinsically positive even if demanding ('testing'), involves humans in engagement with realities which may seduce

---

7. Genesis 22:1 is rendered *ho theos epeirazen ton Abraam*, while Exodus 20:20 is rendered *heneken gar tou peirasai humas paregenethe ho theos pros humas*.
8. Matt. 4:1//Mk 1:13//Lk. 4:2; 1 Cor. 7:5.     9. Matt. 4:3; 1 Thess. 3:5.     10. Matt. 3:16; 4:1.

the human will from obedience to God ('temptation') (not that the Old Testament does not realize the problem, but it formulates it differently). That which seduces the human will from obedience to God is encountered as a force to be resisted – a force which may be construed in terms of inner human processes of 'desire' (*epithumia*, Jas. 1:14–15), which depicts something of what is symbolized by the satan in his challenges to Jesus. The paradox, with the potential for both glory and tragedy, is that the very process which can develop and deepen human life (divine testing) is the one which can stunt, corrupt, and destroy human life (satanic temptation).

However, instead of seeking to describe more fully the nature of this paradoxical process in its biblical context, or in its classic Jewish and Christian appropriations, I wish to move in a different direction. For in a contemporary context, my impression is that the language and conceptuality of divine testing finds little space, even within Jewish and Christian communities; the notion that the life which we live is a time of 'probation' – which is a way of saying that the path to human fulfilment is a moral and spiritual process of learning to respond positively and faithfully to the endless difficulties of life – is a seed on stony ground. This merits some reflection.

We have seen within a biblical context the importance of testing for both Abraham and Jesus. Commentators also regularly note the importance of testing in other religious literature of the ancient world.[11] But it would perhaps be more accurate to say that testing, in one form or another, as a corollary of the recognition that humans need to grow morally if they are to realize and not waste their human potential, is a commonplace of much literature in many cultures throughout history. Although the obvious historical parallels to the testing of Jesus can be found by searching through ancient literature, there are no less real affinities (*mutatis mutandis*) in, say, the great novels of the eighteenth and nineteenth centuries, where heroes and heroines find fulfilment and happiness (if they do find it) primarily through moral growth in the context of a succession of trials of one kind or other. Although late twentieth-century literature generally eschews this classic pattern, it is by no means extinct, and the astonishing popularity of a book such as J. R. R. Tolkien's *The Lord of the Rings* shows the enduring appeal of an imaginative rendering of the classic pattern.

11. So, for example, Gunkel's discussion of Genesis 22 begins with a list of parallels to Buddha, Zoroaster, and St Antony (1997: 234), while John Kloppenborg sets the testing of Jesus within the context of Graeco-Roman biographies (1987: 261–2).

Beyond literature, however, one may note the continuing, and perhaps increasing, phenomenon of people who alone or with few companions in some way seek to accomplish great journeys and feats of exploration and endurance, sometimes in replication of similar past accomplishments. They sail vast oceans in small boats, traverse desert wastes of extreme heat or cold, climb high mountains, descend inaccessible places underground, fly with the aid of unnecessarily small or parlous machines, or enter forms of sport which are kinds of competitive endurance tests. Some of this is no doubt a form of entertainment and escape from boredom. But those who undertake such things often speak in terms of a kind of self-discovery through pushing themselves to limits unknown in advance, and often feel it somehow crucial to the integrity of their selves that they do difficult and dangerous things which are, in certain obvious (and especially utilitarian) senses, 'unnecessary'. The public interest which often attends such feats suggests a possible symbolic and representative significance which may attach to them, that they may somehow symbolize a courage and endurance and self-discovery which for most people happens in far more mundane and less chosen, but still real and important, ways.

From a theological perspective, one may wonder whether some of this activity may not be a kind of displaced religious quest, a deep and inarticulate search whose only apparent means of realization lies in physical and emotional hardship and endurance, which sometimes may ultimately evade rather than touch the heart of the matter. The difficulties of saying something coherent here are enormous. In theological terms, one is instantly plunged into classic debates about 'grace' and 'nature', about divine revelation and initiative and its relationship to human understanding and experience. How far is that which is given in scripture only able to be recognized and realized because it engages with and develops that which is already taking place in human life? And how does the 'outward' dimension of mundane life relate to the 'inward' dimension of moral and spiritual growth?

This issue arose within our exegesis in relation to 'fear of God'. On the one hand, fear of God characterizes Abraham, as it should characterize Israel, and the particular context of divine *torah* gives content. On the other hand, it is something that should characterize humanity generally and its absence is reprehensible; people are expected to know it and practise it without having been told by God what Israel has been told. And, characteristically (though not as such in Genesis 22), it is the 'outward'

mension of treatment of the weak and vulnerable which gives content
, and displays, the 'inward' dimension of responsiveness to God. Most
⌐⌐ the classic issues of 'grace' and 'nature' can be seen in 'fear of God', and
it may be the same with 'testing' also.

It would therefore certainly be incorrect to suggest that the kind of
contemporary phenomena of 'testing' just described are the same as what
the Bible depicts as 'testing'. For it has been central to the present thesis
that context, interpretation, and understanding are in important ways
integral to, and constitutive of, human life. That is, for the study of God
and humanity, and a collection of texts such as the Bible, one must refuse
to turn (reduce) a useful distinction between fact and interpretation into
any kind of positivism, whereby human 'experience' becomes some kind
of brute fact, and moral and theological (and other) thought and practice
becomes some kind of optional extra. What life 'without God' may
become as life 'with God' is not a matter of adding an 'extra religious bit'
to a life whose nature remains otherwise unchanged, but a transformation of the whole.

My present concern, however, is solely to indicate a possible way of
advancing the discussion by suggesting that what the Bible depicts in
terms of divine initiative and human responsiveness and growth may be
something less far removed from the contemporary world than is sometimes supposed. General understanding of the language and symbolism
of the Bible has decayed so badly that people find it hard to recognize it
for what it is. Consequent widespread assumptions about the 'irrele-
vance' of the Bible (as 'mere' history or ideology), with corresponding
(and sometimes misplaced) attempts on the part of believers to demonstrate its 'relevance', may be in some senses beside the point, which is
rather what it means, and what is necessary, to 'learn the language' or
'inhabit the story' or 'discern the mystery'. It may be less a matter of doing
different things or trying to acquire different kinds of experiences than it
is to re-envision, re-interpret, re-contextualize, and re-live that life which
is already under way; though the changes that this involves ('repentance')
will never be straightforward, and it is only by attending to the content of
scripture, and living accordingly ('faith'), that we may begin to find out
what is involved.

# References

Allison, Dale 1993, *The New Moses: A Matthean Typology*, Minneapolis, Augsburg Fortress Press.

Alter, Robert 1981,*The Art of Biblical Narrative*, London, Allen & Unwin.

1992, 'Narrative Specification and the Power of the Literal' in Alter, Robert, *The World of Biblical Literature*, London, SPCK, pp. 85–106.

Amos, C. 1997, 'Review of Saltzman 1996', *Expository Times* 108: 243.

Arberry, A. 1980[1955], *The Koran Interpreted*, London, Allen & Unwin.

Auerbach, E. 1953, *Mimesis*, Princeton University Press.

Baker, David 1991, *Two Testaments, One Bible: A Study of the Theological Relationship between the Old and New Testaments*, 2nd edn, Leicester, Apollos.

Bal, Mieke 1987, *Lethal Love: Feminist Literary Readings of Biblical Love Stories*, Indiana University Press.

Balthasar, Hans Urs von 1990, *Mysterium Paschale*, Edinburgh, T. & T. Clark (ET from German of 1970).

Bar-Efrat, Shimon 1989, *Narrative Art in the Bible*, Sheffield, Almond (ET from Hebrew of 1979).

Barr, James 1973, *The Bible in the Modern World*, London, SCM Press.

1980, 'Does Biblical Study Still Belong to Theology?' in Barr, James, *Explorations in Theology*, London, SCM Press, pp. 18–29.

1983, *Holy Scripture: Canon, Authority, Criticism*, Oxford, Clarendon Press.

1999, *The Concept of Biblical Theology: An Old Testament Perspective*, London, SCM Press.

Barrett, C. K. 1995a, 'What is New Testament Theology?', in Barrett, C. K., *Jesus and the Word*, Edinburgh, T. & T. Clark, pp. 241–58 (reprinted from Hadidian, D. Y. (ed.) 1981, *Intergerini Parietis Septum (Eph. 2.14): Essays Presented to Markus Barth*, Pittsburgh, Pickwick, pp. 1–22).

1995b, 'The Center of the New Testament and the Canon' in Barrett, C. K., *Jesus and the Word*, pp. 259–76 (reprinted from Luz, U. and Weder, H. (eds.) 1983, *Die Mitte des Neuen Testaments: Festschrift für Eduard Schweizer*, Göttingen, Vandenhoeck & Ruprecht, pp. 5–21).

Barth, Karl 1960, *Anselm: Fides Quaerens Intellectum*, London, SCM Press (ET from German of 1930, 1958).

1961a, *Church Dogmatics* III: 3, Edinburgh, T. & T.Clark (ET from German).

1961b, 'An Exegetical Study of Matthew 28:16–20' in Anderson, G. (ed.), *The Theology of Christian Mission*, London, SCM Press, pp. 55–71.

1962, *Church Dogmatics* IV: 3.2, Edinburgh, T. & T. Clark (ET from German).

Barton, John 1993, *The Future of Old Testament Study*, Oxford, Clarendon Press.

Becker, J. 1965, *Gottesfurcht im Alten Testament*, Analecta Biblica 25, Rome, Pontifical Biblical Institute.

Berlin, Adele 1983, *Poetics and Interpretation of Biblical Narrative*, Sheffield Academic Press.

Betz, H. 1967, 'The Logion of the Easy Yoke and of Rest (Matt. 11.28–30)', *Journal of Biblical Literature* 86: 10–24.

1969, 'The Origin and Nature of Christian Faith according to the Emmaus Legend (Luke 24:13–32)', *Interpretation* 23: 32–46.

Bible and Culture Collective 1995, *The Postmodern Bible*, Yale University Press.

Blass, F., Debrunner, A., and Funk, R. 1961, *A Greek Grammar of the New Testament and Other Early Christian Literature*, Chicago University Press (ET of 10th German edn).

Blowers, Paul 1997, 'The *Regula Fidei* and the Narrative Character of Early Christian Faith', *Pro Ecclesia* 6/2: 199–228.

Blumenthal, David 1998, 'Confronting the Character of God: Text and Praxis' in Beal, Timothy and Linafelt, Tod (eds.), *God in the Fray: A Tribute to Walter Brueggemann*, Minneapolis, Fortress Press, pp. 38–51.

Bornkamm, G. 1971, 'The Risen Lord and the Earthly Jesus' in Robinson, J. (ed.), *The Future of our Religious Past*, London, SCM Press, pp. 203–29.

Brown, R. 1994, *The Death of the Messiah*, 2 vols., New York, Doubleday.

Brueggemann, Walter 1982, *Genesis*, IBC, Atlanta, John Knox.

1997, *Theology of the Old Testament: Testimony, Dispute, Advocacy*, Minneapolis, Fortress Press.

Buber, M. and Rosenzweig, F. 1994, *Scripture and Translation*, Indiana University Press (ET by Lawrence Rosenwald with Everett Fox from German of 1936).

Bultmann, R. 1963, *The History of the Synoptic Tradition*, Oxford, Blackwell (ET from 3rd German edn of 1958).

1969, 'What Does it Mean to Speak of God?' in Bultmann, R., *Faith and Understanding*, London, SCM Press, pp. 53–65 (ET from German of 1925).

Campbell, A. F. and O'Brien, M. A. 1993, *Sources of the Pentateuch: Texts, Introductions, Annotations*, Minneapolis, Fortress Press.

Carroll, Robert 1997, 'Clio and Canons: In Search of a Cultural Poetics of the Hebrew Bible', *Biblical Interpretation* 5/4: 300–23.

Caspi, M. M. and Cohen, S. B. 1995, *The Binding [Aqedah] and its Transformations in Judaism and Islam*, Lampeter, Edwin Mellen.

Cassuto, U. 1964, *A Commentary on the Book of Genesis*, pt. II, Jerusalem, Magnes (ET from Hebrew of 1949).

Childs, Brevard 1974, *Exodus*, OTL, London, SCM Press.

1984, *The New Testament as Canon: An Introduction*, London, SCM Press.

1992, *Biblical Theology of the Old and New Testaments*, London, SCM Press.

1994, 'Old Testament in Germany 1920–1940: The Search for a New Paradigm' in Mommer, P. and Thiel, W. (eds.), *Altes Testament – Forschung und Wirkung: Festschrift für H. Graf Reventlow*, Frankfurt, Peter Lang, pp. 233–46.

Clines, David 1990, *What Does Eve Do To Help?* JSOTS 94, Sheffield, JSOT.

1993, 'Biblical Interpretation in an International Perspective', *Biblical Interpretation* 1: 67–87.

1995, *Interested Parties: The Ideology of Writers and Readers of the Hebrew Bible*, JSOTS 205, Sheffield Academic Press.

1997, *The Bible and the Modern World*, Sheffield Academic Press.

Conzelmann, Hans 1960, *The Theology of Saint Luke*, London, Faber (ET from German of 1953).

Cooper, A. 1987, 'On Reading the Bible Critically and Otherwise' in Friedman, R. E. and Williamson, H. G. M. (eds.), *The Future of Biblical Studies: The Hebrew Scriptures*, Atlanta, Scholars Press, pp. 61–79.

Crenshaw, J. 1978, *Gerhard von Rad*, Waco, Word.

1984, *A Whirlpool of Torment*, OBT, Philadelphia, Fortress Press.

Davidson, Robert 1983, *The Courage to Doubt*, London, SCM Press.

Davies, Philip, 1995, *Whose Bible is it Anyway?* JSOTS 204, Sheffield Academic Press.

Davies, W. and Allison, D. 1997, *The Gospel According to Saint Matthew*, vol. III, Edinburgh, T. & T. Clark.

Davila, J. 1991, 'The Name of God at Moriah: An Unpublished Fragment from 4QGenExod$^{a}$', *Journal of Biblical Literature* 110: 577–82.

Delaney, Carol 1989, 'The Legacy of Abraham' in Bal, M. (ed.), *Anti-Covenant: Counter-Reading Women's Lives in the Hebrew Bible*, JSOTS 81, Sheffield, Almond, pp. 27–41.

Derousseaux, L. 1970, *La Crainte de Dieu dans l'Ancien Testament*, Lectio Divina 63, Paris, Cerf.

Dillon, R. 1978, *From Eyewitnesses to Ministers of the Word: Tradition and Composition in Luke 24*, Analecta Biblica 82, Rome, Pontifical Biblical Institute.

Dodd, C. H. 1935, *The Parables of the Kingdom*, Welwyn, Nisbet.

Edgerton, W. 1992, *The Passion of Interpretation*, Louisville, Westminster John Knox Press.

Eichrodt, W. 1967, *Theology of the Old Testament*, vol. II, London, SCM Press (ET from 5th German edn of 1964).

Eliade, M. 1958, *Patterns in Comparative Religion*, London, Sheed & Ward.

Evans, C. 1990, *Saint Luke*, TPINTC, London, SCM Press.

Farrer, Austin 1965, *The Triple Victory*, London, Faith Press.

Fitzmyer, Joseph 1981, *The Gospel According to Luke I-IX*, AB28, New York, Doubleday.

1985, *The Gospel According to Luke X-XXIV*, AB28a, New York, Doubleday.

Fowl, Stephen 1998, *Engaging Scripture*, Oxford, Blackwell.

Fowl, Stephen and Jones, L. Gregory 1991, *Reading in Communion: Scripture and Ethics in Christian Life*, London, SPCK.

Fretheim, T. 1994, 'The Book of Genesis' in Keck, L. et al. (eds.), *The New Interpreter's Bible*, Nashville, Abingdon Press, pp. 319–674.

1995, 'God, Abraham, and the Abuse of Isaac', *Word & World* 15: 49–57.

Fuhs, H. 1990, '*Yare*', in Botterweck, G. and Ringgren, H. (eds.),*Theological Dictionary of the Old Testament* VI, Grand Rapids, Eerdmans, pp. 290–315 (ET from German of 1980–2).

Funk, Robert and Hoover, Roy 1993, *The Five Gospels: The Search for the Authentic Words of Jesus*, London, Macmillan.

Giblin, C. H. 1975, 'A Note on Doubt and Reassurance in Mt. 28.16–20', *Catholic Biblical Quarterly* 37: 68–75.

Gilbert, Martin 1978, *Exile and Return: The Emergence of Jewish Statehood*, London, Weidenfeld & Nicolson.

Gooch, Paul 1996, *Reflections on Jesus and Socrates: Word and Silence*, Yale University Press.

Goshen-Gottstein, M. 1987, 'Abraham – Lover or Beloved of God' in Marks, J. H. and Good, R. M. (eds.), *Love and Death in the Ancient Near East*, Guilford, CT, Four Quarters, pp. 101–4.

Gowan, D. 1994, *Theology in Exodus*, Louisville, Westminster John Knox Press.

Guillaume, J. 1979, *Luc interprète des anciennes traditions sur la résurrection de Jésus*, Etudes Bibliques, Paris, Gabalda.

Gunkel, H. 1997, *Genesis*, Macon, GA, Mercer University Press (ET from German of 1910).

Gunn, D. and Fewell, D. 1993a, *Narrative in the Hebrew Bible*, Oxford University Press.

1993b, *Gender, Power, & Promise: The Subject of the Bible's First Story*, Nashville, Abingdon Press.

Hargreaves, J. 1998, *A Guide to Genesis*, London, SPCK (rev. edn of 1969).

Harnack, A. 1905, *History of Dogma*, vol. 1, London, Williams & Norgate (ET from German of 1894).

Harvey, A. 1982, *Jesus and the Constraints of History*, London, Duckworth.

Hayward, C. T. R. 1981, 'The Present State of Research into the Targumic Account of the Sacrifice of Isaac', *Journal of Jewish Studies* 32: 127–50.

Hengel, M. 1977, *Crucifixion*, London, SCM Press (ET from German of 1976).

Heron, A. 1991, 'The Biblical Basis for the Doctrine of the Trinity' in Heron, A (ed.), *The Forgotten Trinity*, Inter-Church House, London SE1 7RL, BCC/CCBI.

Hickling, C. 1994, 'The Emmaus Story and its Sequel' in Barton, S. and Stanton, G. (eds.), *Resurrection: Essays in Honour of Leslie Houlden*, London, SPCK, pp. 21–33.

Hirsch, S. 1959, *The Pentateuch*, vol. 1, *Genesis*, London, Honig (ET from German of 1867).

Hopkins, David 1980, 'Between Promise and Fulfilment: Von Rad and the Sacrifice of Abraham', *Biblische Zeitschrift* 24/2: 180–93.

Jacob, Benno 1934, *Das Erste Buch der Tora: Genesis*, Berlin, Schocken (repr. New York, Ktav, n.d.)

1992, *The Second Book of the Bible: Exodus*, New Jersey, Ktav (ET from unpublished German of the 1940s).

Janzen, J. G. 1993, *Genesis 12–50: Abraham and All the Families of the Earth*, Grand Rapids, Eerdmans.

Japhet, S. 1994, 'The Trial of Abraham and the Test of Job: How do they Differ?', *Henoch* 16: 153–71.

Jenks, A. W. 1977, *The Elohist and North Israelite Traditions*, SBLMS22, Missoula, Scholars Press.

Jenson, Robert 1996, 'Hermeneutics and the Life of the Church' in Braaten, Carl and Jenson, Robert (eds.), *Reclaiming the Bible for the Church*, Edinburgh, T. & T. Clark, pp. 89–105.

1997, 'Karl Barth' in Ford, David (ed.), *The Modern Theologians*, 2nd edn, Oxford, Blackwell, pp. 19–36.

Jeremias, J. 1966, *The Eucharistic Words of Jesus*, London, SCM Press (ET from German).

1972, *The Parables of Jesus*, 3rd. edn, London, SCM Press (ET of 8th German edn of 1970).

Joüon, P. and Muraoka, T. 1991, *A Grammar of Biblical Hebrew*, Rome, Pontifical Biblical Institute.

Just Jr, Arthur A. 1993, *The Ongoing Feast: Table Fellowship and Eschatology at Emmaus*, Pueblo, Collegeville, MN, Liturgical Press.

Kant, I. 1979, *The Conflict of the Faculties*, New York, Abaris (ET from German of 1798).

Kasper, Walter 1989, 'Revelation and Mystery: The Christian Understanding of God' in Kasper, Walter, *Theology & Church*, London, SCM Press, pp. 19–31 (ET from German of 1987).

Kautzsch, E. and Cowley, A. 1910, *Gesenius' Hebrew Grammar*, Oxford, Clarendon Press (ET from 28th German edn of 1909).

Kilian, R. 1970, *Isaaks Opferung*, Stuttgarter Bibelstudien 44, Verlag Katholisches Bibelwerk.

Kingsbury, J. D. 1975, *Matthew: Structure, Christology, Kingdom*, Philadelphia, Fortress Press

Kloppenborg, John 1987, *The Formation of Q: Trajectories in Ancient Wisdom Collections*, Philadelphia, Fortress Press.

1992, 'Theological Stakes in the Synoptic Problem' in Van Segbroeck, F. et al. (eds.), *The Four Gospels 1992: Festschrift Frans Neirynck*, Leuven University Press, pp. 93–120.

Koester, Helmut 1990, *Ancient Christian Gospels: Their History and Development*, London, SCM Press.

Kuschel, Karl-Josef, 1995, *Abraham: A Symbol of Hope for Jews, Christians and Muslims*, London, SCM Press (ET from German of 1994).

Lane Fox, Robin 1991, *The Unauthorized Version: Truth and Fiction in the Bible*, London, Viking.

Lange, J. 1974, *Das Erscheinen des Auferstandenen im Evangelium nach Matthäus: Eine traditions- und redaktionsgeschichtliche Untersuchung zu Mt 28,16–20*, Forschung zur Bibel 11, Würzburg, Echter Verlag.

Lash, Nicholas 1986, 'What Might Martyrdom Mean?' in Lash, Nicholas, *Theology on the Way to Emmaus*, London, SCM Press, pp. 75–92.

1996, *The Beginning and the End of 'Religion'*, Cambridge University Press.

Layton, Bentley 1987, *The Gnostic Scriptures*, London, SCM Press.

Lerch, David 1950, *Isaaks Opferung christlich gedeutet: Eine auslegungsgeschichtliche Untersuchung*, Beiträge zur Historischen Theologie 12, Tübingen, J. C. B. Mohr.

Levenson, Jon 1985, *Sinai & Zion: An Entry into the Jewish Bible*, Minneapolis, Winston.

1993a, *The Death and Resurrection of the Beloved Son: The Transformation of Child Sacrifice in Judaism and Christianity*, Yale University Press.

1993b, 'Historical Criticism and the Fate of the Enlightenment Project' in Levenson, Jon, *The Hebrew Bible, the Old Testament, and Historical Criticism*, Louisville, Westminster John Knox Press, pp. 106–26.

1994, *Creation and the Persistence of Evil: The Jewish Drama of Divine Omnipotence*, 2nd edn, Princeton University Press.

1998, 'Abusing Abraham: Traditions, Religious Histories, and Modern Misinterpretations', *Judaism* 47: 259–77.

Loisy, A. 1924, *L'Evangile selon Luc*, Paris, E. Nourry.

Louth, Andrew 1983, *Discerning the Mystery: An Essay on the Nature of Theology*, Oxford, Clarendon Press.

Luz, Ulrich 1995, *The Theology of the Gospel of Matthew*, Cambridge University Press (ET from German of 1993).

McGrath, Alister E. 1985, *Luther's Theology of the Cross: Martin Luther's Theological Breakthrough*, Oxford, Blackwell.

McIntosh, Mark 1998, *Mystical Theology*, Oxford, Blackwell.

MacKinnon, Donald 1986, 'The Evangelical Imagination' in Mackey, J. (ed.), *Religious Imagination*, Edinburgh University Press, pp. 175–85.

1987, 'The Inexpressibility of God' in MacKinnon, Donald, *Themes in Theology: The Three-Fold Cord*, Edinburgh, T. & T. Clark, pp. 11–19.

Maimonides, M. 1956[1904], *Guide for the Perplexed*, New York, Dover (ET from Arabic of 12th century).

Mason, Rex 1997, *Propaganda and Subversion in the Old Testament*, London, SPCK.

Meeks, Wayne 1990, 'Equal to God' in Fortna, R. and Gaventa, B. (eds.), *The Conversation Continues: J. L. Martyn Festschrift*, Nashville, Abingdon Press, pp. 309–21.

Michel, Otto 1983, 'The Conclusion of Matthew's Gospel' in Stanton, G. (ed.), *The Interpretation of Matthew*, London, SPCK, pp. 30–41 (ET from German of 1950).

Miller, A. 1990, *The Untouched Key: Tracing Childhood Trauma in Creativity and Destructiveness*, New York, Doubleday.

Miller, P. 1997, *Theology Today* 54/3.

Mleynek, S. 1994, 'Abraham, Aristotle, and God: The Poetics of Sacrifice', *Journal of American Academy of Religion* 62: 107–21.

Moberly, R. W. L. 1988a, 'Did the Serpent Get it Right?', *Journal of Theological Studies* 39: 1–27.

1988b, 'The Earliest Commentary on the Akedah', *Vetus Testamentum* 38: 302–23.

1992, *The Old Testament of the Old Testament*, OBT, Minneapolis, Fortress Press.

1998, ' "God is Not a Human that He Should Repent" (Numbers 23:19 and 1 Samuel 15:29)' in Beal, Timothy and Linafelt, Tod (eds.), *God in the Fray: A Tribute to Walter Brueggemann*, Minneapolis, Fortress Press, pp. 112–23.

1999, 'Toward an Interpretation of the Shema' in Seitz, C. and Greene-McCreight, K. (eds.), *Theological Exegesis: Essays in Honor of Brevard Childs*, Grand Rapids, Eerdmans, pp. 124–44.

Mohrlang, R. 1984, *Matthew and Paul: A Comparison of Ethical Perspectives*, SNTSMS 48, Cambridge University Press.

Moltmann, J. 1974, *The Crucified God*, London, SCM Press (ET from German of 1973).

Murphy, Roland 1992, 'The Fear of the Lord: A Fear to End All Fears' in Charlesworth, J. (ed.), *Overcoming Fear Between Jews and Christians*, New York, Crossroad, pp. 172–80.

Noth, M. 1981, *A History of Pentateuchal Traditions*, Chico, Scholars Press (ET from German of 1948).

Oden Jr, Robert 1987, *The Bible Without Theology: The Theological Tradition and Alternatives to It*, San Francisco, Harper & Row.

Otto, R. 1924, *The Idea of the Holy*, Oxford University Press (ET from 9th German edn of 1923).

Peers, E. 1957, *The Complete Works of Saint Teresa of Jesus*, vol. II, London, Sheed & Ward.

Pelikan, Jaroslav and Hansen, Walter (eds.) 1964, *Luther's Works,* vol. IV: *Lectures on Genesis, Chapters 21–25*, St. Louis, Concordia.

Pritchard, J. B. (ed.) 1969[1950], *Ancient Near Eastern Texts Relating to the Old Testament*, Princeton University Press.

Proksch, O. 1924, *Genesis*, 3rd edn, KAT, Deichertsche.

Rad, Gerhard von 1943, 'Grundprobleme einer biblischen Theologie des Alten Testaments', *Theologische Literaturzeitung* 68: 225–34.

1952, 'Typologische Auslegung des Alten Testaments', *Evangelische Theologie* 12: 17–33.

1965, *Old Testament Theology*, vol. II, London, SCM Press (ET from German of 1960).

1971, *Das Opfer des Abrahams*, Munich, Chr. Kaiser Verlag.

1972a [1952], *Genesis*, 3rd edn, London, SCM Press (ET from 9th German edn of 1972).

1972b, *Wisdom in Israel*, London, SCM Press (ET from German of 1970).

Räisänen, H. 1990, *Beyond New Testament Theology: A Story and a Programme*, London, SCM Press.

Ramsey, A. M. 1949, *The Glory of God and the Transfiguration of Christ*, London, Longmans.

Reid, Barbara 1994, 'Prayer and the Face of the Transfigured Jesus' in Charlesworth, J. (ed.), *The Lord's Prayer and Other Prayer Texts from the Greco-Roman Era*, Valley Forge, Trinity Press International, pp. 39–53.

Rendtorff, R. 1993, 'Christological Interpretation as a Way of "Salvaging" the Old Testament? Wilhelm Vischer and Gerhard von Rad,' in his *Canon and Theology: Overtures to an Old Testament Theology*, OBT, Minneapolis, Fortress Press, pp. 76–91(ET from German of 1991).

Reventlow, H. 1968, *Opfere deinen Sohn*, Neukirchen-Vluyn: Neukirchener.

Ricoeur, Paul 1978, *The Rule of Metaphor: Multi-disciplinary Studies of the Creation of Meaning in Language*, London, Routledge (ET from French of 1975).

Robinson, B. 1984, 'The Place of the Emmaus Story in Luke–Acts', *New Testament Studies* 30: 481–97.

Robinson, James and Koester, Helmut 1971, *Trajectories Through Early Christianity*, Philadelphia, Fortress Press.

Rosenbaum, M. and Silbermann, A. 1972, *The Pentateuch with the Commentary of Rashi: Genesis*, Jerusalem, Silbermann.

Roshwald, Mordecai 1991, 'The Meaning of Faith', *Modern Theology* 7: 381–401.

Rumscheidt, H. Martin 1972, *Revelation and Theology: An Analysis of the Barth–Harnack Correspondence of 1923*, Cambridge University Press.

Sailhamer, J. 1990, 'Genesis' in Gaebelein, F. E. (ed.), *The Expositor's Bible Commentary*, vol. II, Grand Rapids, Zondervan, pp. 1–284.

Saltzman, S. 1996, *A Small Glimmer of Light: Reflections on the Book of Genesis*, Hoboken, Ktav.

Sanders, E. P. 1993, *The Historical Figure of Jesus*, London, Penguin.

Sandys-Wunsch, J. and Eldredge, L. 1980, 'J. P. Gabler and the Distinction between Biblical and Dogmatic Theology: Translation, Commentary, and Discussion of his Originality', *Scottish Journal of Theology* 33: 133–58.

Sarna, N. M. 1989, *The JPS Torah Commentary: Genesis*, Philadelphia, Jewish Publication Society.

Schaberg, J. 1982, *The Father, the Son, and the Holy Spirit*, SBLDS 61, Chico, Scholars Press.

Schubert, P. 1957, 'The Structure and Significance of Luke 24' in Eltester, W. et al. (eds.), *Neutestamentliche Studien für Rudolf Bultmann*, Berlin, Töpelmann, pp. 165–86.

Scullion, John 1992, *Genesis: A Commentary for Students, Teachers and Preachers*, Collegeville, Liturgical Press.

Sheriffs, Deryck 1996, *The Friendship of the Lord: An Old Testament Spirituality*, Carlisle, Paternoster.

Spiegel, Shalom, 1979, *The Last Trial*, New York, Behrman (ET from Hebrew of 1950).

Stanton, Graham 1992, *A Gospel for a New People: Studies in Matthew*, Edinburgh, T. & T. Clark.

Steinberg, N. 1993, *Kinship and Marriage in Genesis: A Household Economics Perspective*, Minneapolis, Fortress Press.

Sternberg, Meir 1985, *The Poetics of Biblical Narrative*, Bloomington, Indiana University Press.

Swartley, Willard 1983, *Slavery, Sabbath, War and Women*, Scottdale, Herald Press.

Thoma, Clemens 1981, 'Observations on the Concept and the Early Forms of Akedah-Spirituality' in Finkel, A. and Frizzell, L. (eds.), *Standing Before God: Studies on Prayer in Scriptures and in Tradition with Essays in Honor of John M. Oesterreicher*, New York, Ktav, pp. 213–22.

Thompson, Thomas 1987, *The Origin Tradition of Ancient Israel*: vol. I: *The Literary Formation of Genesis and Exodus 1–23*, JSOTS 55, Sheffield, JSOT.

Trible, Phyllis 1991, 'Genesis 22: The Sacrifice of Sarah' in Rosenblatt, J. and Sitterson Jr, J. (eds.), *'Not in Heaven': Coherence and Complexity in Biblical Narrative*, Bloomington, Indiana University Press, pp. 170–91.

Tuckett, C. M. 1992, 'The Temptation Narrative in Q' in Van Segbroeck, F. et al. (eds.), *The Four Gospels 1992: Festschrift Frans Neirynck*, Leuven University Press, pp. 479–507.

Vischer, W. 1949, *The Witness of the Old Testament to Christ*, London, Lutterworth Press (ET from 3rd German edn of 1936).

Wanke, J. 1973, *Die Emmauserzählung. Eine redaktionsgeschichtliche Untersuchung zu Lk 24,13–35*, Erfurter theologische Studien 31, Leipzig, St Benno-Verlag.

Watson, Francis 1997, *Text and Truth: Redefining Biblical Theology*, Edinburgh, T. & T. Clark.

Webster, John 1998, 'Hermeneutics in Modern Theology: Some Doctrinal Reflections', *Scottish Journal of Theology* 51/3: 307–41.

Weinfeld, M. 1972, *Deuteronomy and the Deuteronomic School*, Oxford, Clarendon Press.

Westermann, C. 1980, *The Promises to the Fathers*, Philadelphia, Fortress Press (ET of German of 1976).

1986, *Genesis 12–36*, London, SPCK (ET from German of 1981).

Wiesel, Elie 1976, *Messengers of God*, New York, Summit, 1976.

Wolff, H. W. 1966, 'The Kerygma of the Yahwist', *Interpretation* 20: 131–58.

1972, 'The Elohistic Fragments in the Pentateuch', *Interpretation* 26: 158–73.

Wright, C. J. H. 1992, *Knowing Jesus Through the Old Testament*, London, Marshall Pickering.

Wright, N. T. 1991, 'Jesus Christ is Lord: Philippians 2.5–11' in Wright, N. T., *The Climax of the Covenant: Christ and the Law in Pauline Theology*, Edinburgh, T. & T. Clark, pp. 56–98.

1996, *Jesus and the Victory of God*, Philadelphia, Fortress Press.

# Index of scriptural references

# Index of names

# Index of subjects

141 – Updating Vischer w/ some of his
own hermeneutical statements.

RC Poem on p. 168
- "biblical int. may take many other
forms than scholarly monograph and
commentary."

ch. 5 – Discussion of the phenomenon or
practice of suspiciously interpreting
Gen. 22. – Approaching the story
w/ an eye toward dissolving God
and/or the because of the
brutality of the story.

182 – "one primary critical norm is that
✗ which [the story] offers, that is
the fear of God."

183 – The effective tool of suspicion for
interpretation